The
Giant Book
of
Insults

ALSO BY LOUIS A. SAFIAN

*An Irreverent Dictionary of Love
and Marriage*

Just for the Pun of It

THE GIANT BOOK OF INSULTS

comprising
2000 Insults for All Occasions
and
2000 More Insults

COMPILED BY LOUIS A. SAFIAN

CASTLE BOOKS

Arrangement has been made to publish
this edition by CASTLE BOOKS,
a division of Book Sales, Inc., Secaucus, N. J.

Manufactured in the United States of America

September 1981

ISBN NO.: 0-89009-383-0

To my wife Rea
who laughs at all my jokes,
not because they're always clever,
but because she is.

Contents

2000 Insults for All Occasions

2000 More Insults

2,000 Insults
for
All Occasions

Introduction

Repartee has been defined as saying what you think after becoming a departee; saying as quick as a flash what you didn't say until next morning. Everyone, at one time or another, has had occasion to echo the familiar lamentation:

Backward, turn backward, O Time, in your flight,
I've just thought of a wisecrack I needed last night!

How often have you felt the need at a given moment for a whimsical wisecrack or a waggish quip to put a spark in your conversation? Why be caught with your gags down? You can't win in a battle of wits unless you are properly armed with a repertoire of rapid-fire repartee, a capsule caricature, a salty sally, or a snappy comeback.

The unabashed purpose of this compilation is to enable you, at the drop of a gag, to place your comic, laconic stamps on the idiosyncrasies of diverse specimens of the human race. I have endeavored to include the wit of absurdity, analogy, burlesque, cynicism, drollery, epigram, facetiousness, ridicule, thought-play, word-play, and urbanity.

The breezy one-liner, to which I have adhered in this volume, gets your point across in headline form in this age of high speed, sums up a situation in a nutshell, and adds attention-winning punch to your comments. The secret of the success of the epigram is found in its definition—a grain of truth in the twinkling of an eye.

13

The so-called insult gag is, in essence, an epigrammatic wisecrack concerning people's nature, conduct, or appearance. TV and nightclub comedians, who are masters of the insult gag, indulge to their hearts' content in acidulous wit and verbal brickbats, bombshells, and blackjacks with the assurance that no one in their audiences identifies himself as their target. Jonathan Swift expressed this idea skillfully in his definition of satire—"a sort of glass, wherein beholders do generally discover everybody's face but their own."

Aside from its reputation for sportive witticism, the insult gag helps at times to blow off steam and get a pet peeve off one's chest. There is an old saying, "It takes all kinds of people to make a world." In our human relations, many of our irritations and annoyances spring from other people's behavior, dress, or appearance. It often becomes necessary to call a spade a spade without stubbing our toes on one.

Edged with the sharp barbs of truth, this thesaurus of sizzling flipquickies, mad-libs, bright slayings, and tongue-whippers offers you a well-stocked arsenal for the fullest expression of your critical faculties. Alphabetically arranged according to the target of your pointed dart, it is a ready reference for assassinating asses, burying boors, demolishing stuffed shirts, knocking the knockers, putting the kibosh on the kibitzers, prodding the pompous, shrinking egotists' heads, and squelching the pest.

So, for your innocent (and not so innocent) pleasure, I offer this supermarket of sweet (and not so sweet) one-liners with which you can add lustre to your reputation as a wit, a clever epigrammist, and an astute caricaturist. The pins are here in abundance to prick a lot of balloons and baboons. With all this ammunition, you can now crack the quips and let them fall where they may.

May your tongue be your sword and may it never grow rusty.

With my best gratings, I am

Very tartly yours,

LOUIS A. SAFIAN

Big Heads

He has gone the way of all flash.

His head is getting too big for his toupee.

His egotism is a plain case of mistaken nonentity.

Every time he opens his mouth, he puts his feats in.

He doesn't want anyone to make a fuss over him—just to treat him as they would any other great man.

He's a real big gun—of small caliber and immense bore.

He'd need a hole in the ground to shrink to his normal proportions.

Someone should press the "down" button on his elevator shoes.

If he had his life to live over again, he would still fall in love with himself.

He thinks it's a halo, but it's only a swelled head.

If his halo falls one more inch, it will be a noose.

He's so bigheaded, he can't get an aspirin to fit him.

He's so conceited, he has his X-rays retouched.

Every time he looks in the mirror, he takes a bow.

He's carrying on a great love affair—unassisted.

His wife worships him—and so does he.

His egotism is nature's compensation for his mediocrity.

Be careful when you're speaking about him—you're speaking of the man he loves.

He's always letting off esteem.

He thinks he's such a shining light, he hands you sunglasses when you look at him.

His conceit is the tribute of a fool.

He's all wrapped up in himself, but he makes a pretty small package.

He's a fellow of real high-hattitude.

He didn't just grow with responsibility—he bloated.

You could make a fortune renting his head out as a balloon.

Success turned his head. Too bad it didn't wring his neck a little.

He thinks he's a big shot just because he explodes.

It's a wonder how such a big head holds such a little mind.

His ego is the only thing about him that kept on growing without nourishment.

He has a 5 ft. 6 in. height and a 6 ft. 5 in. ego.

He's as pompous as an undertaker at a $10,000 funeral.

He's such a big-shot executive, a spiritualist will never be able to contact him. His secretary will have to be contacted first.

You can't help admiring him. If you don't, you're fired.

You can't get anywhere with him by shaking his hand when he puts it out—you have to kiss it.

He doesn't like yes-men around. When he says "No," he wants them to say "No."

He always tells his staff, "Of course, it's only a suggestion, but let's not forget who's making it."

He likes you to come right out and say what you think, when you agree with him.

He's easily entertained. All his staff has to do is just listen to him.

He's always blowing his No's.

He doesn't mind criticism as long as it's out-and-out approval.

He has a colored self-portrait of himself.

He's suffering from infantuation.

Tell him he's brilliant and he says, modestly, "I'll bet you tell that to everyone who's brilliant."

He's so ostentatious, if he ever became an alcoholic, he'd never be admitted to Alcoholics Anonymous.

He's suffering from I-dolatry.

He's an I-soar.

His I's are too close together.

He's an I-specialist.

He's suffering from I-strain.

He's a fellow with big I's who doesn't think of U.

When he meets another egotist, it's an I for an I.

He's a celebrity—spelled "swellebrity."

He's a self-made man who:
- looks more like a warning than an example.
- would have done better if he had let out the contract.
- has no rivals—in love of himself.
- would have been better off if he hadn't been made at all.
- should have consulted an expert.
- adores his maker.

- is the worst example of unskilled labor you've ever seen.
- makes you wonder why he wanted to make himself like that.
- insists on giving everybody the recipe.
- should never have quit the job before it was finished.
- has relieved the Lord of a big responsibility.
- would have been better off if he hadn't fooled around with those do-it-yourself fads.
- believes in himself. Some people are too easily convinced.
- apparently knocked off work too soon.
- never should have hired such cheap labor.
- makes you wonder whether he's boasting or apologizing.

He claims to be the architect of his own success. It's lucky the building inspectors didn't come around during the construction.

From the time he began to be a self-made man, it was the beginning of a lifelong romance.

He's a self-made man whose wife was the power behind the drone.

He wouldn't have done such a good job as a self-made man if his wife hadn't made a few alterations.

His claim that he's self-made sure relieves the conscience of the rest of the world.

You'd make a fortune if you could buy him for what you think of him and sell him for what he thinks of himself.

On his last birthday he sent his parents a telegram of congratulations.

A glazed look comes into his eyes when the conversation drifts away from himself.

He thinks he can push himself forward by patting himself on the back.

His head is so big they have to pin his ears back to get him through Grand Central Station.

His swelled head is just nature's frenzied effort to fill a vacuum.

He's a small country, bounded on the north, south, east, and west by himself.

He's so egotistical, when he hears thunder, he takes a bow.

His conceit is a gift of Providence to a little man.

Take the air out of that little wheel and all you have left is a flat tire.

He's blown his horn so loud, he hasn't any wind left for climbing.

He's high-hatting everyone on the way up. He's liable to meet them on the way down.

One of these days he'll learn that it's only a matter of eighteen inches between a pat on the back and a kick in the pants.

If he ever gets to Heaven he'll find the front seats occupied by fellows who weren't such big shots down here.

As a swelled-up comer, he's a sure goner.

Birthdaze

She's the demure type—demure she gets older, demure she conceals it.

She looks like a million dollars—after taxes.

There'll be no candles on her birthday cake. She's in no mood to make light of her age.

She never forgets her age, once she's decided what it's to be.

She's discovered the secret of perpetual youth—she lies about her age.

If she put the right number of candles on her birthday cake, it would be a fire hazard.

Hoity-toity? She may be hoity, but she'll never see toity again.

Her husband is pleading with her to have birthdays again. He doesn't want to grow old alone.

The best years of her life were the ten years between twenty-nine and thirty.

She's been pressing thirty so long, it's pleated.

Her age ranges from thirty to secrecy.

She could add years to her life by simply telling the truth.

She claims her age is her own business. Poor thing, she's practically out of business.

She reckons her age by light years—she's sure light a few years.

When the census taker asked her how old she was, she couldn't remember whether she was forty-two or forty-three, so she said thirty-five.

She hasn't lost the years she's subtracted from her age; she's just added them to the ages of her sisters-in-law.

Birthdays are occasions that her child deserves, her husband observes, and she preserves.

Birthdays are anniversaries on which her husband takes a day off, and she takes a year off.

She's very loyal. Years ago she reached an age she liked, and she has stuck to it.

When it comes to telling her age, she's shy—about ten years shy.

At twenty-one, she was chosen Miss America. In those days, there were very few Americans.

She won't put the right number of candles on her birthday cake. It wouldn't be a birthday party—it would be a torchlight procession.

She's not what she was fifteen years ago—she's nine years older.

In her opinion, the seven ages of a woman are: baby, infant, junior miss, young woman, young woman, young woman, young woman.

She's aged more than her husband, but less often.

As long as she's capable of juggling figures, she'll never be old.

She uses the count-down method of calculating age.

She's a nice age—thirty-five, especially since she happens to be forty-three.

She has a twin brother who is practically identical, except for one minor detail—he's forty-nine and she's thirty-nine.

Her husband is a diplomat. He remembers her birthday and forgets her age.

When she hesitated to state her age on the witness stand, the judge said, "Hurry, madam, every minute makes it worse."

She's celebrating the tenth anniversary of her thirty-ninth birthday.

She looks like a million—every year of it.

She doesn't object to men who kiss and tell. In fact, at her age she needs all the publicity she can get.

The only time she ever gave her right age was on a safari when she was captured by a fussy cannibal who never ate anyone past forty.

She's in her early flirties.

She knows how to hang on to her youth—she never introduces him to other women.

She finally admitted she was forty, but she didn't say when.

Forty has been the most difficult age for her to pass—it's taken her eight years.

She's living it up, saying, "You're only young once." It's time she thought up some other excuse.

She was eighteen and her husband thirty when they met. Now he's sixty, so she figures since he's twice as old as he was then, she must be thirty-six.

She's afraid to grow old, but at forty she really need have no fear of aging. She'll outgrow it fifteen years from now—when she's forty-eight.

Her hardest decision is when to start middle age.

She wouldn't be trying so hard to conceal her age if her husband would act his.

Her once dangerous curves have become extended detours.

She has stopped exercising—pushing fifty is enough exercise for her.

She's at the age where any man who looks back looks good.

Old blondes never fade—like her, they just dye away.

She worried so much about growing old, she grew blond overnight.

She knew the Big Dipper when it was just a drinking cup.

She knew Heinz when he had only seven varieties.

She knew Howard Johnson when he had only two flavors.

She doesn't have an enemy in the world—she's outlived them all.

She's just gotten a prospectus from an old-age home marked "Urgent."

Boozers

He's suffering from bottle fatigue.

His friends don't know what to get him for Christmas, because they don't know how to wrap up a saloon.

His wife never worries about germs when he kisses her—he's boiled most of the time.

He can get loaded on Scotch tape.

He's drinking to forget. The way he's going at it, he should have complete amnesia in a week.

Life for him is a matter of urps and downs.

Who says he's a hard drinker? He does that easier than anything.

He's working his way down from bottoms up.

He drinks like a fish—too bad he doesn't drink what fishes drink.

When he drinks, he loses his inhibitions and gives exhibitions.

He enjoys cocktail parties where drinks mix people.

With him, two pints make one cavort.

He'd rather be tight than President.

His favorite drink is the next one.

24

He's a man of high fidelity—staggers home to his wife every night.

He's sot in his ways.

They're going to star him in a movie called "The Unquench-ables."

If it wasn't for the olives in the Martinis, he'd starve to death.

He's spoiling his health, drinking to everyone else's.

He enters a bar optimistically, and comes out misty optically.

He's divorcing his wife because she has a sobering effect on him—she hides the bottle.

He's drinking doubles—and seeing the same way.

With him, every day is an alcoholiday.

He graduated from college *magna cum loaded.*

He's writing his autobiography, but it's a hundred quarts too long.

His wife is sticking to him through thick and gin.

His idea of a corking good time is uncorking.

Drinking doesn't just drown his troubles—it irrigates them.

He doesn't only drink—he drinks between drinks.

He'd be the nicest guy on two feet if he could only stay there.

As a kid they called him "Half-pint," but he grew up to be a full quart.

He can always beer up under misfortune.

He thinks Beethoven's Fifth is a bottle.

He's been classified 4A—he's been turned down four times by Alcoholics Anonymous.

He's never been able to join Alcoholics Anonymous—he's never sober enough to memorize the pledge.

Two Scotchmen are ruining him—Haig & Haig.

He has the cutest trick. He walks down the street and turns into a saloon.

He always staggers home the shortest distance between two pints.

He always makes a New Year resolution to stop drinking that goes in one year and out the other.

The Red Cross rejected his blood donation—his plasma had an olive in it.

Those hiccoughs of his are merely messages from departed spirits.

He approaches you from several different directions at once.

He puts vitamins in his gin so he can build himself up while tearing himself down.

His idea of a balanced diet is a highball in each hand.

He's so high, if you smell his breath you get a nosebleed.

After work, he always stops at a bar for an hour and a quart.

He can empty a bottle as quick as a flask.

He has Saloon Arthritis—every night he's stiff in another joint.

When snakes get drunk, they see him.

He's drinking something called "Old Maid"—it has no chaser.

He's drinking something called "Card Table"—a couple of them, and his legs fold right up under him.

He has a red nose, a white liver, a green brain, a dark-brown breath, and a blue outlook.

Every New Year he resolves not to drink any more, just about the same.

He's so wet, every time you blow on him he ripples.

He consulted a psychiatrist about his drinking and now things are altogether different—he does his drinking on a couch.

He's in a state of melancholism.

First, he drinks when he's pooped to make a new man out of himself, then he drinks to the new man.

He always goes to parties where there's rum for one more.

He has no respect for age unless it's bottled.

His tippling has a wide range: jocose, morose, bellicose, lachrymose and comatose.

He started to write a drinking song, but never got past the first two bars.

He was last seen in a bottle of bourbon.

He never drinks more than he can stand—the minute he can stand, he starts drinking again.

Give him a couple of glasses and he's sure to make a spectacle of himself.

He's following his doctor's advice to stop all drinks—you don't see any getting past him.

He's just broken his pledge never to take another drink. It was the worst afternoon he ever spent.

Nothing makes him drink the way he does—he's a volunteer.

With that 100-proof breath, he breathed on his wife's leopard coat and changed it right back to rabbit.

He has cheeks like roses, and a nose to match.

He won't take his doctor's advice to stop drinking. He claims there are lots more old drunks than old doctors.

The only time he goes to the refrigerator is when he needs ice cubes.

He has a finicky stomach—he can't eat an olive unless it's sterilized in gin.

He's fighting a losing battle trying to keep himself and his business in a liquid condition.

The only way he ever opens a conversation is with a corkscrew.

He saw the ocean for the first time and muttered, "Look at those melted ice cubes."

On board ship, he peered through a porthole all afternoon, finally mumbling, "It'sh a lousy TV show."

On his latest cruise, the weather was so bad he had to be lashed to the bar.

He's thinking of quitting drinking—he's beginning to see the handwriting on the floor.

His head must be made of cork—it's always at the mouth of a bottle.

He thinks he can pull himself out of his troubles with a corkscrew.

He might be able to make both ends meet if he weren't so busy making one end drink.

He's a gin rummy specialist. He drinks so much, he looks like a rummy.

It's a beef-stew marriage. His wife is always beefing and he's always stewed.

It's a nip-and-tuck marriage. He always insists on a nip and his wife has to tuck him in.

If a mosquito bit him, it would die of alcohol-poisoning.

When mosquitoes decide to bite him, they bring along a glass of water as a chaser

If you want him to take notice of you, pretend you're a bartender.

He's been thrown out of so many bars, he now wears nothing but gray, so his suits will match the sidewalk.

He's been dispossessed—they're repairing the gutter.

They're calling him "Cucumber"—he's pickled so often.

They're calling him "Syncopation" because of his irregular movements—from bar to bar.

No wonder his stomach looks like a beer keg—it's all he uses it for.

When he drinks, he feels sophisticated—too bad he can't pronounce it.

The only things he fixes around the house are Manhattans and Martinis.

He only puts on weight in certain places—in saloons, for instance.

All through the day he asks people for the time, and he can't figure out why he always gets different answers.

He magnifies his troubles by looking at them through the bottom of a glass.

He's insulted when you offer him a drink, but he swallows the insult.

He's living proof that there's no fool like an oiled fool.

He reminds you of the proverb "Where there's a swill there's a sway."

He's a perfect illustration of the old saying "A fool and his money are soon potted."

A little blurred never tells him when he's had enough.

He never has a hangover—he stays drunk.

Bores

Only his varicose veins save him from being completely colorless.

If you're enjoying yourself in his company, it's all you're enjoying.

He believes that no matter how crowded a gathering may be, there's room for one bore.

He's so dull, he can't even entertain a doubt.

Monopologues are his specialty.

People and things are here today and gone tomorrow, but he's here today and here tomorrow.

He always has a lot of get-up-and-go except when it's time to get up and go.

As a guest, his shortcoming is his long staying.

As guests go, you wish he would.

He's the kind of neighbor who can get to your house in a minute and out of it in hours.

He comes into a room dragging his tale behind him.

He can stay longer in an hour than most people do in a week.

He's a great athlete—he can throw a wet blanket the entire length of a room.

When there's nothing more to be said, he's still saying it.

He not only monologizes a subject, he monotonizes it.

If you see two fellows together and one looks bored, he's the other.

He has a wide circle of nodding acquaintances.

You have to watch his finger closely—it fits into any buttonhole.

He's hither, thither, and yawn.

There's no doubt he's trying—in fact, he's very trying.

His conversations are on a boast-to-boast hookup.

He deprives you of privacy without providing you with company.

He's interesting to a point—the point of departure.

As his host, you wish he would leave and let live.

He lights up a room when he leaves it.

He says a thousand things, but he never says "good-bye."

He not only encroaches on your time, he trespasses on eternity.

No one is his equal in keeping a conversation ho-humming.

He's full of sayings that should go without saying.

He's as stimulating as a mouthful of sawdust and water.

He's as dull as a fat lapdog after dinner.

The older he gets, the further he descends into his anecdotage.

He can wrap up a one-minute idea in a one-hour vocabulary.

He has a diarrhea of words and a constipation of ideas.

He's such a bore, he couldn't get anyone into his fall-out shelter during a nuclear attack.

You don't know what makes him tick, but you wish it was a time bomb.

He never opens his mouth unless he has nothing to say.

He wearies you with the patter of little feats.

He can get more out of his surgical operation than even Adam did.

It's amazing how he manages to enter a room voice first.

He's very cultured—he can bore you on any subject.

As a host, he makes his company feel at home, and that's where they wish they were.

He throws the kind of party that's a fete worse than death.

His parties are so dull and quiet, you can hear a pun drop.

He's a socialite—one of the Bore Hundred.

He gets offended when others talk while he's interrupting.

He leaves little to your imagination, and even less to your patience.

Chatterboxes

Generally speaking, he's generally speaking.

She must have been vaccinated with a phonograph needle.

He's a sound speaker—and, oh, those sounds!

His idea of conversation is a filibuster.

Her word is never done.

Is she breathtaking! Every few hours she stops talking and takes a breath.

He's the type who approaches every subject with an open mouth.

What he needs is a little lockjaw.

He may be down, but he's never out—talked.

He should rent his mouth out as a fly-catcher.

She not only has the last word, but the last 5,000.

Her vocabulary is small, but the turnover is terrific.

His mouth is so big, he can whisper in his own ear.

He's like a shirt button—always popping off.

She's always giving everyone a preamble to her constitution.

Her tongue is so long, she can seal an envelope after she puts it in the mailbox.

He could talk his head off and never miss it.

Her laryngitis is the wages of din.

He reminds you of a clarinet—a wind instrument.

He has to be eschewed if you don't want to be chewed.

She has a nice, open face—open day and night.

She has a chronic speech impediment—palpitation of the tongue.

He thinks it's more blessed to be glib than to perceive.

The only thing that can cheat her out of a last word is an echo.

Try to argue with him, and his words will flail you.

When you get away from him, you feel like a fugitive from a chin gang.

She's an oft-spoken person.

He's a man of a few words—a few million.

Why, it takes him a half-hour just to say "Hello."

He speaks eight languages, but can't hold his tongue in one.

Everyone calls her "Amazon"—she's so big at the mouth.

They call her "Flo" because she talks in a steady stream.

Her mind is always on the tip of her tongue.

With him, you can't be on speaking terms—unless you're on listening terms.

The last time anyone saw a mouth like his, it had a fishhook in it.

She throws her tongue in high gear before her brain is turning over.

Every time she sets her trap for a man, she forgets to shut it.

If exercise eliminates fat, how in the world did she get that double chin?

What he lacks in depth, he makes up in length—of his tongue.

He knows very little, but he knows it mighty fluently.

She's suffering in silence—her phone is out of order.

He has let his mind go blank, but has forgotten to turn off the sound.

He's a freight train of wordage—with no terminal facilities.

It took her surgeon an hour to perform the operation—it'll take her months to describe it.

He thinks the world will beat a path to his door because he's built a better claptrap.

The way she monopolizes the party line, if anyone needs a doctor they have to put an ad in the paper.

He's very broad-minded—he approaches every question with an open mouth.

You couldn't get a word in with her even if you folded it in two.

His body is getting shorter, but his anecdotes are growing longer.

Her favorite expression is "Oh, I'm speechless!" If she'd only stay that way!

His conversation is as long-drawn-out as the music from an accordion.

When all is said and done—he just keeps on talking.

She talks like a revolving door.

If silence is golden, he must have been born on the silver standard.

He's a real drip. You can always hear him, but can rarely turn him off.

It's no trick for him to put his foot in his mouth—he has a big mouth.

He can hardly ever wait to hear what he's going to say.

He listens to a conversation only when he's talking.

He can be read like a book but not shut up so easily.

When they start a filibuster in Congress, they call him in as an advisor.

What he needs is a yappendectomy.

They call her "A.T. & T."—Always Talking and Talking.

He can even talk for hours about the value of silence.

She's a real vocalamity.

She's getting a double chin—just too much work for one.

The only thing he ever exercises is his tongue.

The best way for her to save face is to keep the lower half shut.

He not only holds a conversation, he strangles it.

She claims to be very outspoken—but she's hardly ever.

She simply loves wordy causes.

He'd be better off if his mind worked as fast as his mouth.

She has a good memory, and a tongue hung in the middle of it.

Chiselers

Whoever molded his character overemphasized the chisel.

He carved his career by first-class chiseling.

He talks on principles and acts on interest.

He's long on promises and short on memory.

In any contract with him, he'll deal from the bottom of the pact.

He always lays his cards on the table, but he has another deck up his sleeve.

He's oilier than a kerosene lamp.

He climbed the ladder of success kissing the feet of the one ahead of him and kicking the head of the one following him.

He's one of those fellows who will pat you on the back before your face and hit you in the face behind your back.

He's a contact man—all con and no tact.

When he says "Good morning," they call the weather bureau to make sure.

He never goes back on his word—without consulting his lawyer.

If he had his conscience taken out, it would be a minor operation.

Ic's a man of promise—broken promise.

He has as much conscience as a fox in a chicken farm.

When he pats you on the back, he's figuring where to stick the knife.

He's a man of convictions—and he has served time for every one.

He claims he was born with a silver spoon in his mouth. It must have had someone else's initials on it.

Everything he touches turns to gold, but the judge is ordering him to put it back.

He talks in stereophonic style—out of both sides of his mouth.

Even the wool he pulls over your eyes is half rayon.

It's easier to hold an eel by the tail than to pin him down.

He's always ready to back his hot tips with your cash.

He changes sides oftener than a windshield wiper.

He goes through life's revolving door on other people's push.

He reminds you of a bee—a hum-bug.

His friends think they're being cultivated—but they're being trimmed.

He's as elusive as a wet fish.

He has the gift of grab.

He prays on his knees on Sunday, and on everybody the rest of the week.

He stands for everything he thinks you'll fall for.

He's going to Saranac for respiratory trouble; his creditors won't let him breathe easy.

If he enters into a verbal contract with someone for $200 a week, he pays off verbally.

He's an expert at handing out baloney disguised as food for thought.

He has a lot of grit. He can take it—no matter who owns it.

He's a human kite. He got where he is with wind and pull.

He's polished—in a slippery sort of way.

He has the human touch; it conceals an itching palm.

He started out in life as an unwanted child—now he's wanted in ten states.

Give him a free hand and he'll stick it right in your pocket.

He was born a mountaineer and hasn't been on the level since.

If you lend him money, you can charge it to profit and louse.

When he pats you on the back, he's trying to get you to cough up something.

He's a big iron and steel man from Pittsburgh. His wife irons and he steals.

The louder he protests his honesty, the more firmly you have to clasp your wallet.

Honesty pays for most people, but it doesn't pay enough to suit him.

When he lays his cards on the table, it's a good idea to count them.

He got his principal entirely without principle.

Watch out when he shakes your hand; he's trying to pump money out of your pocket.

When he left his last apartment, his landlady actually wept— he owed six months' rent.

He got that stoop living up to his ideals.

You're safe while he holds you warmly by both your hands—because you can watch both of his.

His ancestors never made an honest dollar and he's following in their fingerprints.

He's such a phoney, he even gets cavities in his false teeth.

If he was a psychologist, he'd be another Fraud.

He has one of those hydromatic handshakes—no clutch.

Some men marry poor women to settle down. He's marrying a rich one to settle up.

He's so tricky, he could skin a flint.

His paycheck should be gift-wrapped.

His remarks are always more candied than candid.

He's a gentleman to his fingerprints.

The only time he calls a spade a spade is when he stubs his toe on one.

A dollar can never fall as low as the means he adopted to get it.

He gives publicly and steals privately.

When he was a boy, his ambition was to be a pirate. It isn't everyone that realizes his ambitions.

He's always ready to help you get what's coming to him.

He's so sugary, you can get diabetes listening to him.

He claims that once, in Europe, he called on three kings. It must have been in a poker game.

His credit is so bad, he can't even borrow trouble.

He can put the screws on you faster than an undertaker.

He believes in the greatest good for the greatest number, and his idea of the greatest number is Number One.

As far as he's concerned, the voice of Conscience has no telling effect.

He's pulling himself up by his bootlicks.

He was recently voted "Man of the Hour"—but you've got to watch him every minute.

He's one of those get-rich-quick schemers who's always on the lookout for people who want to get poor quick.

He's as hypocritical as a funeral director trying to look sad at a $10,000 funeral.

He likes to eat his cake and have yours too.

He's very generous with his friends. He'll always divide with them—as much as they have.

He's as phoney as a dentist's smile.

He's living from handout to mouth.

He lives by the sweat of his frau.

He's leading a dog's life—creditors are dogging his footsteps.

He gets awfully depressed when he sees his friends spending money lavishly and he can't help them.

The less you have to do with him, the less you'll be worse off.

You can always get from him straight-from-the-shoulder double-talk.

If you pieced together all the bum checks he writes in a month, you'd have a good-sized rubber raincoat.

He married a woman for her pa value.

He has a magnetic personality. Everything he has is charged.

You have to have good blood pressure watching how free he is with the money he owes you.

He never forgets a favor—if he did it.

He's as artificial as manufactured ice.

His wife likes to shop on the sunny side of the street, but he prefers to do his business on the shady side.

He's done a good deal for lots of people. He's kept a flock of detectives, bill collectors, and Treasury men working regularly.

As a young fellow, he once ran away with a circus, but the police caught him and made him bring it back.

He has a lot of hidden charms; his money is in vaults, in Swiss banks, and so on.

He is a master of the art of moving in the best circles without going straight.

He buys lovely period furniture—and it's only a short period before the installment people take it back.

One time he was connected with the police department—by a pair of handcuffs.

He's always selling himself. The trouble is he misrepresents the goods.

He has a positive genius for worming his way out of your confidence.

He claims his furniture goes back to Louis the 14th. It will, if he doesn't pay Louis before the 14th.

He's so full of angles, he's selling haunting licenses to ghosts.

He's a real phoney—a cross between nothing.

If he ever fell over his own bluff, he' be fractured.

He seems to be too good to be true—and he isn't.

He claims he lost a wad at the races. Next time he shouldn't bet chewing gum.

He tells women he's loaded with the green stuff—he's a lettuce farmer.

He claims he has enough money to live on for the rest of his life, and he has, too—if he died next week.

He claims his sofa is French Provincial 1809, but it's Sears Roebuck—$395.

He claims his dad is a Southern planter. For once he's telling the truth—his dad is a Mississippi undertaker.

He claims he's a big man—has several hundred people under him. He's a watchman in a cemetery.

He claims he used to be an organist but gave it up. His monkey must have died.

He claims he was once a lifeguard. It must have been in a car wash.

He claims he comes from a family of standing. They're probably floorwalkers, elevator operators, and policemen.

He claims he comes from a family of rock 'n' rollers. They hit you on the head and then they roll you.

He claims the coat he got his wife is dyed mink. From the looks of it, it must have died a horrible death.

His oily tongue goes with his slick mind.

He's as phoney as a harlot's tears.

He's as deceitful as a crow.

His probity is all right—until someone probes.

If you lend him money, you never see him again—and it's worth it.

If you lend him your garden rake, he comes back for mower.

He believes in free speech—especially long distance phone calls on other people's phones.

He says he has followed the Ten Commandments all his life. Too bad he never managed to catch up with them.

He has the kind of checkered career that's bound to end up in a striped suit.

He left the farm because he was sure that the Man with the Hoe doesn't get nearly as far as the Man with the Hokum.

Crabs

He's so disagreeable, his own shadow won't keep him company.

He's so contrary, he does everything versa vice.

You can't tell him anything—he has a soundproof head.

He follows the straight and narrow-minded path.

He's so narrow-minded, he can look through a keyhole with both eyes.

He's so narrow-minded, he has to stack his ideas vertically.

She's the kind of hostess whom you thank for her hostility.

Arguing with her is like trying to read a newspaper in a high wind.

He's a blower-upper without any countdown.

He has a concrete mind—permanently set and all mixed up.

She's so contrary, if she drowned they'd have to look upstream for her.

He looks through rose-colored glasses with a jaundiced eye.

His tactics are a combination of needles and threats.

He likes people who come right out and say what they think, when they agree with him.

He doesn't like yes-men. He doesn't mind anyone disagreeing with him, even though it costs them their job.

He had three phones installed, so he can hang up on more people.

He's a real lamb; when you ask him for a raise, he says, "Ba-a-a-ah."

Everyone has a good word for him—they all whisper it.

He has an open mind—it should be closed for repairs.

Arguing with him is like trying to blow out an electric-light bulb.

It's as easy to convince him as trying to poultice the hump off a camel's back.

He's always down on everything he's not up on.

He believes in law and order—just so long as he can lay down the law and give the order.

He has a disposition like an untipped waiter.

He claims he never made a mistake in his life, but he has a wife who did.

There's nothing wrong with him that trying to reason with him won't aggravate.

His comebacks are as snappy as his checks.

He thinks the world is against him—and it is.

He's as cross as capital X . . . as irascible as a sick monkey . . . as surly as a butcher's dog . . . as cross as a child denied a sugarplum.

He can make more cutting remarks than a tax examiner.

He's a very determined person. When he puts his foot down, someone is invariably under it.

One of these days he'll really lose his head, and the chances are he'll never miss it.

To a guy with a sour puss like his, you don't say "Good morning"; you say "Unhappy days."

He's as uncompromising as a policeman's club.

He should have been an auctioneer—he looks forbidding.

He's been peevish ever since as a boy he crawled under a tent to see the circus, and found it was a revival meeting.

He's so technical, if you should sneeze at a board meeting and someone said "Gesundheit," he'd put it to a vote.

She's all right in her own way—but she always wants it.

She has the kind of intuition that enables her to put two and two together and come up with an answer that suits her.

She claims to be positive, but she's just wrong at the top of her voice.

The only time she'll listen to an argument is when it's by her next-door neighbors.

First thing in the morning she brushes her teeth and sharpens her tongue.

She belongs to the meddle classes.

She thinks marriage is a good investment if, as a mother-in-law, she puts her two cents in.

He entertains new thoughts as if they were his in-laws.

He pays you a compliment like he expected a receipt.

He reminds you of a crocodile; when he opens his mouth, you don't know whether he's trying to smile or getting ready to chew you up.

Whatever is eating him must be suffering from indigestion.

He has a unique talent for invading an issue.

They call him "Sliver" because he's always getting under everyone's skin.

If he's ever forced to eat his own words, he'll have an acute case of indigestion.

He's always as sore as a porcupine with ingrown quills.

He's as tranquil as a Texas cyclone.

He's temperamental—90 per cent temper and 10 per cent mental.

He's a very sneer-sighted person.

When he wants your opinion, he gives it to you.

He's always sticking his No's in other people's business.

He's running a large-scale operation with a small-scale mind.

When he weighs facts, he's sure to have his thumbs on the scale.

There's an explanation for his disposition—he must have sized himself up recently and gotten awfully sore about it.

When he became the department head, they replaced the office sign reading "Smile" with a new one reading "Smile Anyway."

The way he barks at you, you'd think you were his old father or mother.

He doesn't pull his own weight as much as he throws it around.

His idea of stimulating sales is to stick pins into his salesmen instead of into the maps.

His idea of efficiency is placing signs all over the office: "Remember, you can be replaced by a button."

He doesn't hold an opinion—it holds him.

He won't even listen to both sides of a phonograph record.

He's generous to a fault—when it's his own.

The trouble with him is that someone once told him to be himself.

The more his teeth drop out, the more biting he gets.

He'd find faults even in Paradise.

The less he knows, the more stubbornly he knows it.

The narrower his mind, the broader his statements.

He's a genius at arguing about things he doesn't understand.

The only time he listens to reason is to gain time for a rebuttal.

He's not feeling so well. Something he agreed with is eating him.

He's one of those cynics who thinks the world never changes —just short-changes.

You have as much chance of winning an argument with him as with an umpire.

When he was seven, he found there was no Santa Claus and he's been cynical ever since.

He thinks twice before he speaks, so that he can say something nastier than if he spoke right out.

He thinks he's broad-minded, but he's really thick-headed.

He's always giving you a piece of his mind, and he can least afford it.

You often wonder whether the chip is on his shoulder or in his head—or both.

He must have gotten up on the wrong side of the floor this morning.

They call him "the Compositor"—he has such set ways.

The hardest thing he finds to give is in.

He's as stimulating as a hearse . . . as a graveyard on a wet Sunday . . . as a squeezed lemon . . . as a subpoena.

He has an even disposition—always waspish, cross, crusty, and crabbed.

He's leading his staff such a rat race, they're on a strike for more cheese.

Cream Puffs

He wouldn't even open an oyster without first knocking on the shell.

He's a regular Rock of Jello.

Once he makes up his mind, he's full of indecision.

He does everything the herd way.

He's not a Yes-man. When the boss says No, he says No.

With him, necessity is the mother of tension.

He's so nervous, he keeps coffee awake.

He's never been married—he's just a self-made mouse.

His trouble is too much bone in the head and not enough in the back.

He's living in the present—tense.

He's so tense, his office furniture is overwrought iron.

He's as spineless as a chocolate eclair.

After they made him, they broke the jelly mold.

He's as nervous as a cat up a tree.

He won't wear contact lenses. What would he put on in case a fight started?

He has as much guts as a skeleton.

They call him "Jigsaw." Every time he's faced with a problem, he goes to pieces.

He's so indecisive, when his psychiatrist asked him if he had trouble making up his mind, he answered, "Yes and no."

He works so hard because he's too nervous to steal.

These smoking reports are making him so nervous, he's smoking twice as much.

He reminds you of a weathercock that turns with every wind.

He's in constant fear his last breath will be a hiccough, and he won't be able to say "Excuse me."

He's always on the fence to avoid giving offense.

What he needs more than his intercom system is an inner calm system.

Brave? He'll go into the morgue and offer to lick any man in the house.

Once while hunting in Africa he bagged a lion—he bagged and bagged him to please go away.

He's just found a job that takes a lot of guts—he strings tennis racquets.

He never takes tranquilizers—if he's not tense, he's nervous.

He always stoops to concur.

His ulcers are not from what he eats, but what's eating him.

He's the real decisive type—he'll always give you a definite maybe.

Whenever he feels like disagreeing with the boss, he first looks at both sides—his side and the outside.

His psychiatrist just told him, "You haven't got an inferiority complex—you are inferior."

He has a lot of courage—to bear the misfortunes of others.

He's so timid, he tells an elevator operator, "The 22nd floor, please, if it won't take you out of your way."

He's as nervous as a diner watching the chef handling a racing form.

He's so nervous, he twangs in a high wind.

They call him "Serutan" because he's so backward.

He has a unique talent for making difficulties out of opportunities.

His final decision seldom tallies with the one immediately following it.

He's so indecisive, he has a seven-year-old son he hasn't named yet.

He's as jumpy as a kangaroo, as fidgety as an old maid, and as pliable as wax.

He bows and scrapes like a windshield wiper.

He gives his conscience a lot of credit that belongs to his cold feet.

He's a man of conviction—after he knows what his wife thinks.

Dressed and Undressed

Her gowns are cut to see level.

Give her an inch and she'll soon wear it for a dress.

She wears a $200 gown, but her heart isn't in it.

In choosing her evening gowns, she goes practically all out.

She wears too much of not enough.

She has reached success by attireless effort.

The way she wears clothes, she can't even hide her embarrassment.

Her clothes are based on the assumption that men find a woman least wearing when she wears least.

She wears peek-a-bosom gowns.

She dresses to be seen in the best places.

She wears the kind of dresses that start late and end early.

Her evening gowns are real confusing. You can't decide whether she's on the inside trying to get out, or on the outside trying to get in.

She shows more of a lot of woman than a lot of style.

She wears Texas dresses—with those wide, open spaces.

The way her neckline keeps going down and her hemline keeps going up, the fellows are all hanging around; they want to be there when both ends meet.

She looks as if she was poured into her dress and forgot to say when.

She's a moron with less on.

She's Vogue on the outside and vague on the inside.

She wears atom-bomb dresses—a 50 per cent fall-out.

The way she dresses, every day is the dawn of a nude day for her.

She's fast gaining a reputation for being the less-dressed woman in town.

She wears the kind of gown that is more gone than gown.

She wears so little, farmers want to hire her to shock their grain.

Her clothes are designed not so much to make her look good as to make men look good.

She's dressed like she's fleeing from a burning building.

She wears unmentionables—nothing to speak of.

With those low-cut dresses, it doesn't take much talking on her part to pour her heart out.

She wears more clothes when she goes to bed than when she goes out evenings.

Her clothes fit her—like a convulsion.

Her neckline is so low, you can't tell whether her dress is slipping or she's coming up.

Her clothes are like barbed wire—they protect the property without obstructing the view.

The only time she has something on is when she dresses a wound, or has a coat on her tongue.

She has no more on her body than on her mind.

She made it to the top because her clothes didn't.

Just one false move she'll make in that dress—and the boys will appreciate it.

That strapless gown can never, never survive the next samba.

Her dresses are like racing cars—they hold fast going around the curves.

It would do her some good, once in awhile, to stop, look, and loosen.

She dresses like a bad photograph—overdeveloped and over-exposed.

She's either suffering from clothestrophobia, or she likes life in the raw.

She's penny-wise and gowned foolish.

She's looking for the impossible—a fashion designer who can make a dress both fitting and proper.

She looks as if her clothes were thrown on her with a pitchfork.

She's a regular clotheshorse. When she puts on her clothes, she looks like a horse.

Her wardrobe ensemble is in a clash by itself.

She's not just dressed—she's upholstered.

Nothing is harder on her clothes than another woman's.

She has absolutely nothing to wear, and three closets to keep it in.

Her entire conversation consists of who, what, when, and wear.

She's always at the beach trying to outstrip the other girls.

She goes to the seashore, where she puts on a bikini and takes off her brains.

She goes to the beach with a baiting suit.

She wears two bandanas and an unworried look.

She wears the kind of bikini that's based on the theory that nothing succeeds like nothing.

Her bathing suit is designed to enable her to clink or swim.

A moth would have to be on a strict diet to eat her bathing suit.

She's a living example of a stern reality—a plump dame in shorts.

She wears clinging dresses. The ones she's wearing have been clinging to her for years.

That's a nice dress she's wearing. Her friends wonder if the style will ever come back.

She never follows a new fashion unless it's impractical, uncomfortable, and unbecoming.

She has a passion for clothes, none of which return her affection.

If that's mink she's wearing, some rabbit must be living under an assumed name.

She dresses in season—like an Easter egg or a Christmas tree.

Her hat looks as if it had made a forced landing on her head.

With those silly hats she wears, it's obvious she's the one who wears the plants in the family.

She says that whenever she's down in the dumps she gets a new hat. Obviously that's where she gets them.

She looks as bedraggled as a pigeon who got caught in a badminton game.

She's as up to date as a 1940 calendar.

She dresses to please, and it doesn't take much to please her.

Her slacks are so tight, she has to carry her handkerchief in her mouth.

She's interested in clothes—too bad she's not interesting in them.

As the first duck said to the second duck, "Stop walking like that dame wearing slacks."

She's in her salad days—but she's not very particular about her dressing.

She's dressed like an unmade bed.

She must be wearing those clothes to pay off an election bet.

Her clothes look as though she'd dressed in front of an airplane propeller.

She has a suit for every day in the month—the one she has on.

There's something that won't go with that loud dress of hers—her husband.

She's as seedy as a raspberry.

Her friends hadn't seen her for four years. If it wasn't for her dress they never would have recognized her.

Dumbbells

The closest he'll ever come to a brainstorm is a light drizzle.

Brains aren't everything. In fact, in her case they're nothing.

They've named a town after him—Marblehead, Massachusetts.

He's going to the hospital for a minor operation—they're putting a brain in.

The only thing that can stay in his head more than an hour is a cold.

He doesn't dare be lost in thought. He's a total stranger there.

When she says "Hello," she tells you all she knows.

If he said what he thought, he'd be speechless.

She has no more on her mind than anywhere else.

He spends half his time trying to be witty. You might say he's a half-wit.

They call her "Sanka" because she has no active ingredient in the bean.

It takes her an hour to cook Minute rice.

He'd have to climb Mt. Everest to reach a deep thought.

Every time he gets into a taxi, the driver keeps the "Vacant" sign up.

He lost his mind when a butterfly kicked him in the head.

He's an M.D.—Mentally Deficient.

He's just gotten an idea. He should be real kind to it—it's a long way from home.

A demitasse would fit his head like a sombrero.

Too bad they don't sell toupees with brains in them.

He goes to a chiropodist for psychoanalysis—his brains are in his feet.

His brain is like a politician's speech—mostly empty.

The only reason he manages to keep his head above water is that wood floats.

He can detect a rattle in his car quicker than one in his head.

The only way he'll lose a lot of fat is to cut his head off.

She was hurt while taking a milk bath. The cow slipped and fell on her head.

He's such a blockhead, he gets a sliver in his fingers every time he scratches his head.

He has a brain—but it hasn't reached his head.

He was born stupid, and lately he's had a relapse.

He's brighter than he looks—but then, he'd just have to be.

He couldn't count up to twenty without taking his shoes off.

He's full of brotherly love. He always stops anyone who's beating a donkey.

He has a lot of backbone. The trouble is, the bone is all on the top.

Scientists are studying how long a man can live without brains. They're checking his age.

He claims he just got a bright idea—beginner's luck!

Dieting won't help him—no diet will reduce a fathead.

He may talk like a fool and act like a fool. But don't get the wrong idea about him—he *is* a fool.

He's the living proof of reincarnation. No one could be as dumb as he in one lifetime.

Everything that's said to her goes into one ear and out the other—there's nothing to block traffic.

He'd have to step out of his mind to get an idea.

Everything about her is open—an open mind with a vacant stare.

The last time he stuck his head out of his basement door, they started a hockey game.

He was so excited when he was promoted from the sixth to the seventh grade, he could hardly shave without cutting himself.

She has a soft heart, and a head to match.

At school he had underwater marks—below C level.

He has a photographic mind, but nothing develops.

What he lacks in intelligence he makes up in stupidity.

He has a mind like a defective parachute—it doesn't open when it should.

Everyone keeps telling him to put his best foot forward. The trouble is, he doesn't know which one it is.

He always stops to think. The trouble is, he forgets to start again.

If they ever put a price on his head, he should take it.

She's more concerned with what's on her head than what's in it.

He's a fugitive from a brain gang.

He's just as smart as he can be—unfortunately.

He can never seem to make up what little mind he has left.

He's a man of rare intelligence—it's rare when he shows any.

He's like a blotter—takes it all in but gets it backwards.

He would do well to follow the example of his head and come to the point.

He's a gross ignoramus—144 times worse than an ordinary ignoramus.

He goes through life believing everything; it saves him from thinking.

He says he's going to give up working and live by his wits. Well, half a living is better than none.

Noises in his head never keep him awake. You can't transmit sound through a vacuum.

Every time there's fire in his eyes it's quenched by the water on his brain.

His mind wanders, and he just goes along.

He's a simple man of the people—in fact, the simplest.

He has been educated beyond his intelligence.

Poor guy, in a battle of wits he's completely unarmed.

It's not that he hasn't presence of mind; his trouble is absence of thought.

He's got brains, but they're in dead storage.

It looks like he'll never be too old to learn new ways of being stupid.

On a recent aptitude test, he not only had every answer wrong —he even misspelled his name.

The only fast way he'll ever broaden his mind is to put it under a train.

He's nobody's fool. Poor guy, he couldn't get anyone to adopt him.

He speaks straight from the shoulder. Too bad his remarks don't start higher up.

The breakfast room of a honeymoon hotel isn't as vacant as his head.

She has a heart of gold and a brain of pure meringue.

He isn't a chip off the old block—he's the old block itself.

The programs she watches on TV are a vidiot's delight.

She's even stuck for an answer when someone says "Hello."

Offer him a penny for his thoughts and you're more than liberal.

It's a mystery how his head grew without any nourishment.

He's like an old stove—big belly and no head.

They're trying to find a job for him one step below automation.

He has most situations right in the hollow of his head.

She has a 40 bust and an I.Q. to match.

If there's an idea in his head, it's in solitary confinement.

When he was in the eighth grade he wasn't at all like any of the other kids—maybe that was because he was eighteen.

He was in one class so long, the other pupils used to bring him apples thinking he was the teacher.

At college he was a halfback and away back in his studies. His college education was only pigskin deep.

There's a fable about an ass disguising himself with a lion's skin, but his college did it for him with a sheepskin.

His dad backed his college education with thousands of dollars, and all he got was a quarterback.

He went to college to develop his mind—too bad he's never used it.

He's so gullible, he buys a hair restorer from a bald barber.

He's the exception to the rule that man is the only animal that can't be skinned more than once.

For him, especially, someone should invent a Sucker Fountain Pen—one that runs dry when it comes to signing on the dotted line.

He's as blank as an empty bottle, as dizzy as a goose, and as stupid as a coot.

It takes real talent to be as dumb as he is.

He says he's changed his mind. Too bad his new mind doesn't work any better than the old one.

She's got a terrific stairway, but not much upstairs.

If you want to point out a concrete example, ask him to remove his hat.

He's not exactly dumb, but he was fourteen years old before he could wave goodbye.

If he has a cold or something in his head, it's a cold.

He has an ironclad defense against the impact of new ideas—stupidity.

He kept learning more and more about less and less, until now he knows everything about nothing.

He won't submit to an operation for the removal of excess fat. He refuses to have himself beheaded.

He reminds you in a way of the Beatles—he doesn't have a forehead.

He's at his wit's end, and it hasn't taken him long to get there.

There's one thing you can say for him. He's come a long way —for a nincompoop.

The job interviewer said to him, "Yes, we do have an opening for you—and don't slam the door on your way out."

He was born dumb, and it's amazing how he's expanded his birthright.

He wears blue ties to match his blue eyes, and soft hats to match his head.

The way he plays the market, he's neither a bull nor a bear —just a jackass.

He has a successful substitute for lack of brains—silence.

He comes from a long line of real estate people—they're a vacant lot.

His biggest stumbling block is the one under his hat.

Light travels at the rate of 186,000 miles per second, and it hasn't yet reached his mind.

Whoever said it's impossible to underrate human intelligence must have had him in mind.

They use him as a mold for making dumbbells.

He kept his mouth shut and everyone thought him a nincompoop; then he opened it and removed all doubt.

If he had a little more sense he'd be a half-wit.

He has just taken an aptitude test. Good thing he owns the company.

Anyone can be lost in a fog, but he creates his own.

Human intelligence is said by scientists to be half a million years old. In his case, it still isn't large enough for its age.

She called the Fidelity Insurance Company to have her husband's fidelity insured.

He returned a Louis XIV bed because it was too small, and asked for a Louis XV.

He broke a mirror to be sure he'd live another seven years.

He took out blanket insurance because he smokes in bed.

He won't buy a fall-out shelter now. He says he'll wait and buy a used one later.

She added a TV aerial to her washing machine to get cleaner reception.

He put a cake of ice in front of his safe so burglars would get cold feet.

She was asked what she thought of Red China and she said, "It's all right as long as it doesn't clash with the tablecloth."

She thought she was pregnant, so she swallowed some blank film so nothing would develop.

He'd stick his head in an oven to get a baked bean.

She's been cooking the chicken two days because the cookbook said to cook one half-hour to the pound and she weighs 110 pounds.

She was asked if she liked Kipling and she answered, "I don't know—I've never kippled."

He takes off his coat when he weighs himself—and holds it on his arm to get his correct weight.

The preacher told him to spread some sunshine at every opportunity, so he's going around with a sun lamp.

All he knows about nitrates is that they're cheaper than day rates.

He's been working on an invention—crossing a rabbit with a piece of lead to get a repeating pencil.

He's running around a cracker box because it's wrapping reads: "Tear around the top."

They tell her she has a silly puss and she insists she doesn't have a crazy cat.

He's looking around for a round mailbox so he can post a circular letter.

He dips his finger in the glass first to make sure he's got a soft drink.

He boasts that his kid can already say "Dada"—and he's only eight years old.

People told him they'd like to see some change in him, so he swallowed five pennies.

She called the Community Chest for an appointment to have her chest examined.

He bought a truck farm because he heard there's a lot of money in selling trucks.

He thought his wife had stopped smoking cigarettes because he found cigar butts around the house.

She lists her hats as deductible expenses on her tax returns because they "are overhead."

He listed their unborn baby on his tax report because it was part of last year's work.

He heard that the dollar's value is decreasing and the price of bread is going up, so he saves bread.

He followed a wagon-sprinkler down the street for a mile to tell the driver his wagon was leaking.

She got rid of her refrigerator because it was too much trouble to cut ice into those little squares to fit into the trays.

Watching the toe dancers at a ballet, he wanted to know why they didn't get taller girls.

A fellow told her she'd learn to love him in time, so she's keeping his picture in her watch.

He went to the movies to see "The Desert" and asked for two tickets in the shade.

He won't buy insurance, because his dad had a $50,000 insurance policy and it didn't do him any good—he died anyway.

She was going abroad, and when she went to her doctor for shots, she slapped him when he asked to see her itinerary.

He won't buy an electric toothbrush because he doesn't know whether his teeth are A.C. or D.C.

He found a derby in his apartment and sued for divorce on the ground that he couldn't live with a woman who wears a derby.

He puts starch in his cocktails so that he can have a good stiff drink.

When he heard of short-wave reception, he bought a midget radio.

He went to a nudist camp for a game of strip poker.

He went to a nudist camp to sell subscriptions to a fashion magazine.

He wanted to raise a litter of puppies, so he planted a piece of dogwood.

He took the car out in a rainstorm because it was a driving rain.

She thinks the Ford Foundation is a new kind of girdle.

He tried to buy the hat-check concession in an Orthodox synagogue.

She was insulted because a fellow asked her if she was familiar with *Gray's Anatomy*.

He went to the zoo to see what a Christmas seal looks like.

He didn't stay for the second act of the play because it said on the program: "Act 2, two weeks later."

He left the theater at the end of the second act because the program read: "Act 3: same as Act 2."

He looked for a get-well card in the German language because his friend had German measles.

He doesn't see the need to buy toothpaste because his teeth aren't loose.

She brought her cosmetics for a make-up exam.

He applied for insurance because if his hair fell out, the policy would cover his head.

He sleeps at the edge of the bed so that he can drop right off.

He won't buy Webster's Dictionary until they make it into a movie.

He rejected a nose insurance policy because it wasn't printed on Kleenex.

If someone lifts his coffee cup and says "*Skoal*," he says, "No, it's hot."

He stayed on the phone an hour trying to get "Established 1894."

He had a pair of bloomers tatooed on his chest because he always wanted a chest with drawers.

She told her children they could watch the solar eclipse but not to get too close.

He's afraid to eat an apple because he heard his uncle died of "appleplexy."

Besides being so dumb, he's also a tightwad and a woman-chaser, so he went to Reno because he heard it's a place where women are made free.

She's so dumbly superstitious she turned down a marriage proposal because she was reading *The Birth of a Nation* at the time.

He stands in front of the mirror with his eyes closed to see what he looks like when he's asleep.

He keeps looking down all the time because his doctor told him to watch his stomach.

His bride had to postpone the honeymoon so she could explain to him what it was.

He stuffs his mattress with billiard balls so he can roll out of bed.

He takes a pint to bed with him so he can sleep tight.

Passing through customs, he was asked if he had any pornographic literature, and he said, "I haven't even got a pornograph."

Entertainers

His performance has to be seen and heard to be depreciated.

She acts with as much feeling as a fresh-frozen stalk of asparagus.

He comes from a family with a turn for music—they were organ-grinders.

He should be given mustard gas—it goes good with ham.

He's such a ham, no wonder he's critics' meat.

He's living from ham to mouth.

The entire audience was hissing him, except one man. He was applauding the hissing.

She's a promising singer—she should promise to stop singing.

She has a nice voice. In time it may reach her throat.

Her voice is like a drowned seaman—it dies at C.

Her rendition was a howling success.

Instead of singing "The Road to Mandalay," he should have taken it.

He gave a very moving performance—everyone moved to the nearest exit.

Her singing was mutiny on the high C's.

She claims she insured her voice for $100,000. It would be interesting to know what she did with the money.

The audience called for him after his performance; and if it hadn't been for the riot squad they would have gotten him.

He gave the same performance five nights running—he wouldn't dare giving it standing still.

His audience was with him all the way—no matter how fast he ran, he couldn't shake them.

She's a straight actress—36-36-36.

His audience was real polite—they covered their mouths when they yawned.

He's a mastoid of ceremonies—a pain in the neck.

What a comedian! When he performs, the nightclub waives the amusement tax.

What an ad libber! He couldn't even have an argument with anyone without a TelePrompTer.

He was a pioneer on radio. He was the first to be turned off.

He's an M.C. all right—a Mental Case.

She has a singular voice. Good thing it isn't plural.

The way she hits that high C, it sounds as though the high C hits back.

With a voice like hers, if she sang in a cage full of lions, the ASPCA would get after her.

He put his heart and soul into the rendition. Too bad he couldn't put a little music into it too.

She has a nice voice. She ought to cultivate it—and then plant potatoes in it.

He played Macbeth. Macbeth lost.

Her performance underwhelmed the audience.

The only reason he wasn't hissed is that the audience couldn't yawn and hiss at the same time.

She claims singing warms the blood. Hers makes ours boil.

There's only one explanation for that voice—he gargles with ground glass.

In his last appearance at a theater he drew a line three blocks long, but they took his chalk away.

He developed his singing in the bathtub. Maybe he should take more baths.

As a comedian, he couldn't get a laugh out of a laughing hyena.

You don't dare call for an encore—he might call your bluff.

The only explanation for his being an actor is that he likes to sleep late.

After his performance the audience shouted, "Fine! Fine!"— and darned if he didn't have to pay it.

He has discontinued singing on account of his throat. His audiences have threatened to cut it.

What a ventriloquist! His dummy is quitting him to find a new partner.

As an orchestra conductor, he doesn't know his brass from his oboe.

His audiences are glued to their seats. One of these days he'll run out of mucilage.

If the rumor has any foundation, she was made for the part.

She has no talent for acting but she's too famous to give it up.

She insists she's an artist. Her considerate friends are keeping her secret.

As a nightclub singer, she's worth watching. Too bad she's not worth listening to.

After the final curtain, he held hands with the rest of the cast for fear if they broke loose, one of them would have to take the consequences.

He belongs to a five-piece band—they know only five pieces.

He gives the kind of performance that gives failure a bad name.

His repertoire needs scissors and taste.

Her performance had a happy ending—the curtain finally rang down.

His nightclub act starts at 11:30 sharp and ends at 12:30 dull.

There are said to be only twelve basic jokes. Listening to him, you wonder what happened to the other eleven.

He says he dreams his material—how he must dread going to bed.

He hasn't had a role in three years, but he can't give up acting because it's his living.

With the advent of television, an entire new field of unemployment opened up for him.

Failures

He had a forward spring—and an early fall.

When opportunity knocked at his front door, he was out in the backyard looking for four-leaf clovers.

He has both feet firmly planted in the air.

He has spent his whole life in the development of one part of his body—the wishbone.

He's a jack-of-all-trades, and out of work in all of them.

He has a B.A., an M.A., and a Ph.D., but no J.O.B.

He has always followed the path of least persistence.

He goes through life pushing doors marked "Pull."

When he was young he was determined to climb the ladder of success. He's not so successful, but, boy! can he climb ladders!

He has risen from obscurity and is headed for oblivion.

Years ago he was an unknown failure—now he's a known failure.

He lacks only three things to get to the top: talent, ambition, and initiative.

He has a fat chance to succeed, and a head to match.

He's like a pin without a head—always getting into things beyond his depth.

He's on the right track, but he's getting run over sitting there.

He has more pipe dreams than an organist.

He's very responsible. No matter what goes wrong, he's always responsible.

The way he manages his money—confidentially, it shrinks.

He's broke more often than a New Year's resolution.

He's as broke as a pickpocket at a nudist camp.

Everyone calls him the "Archeologist" because his career lies in ruins.

He's going to the dogs faster than a flea.

He gives failure a bad name.

Some day he's going to find himself—and will he be disillusioned!

His trouble is in trying to run large-scale operations with a small-scale mind.

He's always undertaking vast projects with half-vast ideas.

He always blew his own horn so much, it didn't leave him any wind for climbing.

He's all sail and no anchor.

He's a human dynamo who got short-circuited along the way.

He never makes the same mistake twice. Every day he finds some new mistakes to make.

The only way he'll ever get up in the world is in an airplane.

His mother told him that when he grew up, he would come out on top, and she was right—he's bald-headed.

He has something to fall back on, and it won't be long before he lands on it.

He started business on a shoestring and took a lacing.

If a pickpocket went through his pockets, all he would get is exercise.

He was too busy learning the tricks of the trade to learn the trade.

He has a rare gift of instant decision that's heading his firm for bankruptcy.

Two big firms are fighting for his services. The loser gets him.

He's as necessary as a fence around a cemetery.

His furniture is Early American, but it looks more like Late Depression.

He's been dispossessed so many times, he has drapes to match the sidewalk.

Everyone calls him "Arch" because he always needs support.

He's in a hole more often than a gravedigger.

He's always kept his nose to the grindstone, and today he's famous. He's the only person who can cut a steak with his nose.

He's on a merry-go-round—the way of the whirled.

He would have cooked his goose long ago if he had a pot.

Care isn't killing him—it's don't care.

He not only starts things he can't finish; he starts things he can't even begin.

His business is doing as well as a hat-check concession in a nudist colony.

The only way he'll ever make piles of money is to become a bank teller.

He has a difficulty for every solution.

He tried for a corner on the market—now he has a market on the corner.

Everyone speaks highly of him. They say he's perfect—a perfect nonentity.

He has a Phi Beta Kappa key on his watch chain—but no watch.

His business is looking up—it's flat on its back.

He started at the bottom—and stayed there.

He was born with a silver spoon, but never made a stir with it.

He started out with some money and brains, but all he used was the money.

A successful man is game—he's everybody's game.

The only way he'll ever make a name for himself is as a forger.

He's always itching for money, but never scratching for it.

He has as much chance to get anywhere as a guy with a wooden leg in a forest fire.

He bought a retirement policy from his brother-in-law. He kept up his payments for twenty years and his brother-in-law retired.

They call him "Jigsaw." Every time he's faced with a problem, he goes to pieces.

He can always be counted on to hit the nail squarely on the thumb.

The only thing he's ever achieved on his own is dandruff.

He's an early bird who never catches the worm.

He left his home town to set the world on fire. He's going back now for more matches.

He's like a cow that goes dry—udder failure.

They want to pay him what he's worth, but he won't work that cheap.

He left his job because of illness and fatigue—his boss got sick and tired of him.

He was fired with enthusiasm because he wasn't fired with enthusiasm.

He's very well-rounded—too bad he isn't pointed in any direction.

Financially, he's as flat as a rubber doormat.

If he quit work today, he'd have enough to live on for the rest of his life if he died tomorrow.

He's a genius—he can do almost anything except make a living.

He's sliding down the ladder of success so fast, he's getting splinters on his backside.

He's the bustling, rushing, hurrying kind who has never stood still long enough to give life a chance to rub a little sense into him.

The only time he's sure where he's going is when he takes castor oil.

He's always down on something he's not up to—and there's plenty he's not up to.

He had to quit the prize ring because of bad hands—the referee kept stepping on them.

He was knocked out so often, he sold advertising space on the soles of his shoes.

He failed as a druggist—always made his chicken salads too salty.

He's as useful as a pin that has lost its head . . . as a bale of hay in a garage . . . as an umbrella to a hippopotamus . . . as a comb to a baldhead . . . as a fan to an Eskimo . . . as an alarm clock on a Sunday morning . . . as a glass eye at a keyhole . . . as a mustard plaster on a wooden leg . . . as a tire pump in a canoe.

Fair-weather Friends

If you have him for a friend you don't need any enemies.

He sticks with his friends until debt do them part.

He sees that you are through when your real friends see you through.

He's always around—when he needs you.

He picks his friends—to pieces.

He always does his best—including his best friends.

His health is endangered when you lend him money—it damages his memory.

In times of trouble he's waiting to catch you—bent over at the right angle.

If he ever needs a friend, he'll have to buy a dog.

He has friends he hasn't even used yet.

He's a close friend—real close when it comes to helping you out with a loan.

He's a very close friend. Too bad he isn't a generous one.

He'll share your lot with you—if it's a good-sized one.

He claims he's the kind of friend who is hard to find. He's harder to lose.

He has neglected his friends in his drive to make a name for himself. He'd be surprised to know the name they have for him.

He hasn't an enemy in the world and none of his friends like him.

A friend who isn't in need is his friend indeed.

He makes friends fast but never makes fast friends.

He just went out to visit all his friends in the city. He should be back in a few minutes.

You're safe when he holds you tenderly by both hands—because you can watch both of his.

He has perfected the surest way to wipe out a friendship—he sponges on it.

He rolls out the carpet for you one day, and pulls it out from under you the next.

He's only interested in the kind of friends whose inferiority he enjoys.

They tried to get him on the "This Is Your Life" program, but had to give it up. They couldn't find a friend.

You can always depend on him—to depend on you.

He has some very good friends. He never stabs them in the back without a twinge of regret.

You'll always find him on the dock whenever any of his friends' ships come in.

He uses his friendships as a drawing account, but he neglects to make deposits.

The only use he has for a friend is to use him.

He's a real fair-weather friend. He'll always lend you his umbrella on a sunny day.

He's one of those guys who is always close to you until you try to touch him.

He remembers what he gives and forgets what he gets.

He only likes you if you dislike the same people that he dislikes.

In your pursuit of happiness don't expect him to run interference for you.

Fallen Angels

She was very grateful when a fellow gave her that fine undie for her birthday—it was her first slip.

She once let her shoulder-strap slip. It was her first undoing.

She was a pert little thing who went out to flirt and came back ex-pert.

She had no horse sense—she didn't know when to say "Neigh."

She had a slight impediment in her speech—she couldn't say No.

It was soft-soap that made her slip.

She worked on a farm as a milkmaid and the boys gave her a bum steer.

She was a lady's personal maid in a wealthy home. She entered via the servant's entrance and came out in a family way.

She went out on a lark and ended up in a bird's nest.

She's charging the stork with something that should be blamed on a lark.

Apparently she never heard of Mason & Dixon or she might have drawn the line some place.

Her parents didn't worry about her until she was out all night one time, and then it was too late.

They call her the "Baseball Girl" because she was thrown out at home.

It was a country romance. It started out with a pint of corn and ended with a full crib.

Her baby is descended from a long line that she listened to.

She won't see a psychiatrist because a couch is a large part of her trouble.

She sowed wild oats hoping in vain for crop failure.

She drew the line at petting, but he was a football hero so she let him cross the line.

She said she'd do most anything for a fur coat, and when she got it she couldn't button it.

She pursued the wrong policy, so now she needs accident insurance.

Her boy friend's car stalled and she didn't.

She's a brainless beauty who is a toy forever.

She's a dumb girl who didn't turn a deaf ear to a blind date.

She tried to brighten things up for a man by sitting in the dark with him.

Every time the boys take her out, they really take her in.

A fellow offered her a couple of drinks in his apartment and she reclined.

She's more to be petted than censured.

She should have followed the advice "No thyself."

She says the baby's father was deaf and dumb, and by the time she spelled "Stop" out on her fingers it was too late.

At school she was voted the girl most likely to concede.

Her grammar is awful—she can't decline.

She's a Hollywood starlet, and she owes everything to the director who made her.

She collected that expensive wardrobe by starting with a little slip.

She's the kind of pushover you can seduce even if you play your cards wrong.

She goes out with football players but still hasn't learned how to intercept passes.

Everyone calls her "Flour" because she's been through the mill.

She's a May bride—she may be pregnant.

Her trouble started when she got into something light for a heavy date.

Her boy friend is called "Pilgrim" because of the way he makes progress with her.

Her father was so surprised when the fellow said he wanted to marry her, the gun fell right out of his hand.

Her trouble is that the fellows take her with a grain of assault.

A fellow invited her into the woods to hear a nightingale, and it turned out to be a lark.

Features

When she comes into a room, the mice jump on chairs.

She walked into a bar one time, and seven guys took the pledge.

She's good-looking in a way—away off.

She could make a good living renting herself out for Halloween parties.

He's dark and handsome. When it's dark, he's handsome.

He should have been born in the Dark Ages. He sure looks awful in the light.

She looks like a professional blind date.

She looks like a million—every year of it.

Some people can live alone and like it, but she lives alone and looks it.

She loves nature—in spite of what it did to her.

Her boy friend drinks ten cups of coffee a day to steady his nerves so he can look at her.

Her name is Alice, because her German parents took one look at her when she was born, and cried, *"Das ist Alles!"*

The day he was born, his father took one look at him, and ran down to the zoo to throw rocks at the stork.

She could make a good living renting herself out to scare people with the hiccoughs.

Before she introduced him to her family, she told them ghost stories so they wouldn't be scared stiff when they saw him.

A Peeping Tom reached in and pulled down her window shade.

He's the kind you have to look at twice. The first time you don't believe it.

As a bathing beauty, she's hardly worth wading for.

She has the kind of charm that rubs off with a damp cloth.

She looks like a dream—in fact, more like a nightmare.

She has Early American features—she looks like a buffalo.

He looks like an accident going somewhere to happen.

She has everything a man would desire, including heft, bulging muscles, and a moustache.

She has long black hair—and wears long gloves to cover it.

He has as much expression as a smoked herring.

She says she's just back from the beauty parlor—was there two hours. Too bad she wasn't waited on.

She's a vision—a real sight.

There's a good reason why she's been overlooked—she's been looked over.

She'd be safe from advances even if she cooked naked in a lumber camp.

She told a cop, "A man is following me. I think he must be crazy." The cop agreed.

He looks like the first husband of a widow.

At her wedding everybody kissed the groom.

She's the type who thinks it's dishonest to look anything but her worst.

The only thing that can ever make her look good is distance.

Once she asked her husband, "Look me right in the face." He answered, "I can't. I've got my own problems."

She's becoming an operating-room nurse because she's better off wearing a mask.

If that isn't her face, how come it looks like it's done up in curlers?

Once, having lost her wrist watch, she accurately advertised: "Lost, wrist watch by a lady with a cracked face."

She's had so many face-lifting jobs, every time she raises her eyebrows, she pulls up her stockings.

She's had her face lifted so many times, it's out of focus.

She's all dressed up and no face to go.

He has a face you don't want to remember and can't forget.

She has a face that looks like it wore out six bodies.

He has a face like a saint—a Saint Bernard.

Her face isn't her fortune—it's her chaperone.

She has a winning smile and a losing face.

He has the kind of a map only Rand McNally could love.

Only an auctioneer would be pleased with her face—it's forbidding.

You can't blame her for lying about her face, now that her face is being truthful about it.

You have a very striking face. How many times have you been struck there?

If I had your face, I'd hire a pickpocket to lift it.

I recall your name all right, but I just can't think of your face.

She has the kind of a face that once seen is never remembered.

She's had her face lifted so many times there's nothing left inside her shoes.

If Moses had seen *his* face, there would have been another commandment.

She looks like she just stepped out of Vogue, and fell flat on her face.

She's not really two-faced. If she had two, why would she be wearing that one?

I never forget a face, but with yours I'll make an exception.

A kind man said to her, "When I look at you, time stands still." What he really meant was that her face would stop a clock.

He has a face that really grows on people. But if it grew on them, they'd chop it off.

Is that your face, or did you block a kick?

At bedtime, her face is as greased as an English Channel swimmer's.

Her photographs do her an injustice—they look like her.

It hasn't helped her to have her face lifted, so she's thinking of lowering her body instead.

Two weeks ago she put mud on her face to improve her looks. It improved her looks so much, she hasn't taken it off yet.

The only way he can get some color in his face is to stick his tongue out.

She packs so much mud on her face at bedtime, her husband would be at home if he was lost in a swamp.

He has a fairly good nose, as noses run.

He can't run for President. They couldn't get his nose on a stamp.

Her nostrils are so big, when you kiss her it's like driving into a two-car garage.

Is that your nose—or are you eating a banana?

He can overlook everything—except his nose.

She has a nice chin, and for her mother that goes double.

She has two chins, going on three.

He could go through life taking it on the chin if he knew which one it was.

He would have been a great violinist, but he couldn't figure out which chin to put the fiddle under.

She has stopped patting herself on the back and started patting herself under the chin.

His lower jaw recedes so much, he has to use his Adam's apple for a chin.

He has so many cavities in his teeth, he talks with an echo.

Her teeth are like pearls—they need stringing.

Her teeth are so far apart, every time she opens her mouth she looks like a picket fence.

He has only three teeth, and one of them he got when he joined the Elks.

She has two beautiful eyes. Too bad they're not mates.

The way she keeps her eyebrows it certainly takes a lot of pluck.

She lost her job as a cook. She's so cockeyed, the folks never knew where their next meal was coming from.

He has watchman's eyes. They both keep watching his nose.

He's a store detective. He's so cross-eyed, nobody knows whom he's watching.

He's so nearsighted, he once lost a bass fiddle in a one-room apartment.

He was turned down for an operator's license on account of nearsightedness—he had his wife along.

He's as nearsighted as a mole.

He sleeps quite comfortably—he has such big pillows under his eyes.

When she cries, the tears from her right eye fall on her left cheek.

She has dyed by her own hand.

They call her "Kitty" because she has dyed nine times.

She's a cross between a brunette and a drugstore.

Some women are blond on their mother's side, some on their father's side, but she's blond on the peroxide.

She's an established bleachhead.

There's one trouble with her upsweep hair-do. It's hard to tell where she swept it up from.

With that hair-do, it's like looking for a noodle in a haystack to find her.

At the movies, they have to ask her to take off her hair.

She has one of those new hair tints—hue-it-yourself.

As a blonde, she's chemistry's greatest contribution to the world.

She's showing her true colors. She hasn't been to the hair-dresser's for three weeks.

Was she embarrassed when she was asked to remove her mask at the masquerade party! She didn't have one on.

Her wrinkles are all where her smiles should have been.

She has enough wrinkles in her face to hold a three-day rain.

She has more wrinkles than a dried plum.

He's a man of polish—mostly around his head.

He combs his hair with a sponge.

He sure has blown his top.

He has less hair to comb, but more face to wash.

It's not that he's bald-headed—he just has a tall face.

Get a load of that head of skin.

He gets less for his money every time he goes to the barber.

His mouth is so big, he can eat a banana sideways.

He has something to snicker at every day—he shaves daily.

He has such a receding chin, he has no trouble eating corn on the cob.

Figures

She's losing her girlish figure and her boyish husband.

She not only has kept her girlish figure—she has doubled it.

She has a Supreme Court figure—no appeal.

She's pretty well reared. She doesn't look so good in front either.

Now that her husband is rich enough to buy her dresses for a fancy figure, she no longer has one.

Not only isn't her face her fortune, but the other parts don't draw interest either.

She doesn't have the figure for a bikini—just the nerve.

She boasts she got that dress for a ridiculous figure. Obviously.

She's far from her old sylph.

Anatomy is something every woman has, but on her it doesn't look so good.

She has a figure like an hourglass. It takes an hour to figure out what it is.

The only way she could cut quite a figure is by sitting down on a broken bottle.

Too bad she isn't as well-formed as she is well-informed.

She's too lazy to watch her figure, so the boys don't either.

The fellows look up to her rather than around.

The only thing that saves her from being figureless is her Adam's apple.

He's in the punk of condition.

He's so anemic, he has to get a transfusion in order to bleed.

He's so anemic, the only way he can get any color in his face is to stick his tongue out.

He's so emaciated, if he were alive he'd be a very sick man.

He can get a $200 advance from any undertaker.

The shape he's in, his insurance agent is demanding his calendar and blotters back.

It's lucky for him he's not a building or he'd be condemned.

With those varicose veins, she could win first prize at a costume party by going as a road map.

He retired after twenty-five years of service—he received a silver ulcer.

I wouldn't say his condition's critical, but I wouldn't advise him to start a magazine serial.

He has such high blood pressure, if it wasn't for his skin he'd be a fountain.

He's the cave-man type—one hug and he caves in.

He's as flabby as a sponge.

He has such a bad case of insomnia, the sheep are picketing him for shorter hours.

He doesn't sleep because of worry—worry about not sleeping.

He suffers from insomnia worse than a bedbug.

Even when he sleeps, he dreams he doesn't.

He's so thin, his muscles look like flea bites on a piece of spaghetti.

She's as thin as a whisper.

He can make a good living doing scarecrow work.

The only thing a sweater does for her is keep her warm.

She's so thin, she could walk through a harp.

He's getting so thin, the watermelon he had tattooed on his chest looks like an olive now.

She's so thin, she can take a bath in a fountain pen.

Every time she yawns, her dress falls down.

She has an income tax figure. The Internal Revenue is after her for not filling out her form.

She's so thin, she doesn't have enough on her to itch.

You have to look at her twice to see her once.

When her husband takes her to a restaurant, the headwaiter asks him to check his umbrella.

A real estate man jilted her because of her unattractive frontage.

They call her "Seven-Eleven" because when she walks you can hear her bones rattle.

She recently swallowed an olive and was rushed to a maternity hospital.

She has to pass a place twice to cast a shadow.

He has an outstanding personality. It's centered in his bay window.

She's a perfect model—for a shipbuilder.

It would do her good to practice girth control.

She has to put on a girdle to get into a kimono.

His opulence is only exceeded by his corpulence.

If he ever gets into an elevator it had better be going down.

He has an easygoing nature. He's too heavy to run and too fat to fight.

He's living way beyond his seams.

The only thing about him that's getting thinner is his hair.

He's so fat, when he falls down he rocks himself to sleep trying to get up.

He used to be spic and span, but now he's more span than spic.

I knew him when he had only one stomach and one chin.

He's too fat to play golf. If he puts the ball where he can hit it, he can't see it, and if he puts it where he can see it, he can't hit it.

The way he eats, no wonder he gets thick to his stomach.

Success has brought him not only poise but avoirdupois.

The lines of her body are the lines of real resistance.

The way she overeats she'll never break the pound barrier.

She can eat anything and never gain a pound—over 175.

She's the living proof that you can't eat your cake and have "It."

She's living in a food's paradise that is fast putting an end to her.

When it comes to her wearing slacks, the end doesn't justify the jeans.

The only way she reigns superior is with her jutting posterior.

The way she's putting on weight, she'll never be her old sylph again.

The trouble with her is she's not sylph-conscious.

With all that food going to waist, she's a real hippochondriac.

It wouldn't hurt her to go to some length to change her width.

The trouble with the bulk of women like her is where it shows.

She keeps forgetting that a moment on the lips is a lifetime on the hips.

She's one of those women who eat too much sweets and have too much seats.

She'll never realize woman's fondest wish—to be weighed and found wanting.

She could help herself more by helping herself to less.

She was recently on a strict diet—all she lost was her temper.

When she wears slacks she reveals stern facts.

She claims she lost five pounds but she should take a look behind her.

Her bathing suits let her swim but not slink.

The photographer couldn't show her most outstanding side. She was sitting on it.

She's enlarging not only her sphere but her circumference.

She sure stretches the truth when she wears those tight ski pants.

Her obesity is a matter of just deserts—only a bulge in a girdled cage.

Her obesity is surplus gone to waist.

Her waistline is definitely of her own chewsing.

She weighs one hundred and plenty.

She's no good at all at counting calories and she has the figure to prove it.

She's one of the five million overweight women. These, of course, are round figures.

All the exercise he ever gets is moving food from the plate to the palate.

His idea of interior decoration is an enormous meal.

He lives by dinner time instead of inner time.

He must be eating army food. Everything he eats goes to the front.

His wife got rid of 235 pounds of ugly fat—she divorced him.

When it comes to food, he's all will and a yard wide.

He has no trouble at all watching his waistline—it's right there in front where he can see it.

On account of his unrestrainable appetite, everyone is having fun at his expanse.

He might lose some weight if he kept his mouth and the refrigerator closed.

His doctor put him on a seven-day diet, but he ate the whole thing in one meal.

He'll eat anything that won't bite first.

The way she indulges explains her bulges, and she can blame the platter as she gets fatter.

That cheese cake she likes so much is fast turning into pound cake.

It's a crime the way she overeats; her girdle is the punishment that fits the crime.

She eats so much, no wonder her shape is like a figure ate.

Her clothes are designed to make her look younger, but she'll never fool a flight of stairs.

She has lost in youth what she has won in weight.

She has a real shady background. She has hips like a beach umbrella.

She has switchboard hips—every line is busy.

She has a figure like a pillow.

He's so fat in shorts, he looks like a chiffonier—a big thing with drawers.

He's so fat, his wife gave him a belt for Christmas and he's using it for a wrist watch.

He's so paunchy, his wife would like him better the more she saw him less.

The only good thing you can say for his obesity is that a great deal of him is having a good time.

Her figure reveals that she could help herself more by helping herself to less.

The only well-rounded thing about her is her figure.

She's like a foreign car—she has all her weight in the rear.

Her figure indicates a need for exercise—like shaking her head from side to side when offered a second helping.

She'd do well to follow that fine slenderizing advice: "Don't chew—eschew."

It would do her good to go to the beach. Last year's bathing suit will induce her to go out of her weigh to be slimmer.

Flat Tires

Some women get orchids—all she gets are forget-me-notes.

Girls return his letters marked "Fourth Class Male."

She hasn't a gent to her name.

She's not fussy. If she can't get a man 6 foot 3, she settles for one 3 foot 6.

She'll never be the center of Ah-traction.

He sent his picture to the Lonely Hearts Club. The reply came back, "We're not that lonely."

He always looks as uncomfortable as a centipede with athlete's foot.

She's so unattractive, when the boss chases her around the desk, he walks.

She's two-thirds married—she's willing and so is her mother.

She's working like a horse to get a groom.

When she swears she's never been kissed, you can't blame her for swearing.

His idea of an exciting night is to turn up his electric blanket.

When he hears a girl singing in the bathtub, he puts his ear to the keyhole.

If he took up burglary, he couldn't even steal a kiss from an old maid.

He could get lost in a crowd of two.

She's studying to be a contortionist so she can sit in her own lap.

The only man she ever had at her feet was a chiropodist.

The only time she's ever squeezed is when she wears tight shoes and girdles.

She's such a wallflower, she comes home wearing the same lipstick she started out with.

After the boys look her over, they overlook her.

She dated him because he was an old flame, but he turned out to be a silly ash.

He's a real Don Juan with women—they *Don Juan* to have anything to do with him.

He's the type who talks astronomy to a luscious blonde on a moonlit night.

He's a real nature lover—he goes into the woods at night without a girl.

The only time he ever raves about nylon stockings is when they're empty.

Until you've met him, you're sure that the largest prune is six inches in diameter.

He has the personality of the back wall of a handball court.

He was the life of the party. This gives you an idea of how dull the party was.

His life is so dull, he actually looks forward to dental appointments.

He's the kind you ask to stay with you when you want to be alone.

He went out for football, because when he was born his parents took one look at him and shouted, "That's the end."

The fellows wind her up but she doesn't spin.

She has as much sex appeal as a bedtime story over the radio.

Her parents warned her that life is full of temptations, but so for no one has tempted her.

She hasn't had mush experience.

She's smart—a regular encyclopedia. One thing she doesn't know —reference books are never taken out.

Life for her has been a hit-or-miss proposition. She doesn't make a hit, so she remains a miss.

She's as lonesome as a bachelor's toothbrush.

She's been engaged to some promising men—too bad they didn't keep their promises.

Landing a man on the moon doesn't worry her nearly as much as landing one right here on earth.

She has decided to be an airline hostess—it's the only job where she can strap a man down.

Oh, the youthlessness of her existence!

She knows all the answers but nobody asks her the question.

If she found a man in her bedroom, she'd give him twenty-four hours to get out.

She could have married any man she pleased. Trouble was, she never pleased one.

Given the choice of a man with brains, money, or appearance, she would unquestionably pick appearance—and the sooner the better.

She's unhappily unmarried.

She went to college for four years—and whom did it get her?

She's an unemployed schoolteacher—she has no class.

She'll die quite happily; she just heard that marriages are made in heaven.

They call her "Dusty" because she's been on the shelf so long.

They call her "Checkers" because she jumps when the boys make a wrong move.

They call her "Lily" because she likes to go out with dead ones.

They call her "Appendix"—if you take her out once, that's enough.

They call her "Poison Ivy" because she's an awful thing to have on your hands.

Goat-Getters

He's a pain in the neck, and some people have even a lower opinion of him.

He thinks the world is against him. What's more, he's right.

The more you think of him the less you think of him.

When you first meet him, you don't like him; but after you get to know him better, you detest him.

When he was born, something terrible happened—he lived.

He's called a big thinker—by people who lisp.

He's a buried treasure. Too bad they dug him up.

When he was a child, his parents almost lost him; but they didn't take him far enough out in the woods.

Everyone has as much use for him as a duck for a life preserver.

He makes you wish birth control could be made retroactive.

He's not only a bachelor—he's a bachelor's son.

There's something about him that definitely attracts women— to other men.

Man is said to be only a little lower than the angels. If he's an example, they'd better start checking on the angels.

Someone once told him to be himself. He couldn't have been given worse advice.

We all spring from monkeys, but he didn't spring far enough.

He descends from the early Boons. His ancestors were Baboons.

He does serve at least one useful purpose in life—as a horrible example.

He lacks only a few more obnoxious traits to be perfect.

It's not the ups and downs in life that bother the average person; it's the jerks—like him.

Lots of people would enjoy working for him—gravediggers, for instance.

He may be a tonic to his family—he's a pill to everyone else.

He acts that way because he's repressed. In his youth, his mother slapped him—because he set fire to his grandmother.

He's mean, selfish, loudmouthed, and uncouth, but in spite of all that, there's something about him that repels you.

He's high-strung, but not nearly high enough.

He was born in the United States. Terrible things happen in other countries too.

His staff threw him a big dinner. Unfortunately, it didn't hit him.

He doesn't have an enemy. All his friends hate him.

He has a fine personality—but not for a human being.

If he ever finds himself out, he's not going to like it.

He has very winning ways—to make himself disliked.

Everyone calls him "Webster." Words can't describe him.

He once asked a girl if she could learn to love a guy like him, and she answered, "Yes, if he isn't too much like you."

It's not his money that counts. People just hate him for himself alone.

It wouldn't do him a bit of good to see himself as others see him. He wouldn't believe it.

He was a premature baby. He was born before his parents were married.

He hasn't been himself lately. Everyone wishes he would stay that way.

His parents never struck him, except in self-defense.

There's nothing wrong with him that reincarnation won't cure.

Even if he spent $1,000 on a halitosis cure, no one would like him anyway.

He's like a male baby bee—a son of a bee.

Someday he's going to go too far, and everyone hopes he'll stay there.

His family and friends don't mind if he smokes. In fact, they don't mind if he burns.

He hasn't many faults, but he sure makes the most of the ones he has.

Everyone has the right to have some faults, but he abuses the privilege.

Nobody has a higher opinion of him than his closest friends; they think he's a first-class louse.

They're speaking well of him lately—he must be dead.

He's just what the doctor ordered—a pill.

If he could only see himself as others see him, he'd never speak to them again.

He's marrying a female X-ray specialist. No one else can see anything in him.

He has one very highly developed instinct—for being obnoxious.

He's not really his own worst enemy—not while anyone who has anything to do with him is still living.

It's useless to ask him to act like a human being. He doesn't do imitations.

He'll improve himself when crows turn white.

He's a genius. He not only takes infinite pains with what he's doing—he gives them.

He hates the human race. That's because he thinks he's as good as anybody, and he's repulsive.

He'll leave everything to his heirs—except regrets.

He once belonged to a fife-and-drum corps. They kicked him out because he was rotten to the corps.

Some day he's going to need a friend, and he's going to find it hard to get one.

He's very fastidious—fast and hideous.

You can always count on him to display his pest manners.

Someone ought to rent him out to a near-sighted knife-thrower.

His country club is having a membership drive next week—they're going to drive him out.

He's so unpopular, he's developing B.O. to attract attention.

Most of his remarks belong in the dead-letter office—they're uncalled for.

At first people don't care much for him; but he grows on them—the little wart.

His folks didn't know the meaning of "quit" until he was born.

He was left $50,000 in the will of a woman he once jilted—a case of real, heartfelt gratitude.

Years pass, but he doesn't—more's the pity.

Life is what you make it—until he comes around and makes it worse.

His mother-in-law calls him "Son," but she never completes the sentence.

Gold Diggers

So far as men are concerned, she can take them or leave them. After she takes them, she leaves them.

She has a million-dollar smile. She only smiles at guys with a million dollars.

Her motto is: "Dough or die."

She buys spring clothes in the middle of the winter for summer romances with fall guys.

The only man she'll go out with is one who is tall, dark, and has some.

Men of means are worth her wiles.

She spells "Matrimony" "Matter-o' money."

The only love nest she's interested in is an eight-room apartment feathered with cash down.

She's always ready to go out for a little fund.

She doesn't mind whose means she lives beyond.

When it comes to men she prefers the strong, solvent type.

It's hard to figure what she would have found attractive about men if she had lived before money was invented.

It's not too difficult to find her. Just open your wallet, and there she is!

She's climbing the ladder of success lad by lad and wrong by wrong.

She's the cream in a guy's coffee as long as he has plenty of sugar.

She's getting alone fine—by lips and bonds.

A guy never knows the worth of her love until she sues him for breach of promise.

Her motto is: Think—Mink!

She's looking for a rich guy to make her dreams come through.

She's a good listener—when money talks.

She may get married someday. She's just waiting for the right amount to come along.

In her estimation, a man doesn't have to be much if he has much.

All she looks for in a man is brown eyes and green money.

She brings out the animal in men—Mink.

What she looks for in a man is fiscal fitness.

She knows how to stay in the mink of condition.

She doesn't believe in love blindfolded—she wants it billfolded.

Her hobby is collecting romantic antiques—rich old geezers.

Men call her "Sugar" and wind up paying her a lump sum.

She meets a wolf at the door and appears next day in a fur coat.

She'll go out with every Tom, Dick, and Harry, provided they bring jack along.

She sure knows how to mine her own business, especially where diamonds are concerned.

A fellow starts out by calling her "Sugar" and winds up a sad saccharine.

She prefers men who have something tender about them—legal tender.

She's looking for a generous man—one she can take to, and from.

She hails from the corn belt, but all she's interested in now is the money belt.

She gets a grand and glorious feeling when a fellow makes love to her—especially a grand.

When money stops talking, she starts walking.

She falls in love at purse sight.

She speaks only in moneysyllables.

Some girls keep their love letters, but she lets the love letters keep her.

The only thing she's ever been taken in by is a girdle.

She takes everything that a guy can buy; then she takes another guy.

A fellow's love letters are her jilt-edge securities.

She's the one exception to the law of gravity. It's easier to pick her up than to drop her.

Some girls frame the first dollar they ever made. She framed the first man.

If you spoon around with her you have to fork over.

She gets her mink by being like a fox and playing cat-and-mouse with a wolf.

She gets her men by using her come-on sense.

She's a vegetarian. She only goes out with men with plenty of lettuce.

She measures a man's love by the carat.

She loves a man for all he's worth—after he passes the assets test.

Whenever she sued for breach of promise she was calm—and collected.

She dresses on credit, but she'll only undress for cash.

She defrauds the males by using them.

A fellow said he would go through anything for her, so she started right off with his bank account.

She's going out with a sugar daddy. He met her thirty-five checks ago.

Her motto is: "Every man for myself."

She may be good for nothing, but she's never bad for nothing.

She has a great talent for womaneuvers.

Her favorite book is Dun and Bradstreet.

She's a human gimme-pig.

When she threatens to tell a guy's wife, the furs really fly.

Her crowning glory is a rich guy's scalp.

She loves everything about America—the people of America, the songs of America, the Bank of America.

When she gives you that baby stare, you're safer in the electric chair.

She's a female wolf in chic clothing.

She's as true as steel—provided it's U. S. Steel.

Her beautiful eyes have put many a man on the blink.

She pulls the wool over men's eyes, by wearing sweaters that pull their eyes over the wool.

It's the little things about a husband that she likes, like small penthouses, small yachts, small racing stables, and small life expectancies.

She's interested in do-re-mi and she's going fa'.

She started out with a full knowledge about the birds and bees —and she learned fast about the minks.

She likes a guy whose conversation sparkles—with things like emeralds, rubies, diamonds, and sapphires.

She sure has the gift of grab.

She never sells herself for cash—she takes checks, stocks, bonds, and shares in oil wells.

Magic is her hobby—like getting mink off an old goat.

Around town they call her "Cinderella"—the fellows have to slipper fifty, slipper a hundred.

She paints the town red with a guy with a bankroll—she gives him the brush when it's gone.

She's one tomato who knows her onions. She knows how to get guys with lots of lettuce.

It doesn't take long to find there's method in her badness.

She once married a guy for money. She divorced him for the same reason.

Once she gets a guy on the spot, she takes him to the cleaners.

She's sure she has the right dope, that her latest boy friend makes $25,000 a year—at least until a better dope comes along.

She worships the ground where her Texas boy friend discovered oil.

She prefers men who go in for the refined things in life—like oil.

It's the thought—not the gift—that counts with her and the bigger it is the more it counts.

She never kisses a man with beer on his breath—it has to be champagne.

She had a hard row to hoe, so she got an old rake to make it easier for her.

She's working at loving—for a living.

She's great at getting not only the seal of a man's approval, but the mink as well.

She doesn't offer much resistance, so she leads a very nice existence.

She even purses her lips when she's kissed.

She's a great after-dinner speaker. When she speaks to a man, she's after a dinner.

She's always trying to break her boy friends of a bad habit— eating alone.

She's looking for a man with a green thumb—green from peeling off hundred-dollar bills.

She always has lots of men on her arm, but none in her heart.

She has been tried and found wanting—everything money can buy her.

After a guy has spent all his dollars, she recovers her sense.

She loves a man for his money up to a certain point—the decimal point.

She doesn't mind men who love her and leave her, provided they leave her enough.

She doesn't mind if a man doesn't fit the bill so long as he foots it.

She knows how to write letters that speed up the males.

She's looking for a rich man who wants to take her away from it all. Then she'll take it all away from him.

Her idea of a steppingstone to success is a 20-carat stone.

Her concern is not so much what a man stands for as what he falls for.

She doesn't look for too much in a man—just someone to spend with the rest of her life.

She met a man who had more money than he knew what to do with. Now she has it—and he's had it.

She knows how to make feminine capital out of masculine interest.

Her men friends think they're being cultivated, but they're being trimmed.

She'll never be happy until she meets John Dough.

She's a human dynamo. She charges everything—to her sugar daddies.

If a guy takes her for two weeks on the sands, he's sure to spend the next fifty weeks on the rocks.

She couldn't decide what to give a guy who had already given her everything, so she gave him the air.

Her resistance at the start is not so much a proof of her virtue as her experience.

She took her last three husbands not for better or worse, but for good.

There isn't a man who can pin anything on her—not made of diamonds, or hang anything on her—not made of pearls.

Gossips

Tell her a secret, and she's sure to chin and bare it.

She's always letting the chat out of the bag.

His business is what's none of his business.

Anything you tell her goes in one ear and over the back fence.

She's a slight-of-tongue artist.

Her gossip is strictly her-say.

She dotes on cocktail parties where sandwiches and acquaintances are cut into little pieces.

She has a tongue that could clip a hedge.

Wind him up and he's sure to run someone down.

She picks up more dirt with the telephone than she does with the vacuum cleaner.

He has passed from his formative to his informative years.

He likes to be first with the worst.

She's known as "Dame Gossip"—and some folks omit the "e."

There are three quick ways of spreading news: telephone, telegraph, and tell-her.

He can sling dirt faster than a gravedigger.

She burns her scandals at both ends.

He's on spiking terms with everyone.

Her tongue is her sword, and she makes sure it never gets rusty.

He's the type of eavesdropper who gets in your hear.

She clucks like a hen over her grains of gossip.

A good description of her would be fair to meddling.

She never repeats gossip—she's always the one who starts it.

She has a keen sense of rumor.

She doesn't know certain people well enough to talk to, but well enough to talk about.

In a beauty parlor, her gossip alone can curl your hair.

She joined a sewing circle—it was the ideal place to needle everyone.

Keeping a secret from her is like trying to sneak daybreak past a rooster.

With her, a rumor goes in one ear, and out through her mouth.

He's an expert in hintimation.

He has more inside information than a surgeon.

They call him "Stretch" because he has an elastic conscience and a rubber neck.

Automobiles don't run down as many people as he does.

Her motto is: "One touch of scandal makes the whole world chin."

She's the vacuum-cleaner type—she purrs and takes in the dirt.

Most of the rumors he spreads are over the sour grapevine.

She listens in haste and repeats at leisure.

She'll gladly listen to both sides of an argument—if it's her neighbors, talking on a party line.

She has a way of saying nothing that leaves practically nothing unsaid.

He'll never tell a lie—when the truth will do more damage.

He thinks he's polished because everything he says casts a reflection on someone.

She has a good memory, and a tongue hung in the middle of it.

She's such a busybody, she had her appendix removed so she could see what it looked like.

She constantly goes to an ear specialist to prevent overhearing trouble.

She can keep a secret—with telling effect.

Her plastic surgeon was able to do everything with her nose except keep it out of other people's business.

She's terrific at putting one and one together—to make talk.

He's a sociologist on a petty scale; he's always pouring social sewerage into people's ears.

He's the knife of the party.

You can always depend on him to give you the benefit of the dirt.

If one half of the world doesn't know how the other half lives, it isn't his fault.

He doesn't knock before he enters your home, but he knocks plenty after he leaves it.

Her tongue hangs out like a pump handle.

She's suffering from acute indiscretion.

She's as inquisitive as an X-ray.

She has the words of a saint and the claws of a cat.

She seldom repeats gossip—the way she heard it.

She always talks about things that she says left her speechless.

She just can't leave bad enough alone.

She's unhappiest when every member of her women's club shows up.

They call her "Olive"—the way she sticks her nose in other people's business.

She detests gossip—but only when it's about herself.

Her acquaintances may not be the best informed people, but they certainly are the most informed.

Her gossip is an ill wind that blows nobody good.

Her tongue is like a pink dart.

Husbands
(Henpecked)

He brags that he's the boss in his home, but he lies about other things too.

She leads a double life—hers and his.

When she wants his opinion, she gives it to him.

He wears the pants in the house—under his apron.

He comes right out and says what she tells him to think.

They are two minds with but a single thought—hers.

He has been married twenty awed years.

Everything he owns is hers—especially his nerve.

He has the courage of her convictions.

He has two chances of winning an argument with her—slim and none.

She has her way when they agree, and he has her way when they disagree.

She doesn't have to raise the roof. All she has to do is raise an eyebrow.

Whenever he has a contented look on his face, she wipes it off with a dish towel.

The only time he opens his mouth is to ask her for the apron and the vacuum cleaner.

He doesn't snore in his sleep—he cackles.

He always has the last word—he says, "I apologize."

She snaps, "Are you a man or a mouse—squeak up!"

He was a man-about-town, but she turned him into a mouse-around-the-house.

The last big decision she let him make was whether to wash or dry.

She tames to be pleased.

She lost her thumb in an accident and sued for $100,000, because it was the thumb she had him under.

She jumps when he speaks—all over him.

He's very cooperative—he washes up when asked and dries up when told.

He's grateful to be living in a free country where a man can do as his wife pleases.

She's his solace, but if it wasn't for her he wouldn't need any solace.

He put a ring on her finger and she put one through his nose.

She always forgives him when she's in the wrong.

He's her altered ego.

She's his booin' companion.

He can't even open his mouth to yawn—she complains it causes a draft.

He married her for her looks, but not the kind he's getting now.

He was a dude before marriage—now he's subdued.

He even has to ask permission to ask permission.

His parakeet gets to talk more than he does.

She even complains about the noise he makes fixing his own breakfast.

They had a big difference of opinion about getting a dishwasher. She says he doesn't need one.

He goes to a woman dentist. It's a relief to be told to open his mouth instead of shut it.

On an application blank asking his marital status, he wrote, "Below wife."

He worships the ground she gives him the run-around on.

He has his will, but she has her way.

He's definitely not a yes-man. When she says No, he says No.

He's a man of strong determination. Whenever he makes up his mind to tell her to do something, *he* does it.

He gave her an inch and now she's the ruler.

They had a very amusing argument recently. When she threw the axe at him, he thought he'd split.

He walks with his head high and erect—he has a stiff neck.

Once he complained, "You're driving me to my grave." In a minute, she had the car in front of the house.

When he's late for dinner, he gets two kinds of meat—hot tongue and cold shoulder.

He should have been warned, when he carried her over the threshold after they were married, that she couldn't wait to put her foot down.

He should have known he was in for it when right after they were married she took charge of the electric blanket controls.

He should have caught wise at the altar. When he said, "I do," she snapped, "No, you don't."

Every once in awhile she comes to him on her bended knees. She dares him to come out from under the bed.

He keeps his teeth in perfect condition—he doesn't argue with her.

He holds his pay envelope up to the light to see if he got a raise.

They've been married five years and she still hasn't told him how much money he's earning.

She instructed his firm's paymaster to mail his check home and eliminate the middleman.

She denies he's henpecked. She sometimes gives him permission to smoke a big black cigar while he washes the dishes.

He spends his evenings solving crossword puzzles—she hands him the cross words.

He never argues with her. He might win—and then he'd really be in trouble.

It's a mutual partnership—he's the mute.

His name is Alexander, but in his home he's Alexander the Great. Whenever the furnace gets low, she hollers, "Alexander! the grate."

She wants to go to the seashore, claiming that mountain air disagrees with her. He can't see how it would dare.

It doesn't take much to make her purr like a kitten. All he has to do is rub her the right way.

Despite the statistics, he denies that married men live longer than single men—it only seems longer.

He says he runs his house like a ship, with him as the captain. The only trouble is, she's the admiral.

It's his second marriage, and now he has a new leash on life.

She's very thoughtful. She asks him what he would like for dinner—then she picks out a restaurant that serves it.

In a restaurant, out of force of habit, she makes him help the waiter with the dishes.

When she suggests going out to eat, he says forcefully, "We're not going to a restaurant—and that's semifinal."

In their home, she's the chairman of the ways-and-mean-it committee.

He's a very tender husband. No wonder. She always keeps him in hot water.

He's a very agreeable husband—he's always agreeing with her.

He's very forceful—he can make her do anything she wants to do.

He wishes Adam had died with all his ribs in his body.

They always compromise. He admits he's wrong and she forgives him.

The story of his courtship and marriage: He came, he saw, he concurred.

When he asks her to darn his socks, she knits her brow.

She not only wears the pants in the family, she wears the whole suit.

He never knows when he's well off because he never is.

When she takes him to the supermarket, he looks exactly like a man being led to the shopping block.

She always reminds him that he can be replaced, now that machines are being developed that respond to spoken commands.

She uses a very efficient weed-killer in the garden—him.

Their marriage is harmonious so long as he plays second fiddle.

This guy is really henpecked. She even makes him wash and iron his own aprons.

For Easter, she gave him a rabbit punch.

He has a soft spot in his head for her.

The only time she runs her fingers through his hair is when she can't find the towel.

When the traffic cop asked him if he got the number of the hit-and-run driver who had bowled him over, he said, "No, but I'd recognize my wife's laugh anywhere."

It's a perfect love match. He loves her and so does she.

It would be nice if she thought more *of* him than *for* him.

She's made a lasting impression on him. The doctor says the scars will never disappear.

He's the Sovereign, Unconquerable, Supreme, Grand Potentate of his lodge, but he's missed three meetings because she won't let him go.

She telephoned a friend, "I have marvelous news—what a break! My husband had a heart attack and we have to go to Florida for the winter."

He married her to have someone to tell his troubles to, and now he certainly has plenty to talk about.

She's all preaches and scream.

She's a real womanacle.

He's real spousebroken.

Husbands (The Bitter Half)

They were married for better or for worse. He couldn't have done better and she couldn't have done worse.

Whoever said women can't take a joke evidently hasn't seen the specimen she married.

It was love at first sight. She should have wiped her glasses for a good second look.

It must have been love at first sight. If she had taken a second look, she'd have turned and run.

She must have had a real open mind to fall in love with him—a big hole in the head.

It's her second marriage, and now she has a new louse on life.

All she's gotten out of their marriage is bed and boredom.

It's a trial marriage—nothing could be more of a trial.

She has a fine prospect of happiness behind her.

It's not at all true that everyone has a sane spot somewhere—wait till you meet him.

She'll never forget the first time they met, but she's trying hard.

She married him to reform him, and then found that the rites didn't right him and the altar didn't alter him.

122

He was her ideal before marriage—now he's an ordeal.

She married him for his money, and she's earning every dollar of it.

The only reason she's had nine children by him is that she's trying to lose him in a crowd.

Just before his birthday, her friends asked what she was getting for him, and she said, "Make me an offer."

He's made her so nervous she's losing weight, but she won't leave him. She's waiting till he gets her down to 125 pounds.

Their marriage is like baking bread. She's got plenty of dough and he's got plenty of crust.

He married her for her money, and he's giving her everything her money can buy.

He's a go-getter. His wife has a lucrative job, and on payday he makes sure to go get 'er.

He lives by the sweat of his frau.

She married a dreamer, and found he's just a sleeper.

She thought she was getting a model husband—but he's not a working model.

He has a certain something, but she wishes he had something certain.

He isn't a self-starter, so she's become a crank.

She's the driving force in the household, so he bought her a hammer and nails.

He steadies the stepladder for her while she paints the kitchen ceiling.

He likes to mow the lawn in the winter and shovel snow in the summer.

She banks her hard-earned dollars, while he deposits his quarters in an easy chair.

The only exercise he gets is prying frozen ice trays out of the refrigerator.

Although he loafs half the time, she hasn't left him. She feels half a loafer is better than none.

He boasts that he never made a mistake—but he has a wife who did.

She avoids getting up with a grouch—she rises before he does.

When she asks him a question, she has to take a lot for grunted.

He takes his troubles like a man—he blames them on her.

She says he doesn't carry life insurance, just fire insurance— he knows where he's going.

When she accuses him of being a cross, grouchy, ill-mannered brute, he wheedles, "Look, honey, you know no man's perfect."

He needed a wife because sooner or later something was bound to happen that he couldn't blame on the government.

"You say you loved me," she tells him. "If you really did, why didn't you marry someone else?"

The gift she'd appreciate most is something he made himself —like money.

When she asks him for clothes money, he tells her to "go to the best shops and pick some nice things—but don't get caught."

She didn't realize when she sank into his arms, that she would wind up with her arms in the sink.

He promised her a convertible after they were married and he's kept his promise. She's wheeling a baby carriage with the top down.

She wanted a mink coat, so he got her a trap and a gun.

She's demanding a harness. If she works like a horse, she wants to look like a horse.

He treats the money he gives her like horse-radish—he parts with it with tears in his eyes.

He hates to see a woman in cheap clothes—unless, of course, she's his wife.

She bought him underwear initialed B.V.D., and he shot a neighbor whose name was Bernard V. Donaldson.

When he saw the twins for the first time, he insisted that one looked like the milkman and the other like the plumber.

He threatens to divorce her because she said she loved him more than anybody else in the world; that proved to him she was experimenting.

He's studying to be a trapeze artist so he can catch her in the act.

She keeps saying, "Tell me again what a good married life we're having—I keep forgetting."

He's supporting her in the manner to which she was accustomed—he's letting her keep her job.

He called her his cute little dish—now she's his cute little dishwasher.

The doctor says she needs sea air, so he's fanning her with a mackerel.

A fortuneteller told her she'd be a widow soon—that her husband would die by poisoning—and she asked, "Will I be acquitted?"

All she wants is to see his name just once in the obituary column.

He threatened to divorce her once, and she couldn't help shedding a few cheers.

She's leaving her money to charity and her brains to him.

When a neighbor told her she was getting a divorce from the meanest, crossest man in the world, she scoffed, "How can you get a divorce from my husband?"

She refuses to give him a divorce. She says, "I've suffered with the bum for fifteen years, and now I should make him happy?"

He brings home the bacon, but forgets the applesauce.

He forgets his wife's birthdays, but remembers her age.

When she married him, she exchanged the attentions of many men for the inattention of one.

He hasn't paid any attention to her in years, but he'll shoot any man who does.

The only time he shows her any real loving is when he takes her to a drive-in movie and lets her look in other cars.

Once he showed her some attention and it frightened the poor woman half to death.

Once a cyclone ripped their roof off and whirled them a half-mile through the air. It was the first time in years they were out together.

He's a perfect gentleman. When she drops something, he kicks it to where she can pick it up easier.

He's very thoughtful. He holds the door open for her when she staggers in with a load of groceries.

He's very considerate. He hasn't made his garden any bigger because she tires easily.

He's her greatest admirer. He places her on a pedestal—so she can reach the ceiling with her paint-roller.

She's sticking to him through thick and gin.

He has her do her reading in the closet so his sleep won't be disturbed.

As soon as she starts giving her side of an argument, he shuts off his hearing aid.

His timing is perfect—so is his two-timing.

He has circles under his eyes from keeping a triangle under his hat.

He doesn't mind his wife keeping her beauty secrets as long as he can keep his beauties.

Give him enough rope, and he'll be tied up at the office with his blond secretary.

He has found real happiness in marriage—his wife doesn't watch him too closely.

He gave his secretary a fur coat to keep her warm, and then had to give his wife one to keep her cool.

He thought he was pulling the wool over his wife's eyes, but he used the wrong yarn.

He's a homeless individual. Nobody is ever home less than he is.

His wife has two problems—him and the fire. Every time she turns to look at one, the other has gone out.

She married him in the belief that marriage is a union of two souls, but she finds herself hitched to a heel.

She spent the first part of her life looking for a husband; now she's spending the second part wondering where he is.

He's been in love with the same woman for fifteen years. If his wife finds out, she'll kill him.

He has a wife who appeals to his finer side, his loftier instincts, and his better nature—and a mistress who helps him forget them.

As a husband, he's the world's greatest lover—he has five mistresses.

If she ever catches him, the game won't be worth the scandal.

Hypochondriacs

He has an infinite capacity for faking pains.

He wants to have his ache and treat it too.

She always gives you a preamble to her constitution.

When he smells flowers, he looks around for a funeral.

If he finds a feather in his bed, he's sure he has chicken pox.

He always feels like a sick oyster at low tide.

He won't use ice cubes because he can't boil them.

She's always on pills and needles.

He won't kiss his wife unless her lipstick has penicillin in it.

She's always brooding over her health, but never hatches.

He takes so many different-colored sleeping pills, he dreams in Technicolor.

He has taken so many tranquilizers for the butterflies in his stomach, they're playing Ping-pong with them.

He's so afraid of surgery, he won't even read the opening pages of a book.

He always carries a thermometer behind his ear. He even stirs his drinks with it.

He's a stew going to pot.

She's taking drugs that haven't even been written up yet in *Reader's Digest*.

She not only complains of diseases for which there are no known cures, but of some for which there are not even known names.

He won't even talk on the phone to anyone who has a cold.

He's doctoring himself out of medical books. One of these days he's going to die of a misprint.

He's a manic-depressive type—easy glum, easy glow.

He's so full of penicillin, every time he sneezes he cures a dozen people.

She's unhappy because she has no troubles to speak of.

He's like a bus straphanger—he has complaints of long standing.

He'll never die in his sleep—he doesn't sleep that well.

He always feels bad when he feels good for fear he'll feel worse when he feels better.

She eats so much wheat germ to stay healthy that she sways in the breeze.

She calls a doctor when all she wants is an audience.

He collapses at the first twinge, pain, or ache like a dollar umbrella in a storm.

He's so impressionable that if he should come across the same name as his in an obituary column, he'd shoot himself.

She just can't leave being well enough alone.

He's leaving instructions in his will to be buried alongside of a physician.

She never takes a tranquilizer. She gets awfully agitated if she's not high-strung.

He's taken so many green and red pills, they're hiring him to direct the traffic.

She's a real woebegonia.

He has the same effect on you as a wet holiday.

He's as glum as a bankrupt undertaker.

You can never possibly know how she suffers—if you're way out in the woods somewhere, away from telephone, mail, or telegraph.

He can get into a stew faster than an oyster.

She spends most of her life at the complaint counter.

She has such a sour look that when she puts face cream on, it curdles.

His expression is as woebegone as a centipede's with bunions.

He has such a long face, his barber charges him twice as much for shaving him.

With that long puss, she'd be sure to win first prize in a cat show.

She's a misfortuneteller.

Idlers

He's a two-dimensional guy—he has loungitude and lassitude.

The only thing he grows in his garden is tired.

He heard that hard work never killed anybody, but he's taking no chances on being its first victim.

He's not afraid of hard work—he's fought it successfully for years.

He's stopped drinking coffee in the morning because it keeps him awake the rest of the day.

His wife is the power behind the drone.

Regularly every day he does his daily dozing.

He's too lazy to walk in his sleep—he hitchhikes.

He claims he's superstitious—he won't do any work in any week that has a Friday in it.

He puts off until tomorrow everything he has already put off until today.

He has a great laborsaving device—tomorrow.

Every morning he scans the obituary column; if his name isn't there, he goes back to bed.

He always looks forward to the yawn of new days.

131

He gets dizzy spells, which he attributes to his "prostrate" gland.

He complains of a bad case of insomnia—he keeps waking up every few days.

His wife has posted signs that read: "Hunters: Don't shoot anything in these parts that's not moving. It may be my husband."

The only difference between him and the Sphinx is that he moves when the dinner bell rings.

He's having a great life so long as he doesn't waken.

He's the idol of his family. He's been idle for five years.

His idea of roughing it is to turn his electric blanket down to medium.

He's rusting on his laurels.

He has a malady that malingers on.

Nothing is impossible to him—so long as he doesn't have to do it himself.

He needs two desks—one for each foot.

It would be interesting to know what his ambition in life is besides breathing.

He walks in his sleep so he can get his rest and his exercise at the same time.

His motto is: Whatever is worth doing is worth asking somebody to do it."

He does most of his work sitting down—that's where he shines.

When he left his job, his fellow workers got together to give him a little momentum.

He discarded his How-to-Succeed books because they said you have to work for it.

With him, getting up in the morning is a conflict between mind and mattress.

The only things he fixes around the house are Martinis and Manhattans.

He doesn't like gardening because soil rhymes with toil.

He even hires a gardener to take care of his window-box plants.

If he lives long enough, he'll beat Rip van Winkle's record.

He bought a book, How to Conquer Laziness, and has his wife read it to him.

He smokes a clay pipe so that when it falls and breaks he doesn't have to stoop to pick it up.

He even gets winded playing chess.

He doesn't know how long he's been out of work—he can't find his birth certificate.

He's as active as a leftover fly in January.

He's as lively as a galvanized corpse.

There's as much life in him as in a mummy.

He's as torpid as a toad at the bottom of a well.

He's deader than a three-day-old bus transfer.

He's as indolent as an old bachelor.

He's as active as an oyster on the beach in August.

He has a very good background, and he's always leaning on it.

He wakes up in the morning with nothing to do, and goes to bed with it only half done.

Whenever he feels like exercising, he lies down on a couch until the desire passes.

He's always starting to begin to commence to get ready to do something.

He has become so lazy that even loafing is now hard work.

He has the seven-year itch, and he's three years behind in his scratching.

He's college-bred. He made a four-year loaf with his father's dough.

Asked by the census taker whether he was alive, his wife answered: "That's a matter of opinion."

His wife can't say how tall he is. It's been years since she's seen him standing up.

At the altar, he vowed their marriage would be for life. Now his wife wants to know why he doesn't show some.

He sleeps as soundly as a night nurse on duty.

He never puts off until tomorrow what he can put off indefinitely.

His greatest pleasure in life is having lots to do, and not doing it.

He claims he's a victim of mental anguish. Mental languish is more like it.

He does push-ups three times a day—from his big leather chair for meals.

Juvenile Delinquents

He carries a blackjack in his pencil box.

He's playing jacks—Jacks or better to open.

He's playing that nice old game of hopscotch. Only trouble is, he's playing it with real Scotch.

It's not bad enough that he's the toughest kid in the school, but he also has a perfect attendance record.

He's very careful about his health. He smokes only filter-tipped marijuanas.

He would rather steal hub-caps than third base.

His parents give him a free hand, but not in the proper place.

It takes more than understanding for his dad to be a pal to him—it takes stamina.

Instead of being coddled at school, he should be paddled by the Board of Education.

He's a real sadist. He locks the bathroom door on the nights of his grandfather's beer parties.

A good thrashing might get the wild oats out of him.

He's an honor student. He's always saying, "Yes, your Honor," "No, your Honor."

Everything in his home is controlled by switches—except him.

He was a lovable kid. They gave him a sandbox to play in. It should have been filled with quicksand.

He's too young to drive, so he's stealing chauffeured limousines.

He has just joined a union—a teenage mugger's union.

Today's accent may be on youth, but the stress is on the parents.

He has no respect for age unless it's bottled.

He belongs to a gang of boys who are alike in many disrespects.

He'd be smarter if he smarted in the right places.

Liars

He's a man of proven liar-bilities.

He's like a harp struck by lightning—a blasted lyre.

He's a confirmed liar—nothing he says is ever confirmed.

Some people take the bull by the horns—he shoots it.

He's a second-story man. No one ever believes his first story.

He's full of soft soap—mostly lye.

At college, he majored in alibiology.

He not only kisses and tells—he kisses and exaggerates.

He's such an exaggerator, he can't even tell the truth without lying.

A lie never passes his lips—he talks through his nose.

He needs a partition between his imagination and his facts.

He tells more lies than falsies.

He lies like an affidavit.

At a party he's the guy who always starts the bull rolling.

He couldn't even tell the truth in a diary.

You can't believe him, even when he swears he's lying.

He makes his bed and then tries to lie out of it.

He lies like a fellow with a secondhand car to sell.

His conversation is like a dice game—a lot of crap.

He lies on the sand in Miami Beach—about how important he is in his home town.

The only thing that keeps him from being a barefaced liar is his moustache.

He's like a microscope expert—he magnifies everything.

His lies aren't just white lies. As far as the truth is concerned, he's color-blind.

The trouble with his cooked-up excuses is that they're half-baked.

Marriage—
Present Tense

Marriage made the two one, but it's been a constant struggle to establish which one *is* that one.

She's a rag, a bone, and a hank of hair—and he's a brag, a groan, and a tank of air.

He got married because he was tired and she got married because she was curious. They're both disappointed.

They're well matched. He has a furtive look and she has a flirtive look.

It's a beef-stew marriage. She's always beefing and he's always stewed.

The only time they're stuck on each other is when they're plastered.

They make a good match—they're both always lit.

Television is a blessing for them. They would rather look at anything than at each other.

On Valentine's Day they follow their usual custom. They eat each other's heart out.

They're inseparable; it takes several people to pull them apart.

They have their little scraps, but nothing too serious. It doesn't need more than a couple of policemen to break them up.

No sooner did they say "I do" at their wedding than they started to look around to see if they could do better.

When he's in, she's out; when she's in, he's out. They can't find each other to discuss a divorce.

Marriage may be a 50-50 proposition. Unfortunately, they don't understand fractions.

They're petitioning the government to put all matters pertaining to marriage under the jurisdiction of the War Department.

Their unhappiness is due to illness—they're sick of each other.

They're a pair of lovebirds—always flying at each other.

They're incompatible. He has no income and she has no patibility.

They're very compatible. They both dislike each other.

They're as companionable as a cat and a goldfish.

They're as compatible as ham and matzos.

They're as unlike as a yacht and a coal barge.

They quarrel like two halves of a Seidlitz powder.

They get along like two peeves in a pod.

It started out as puppy love, and has since gone to the dogs.

You never hear an angry word from them—their apartment is soundproof.

They're proving that two can live as bitter as one.

Their home is frequently closed for altercations.

They've stopped dating and started intimidating.

They're always holding hands—if they let go they'd kill each other.

They're not just drifting apart—they're under full sail.

They used to keep a diary of their lovers' quarrels, but they had to give it up—it's become too big a scrapbook.

They'd be ashamed to sell their family parrot to the town gossip.

For years they've been racing for supremacy. It's high time they settled down to neck and neck.

They once swore to love—now they love to swear.

One marriage in four ends in a divorce—they're fighting it out to a finish.

If they had to do it over again, they'd still marry each other—at the point of a gun.

Marriage—Past Tense

She's suing him for divorce because of reckless driving. He drove by her with a blonde.

He's being sued for divorce on account of a chronic ailment. He suffers from high blonde pressure.

She's getting a divorce on the ground of mental cruelty—like a couple of times he tried to kill her.

For years she's been suffering from a pain in the neck, so she's getting rid of him.

He's divorcing her because she has a sobering effect on him—she hides the bottle.

She's suing him for divorce and naming his mirror as correspondent.

She's asking for a divorce because he's more interested in spice than spouse.

She's divorcing him because he's just gotten out of a sickbed—his girl friend had the flu.

He was busy earning his salt, but she divorced him because he forgot the sugar.

She's suing for divorce because the man who was once her suitor no longer suits her.

She wants a divorce on the ground of desertion. She gave him enough rope, and he skipped.

He's asking for a divorce on the ground that he couldn't give her the world with a fence around it, so she gave him the gate.

He's suing for divorce on the ground that she threw his coat out. He happened to be in it at the time.

He wants a divorce on the ground that her upkeep is his downfall; he was fast on the deposit, but she was faster on the draw.

He divorced her because life with her was one canned, undarned thing after another.

His ground for divorce: for their anniversary she gave him a set of luggage—packed.

She's not divorcing him because there's any other man in her life. It's just that she's determined there will be.

They're in the divorce court because they regard their marriage tie as a forget-me knot.

They took the "for better or worse" vow, but they didn't say for how long.

They forgot that in "wedding" the we comes before the I.

It was love at first sight and ended at the first slight.

Their "I do" turned out to be much "I do" about nothing.

The trouble with their wedlock was that they misplaced the key.

The grave of their love was excavated with little digs.

Their divorce is hash made of domestic scraps.

The minister gave them a life sentence, but it was suspended in the divorce court for bad behavior.

Common sense might have avoided their divorce—and their marriage too.

She's on her way to Reno, the land of the free and the grave of the home.

Their married life was tense and their divorce the past tense.

Their marriage was a drama in three acts: Announced, Denounced, Renounced.

Their courtship was a quest, their marriage a conquest—the Divorce was the inquest.

They're pressing their divorce suit with the seamy side out.

Their marriage was like a card game. It took two to open, and could have ended up with a full house if they hadn't thrown in their hands.

They're in the midst of a custody battle. She refuses to allow him to keep his mistress.

He got custody of the children and she got custody of the money.

She's a remarkable housekeeper. Every time she gets a divorce, she keeps the house.

It was a long-drawn-out divorce suit. His wife got half and her lawyer the rest.

She's been married three times and getting richer by decrees.

He had no idea when the judge granted the divorce that he had such a high cash-surrender value.

They're separated physically, but not financially.

They finally came to financial terms—hers.

As they left the divorce court, she whispered to him, "Bye now—pay later."

Ever since their divorce, he's getting the billing without the cooing.

The alimony payments are giving him a splitting headache.

She was unhappily married, but with her alimony she's happily unmarried.

Their marriage was a declaration of war, their divorce a declaration of peace, and the alimony is taxation without representation.

He married her in haste and is repenting insolvent.

Before the divorce, he complained of the high cost of loving. Now he's concerned with the high cost of leaving.

It was such a stiff alimony award in her favor, no wonder he calls it "alimoany."

Every time he has to meet an alimony payment, it's a case of wife or debt.

Although they're divorced, she still insists marriage has its compensations—alimony, for instance.

Meanies

If you kicked him in his heart, you'd break your toe.

He'll cry over your wounds so he can get salt in them.

He'd steal a dead fly from a blind spider.

He has as much use for anyone living as an undertaker.

He has a testimonial plaque from Simon Legree.

The only way he can hear any good about himself is to talk to himself.

He's applying for a job as a prison warden so he can put tacks in the electric chair.

He dreamed that he died and the heat woke him up.

His rough exterior covers a heart of flint.

He'd make dice out of his mother's knucklebones.

The only thing he'll share with you willingly is a communicable disease.

He heats the knives so his family won't use too much butter.

He shuts off his hearing aid when his wife offers her side of an argument.

He got his parents a fifty-piece dinner set for their golden anniversary—a box of toothpicks.

146

He's suffering from hardening of the hearteries.

He's taking up ventriloquism so he can go around throwing his voice under old maids' beds.

He's deaf and has never told his barber.

He sends get-well cards to hypochondriacs.

He told his children Santa Claus is too old to get around any more.

He'll give you the shirt off your back any time.

He takes sparrows, dips them in peroxide, and sells them as canaries.

He knifes you in the back and then has you arrested for carrying concealed weapons.

His wife wanted pearls for her birthday, so he gave her an oyster and a rabbit's foot.

He's buying a motel so he can rent cabins to old maids between honeymooning couples' cabins.

He'll throw a drowning man both ends of a rope.

He'd put his pet dog in a sputnik.

The last place he lived in, he campaigned for a dry law, got it passed—and then moved away.

Every time a scaring cigarette report comes out, he goes around blowing smoke in people's faces.

He's very sympathetic. He buries his head in his hands in the subway—he can't bear seeing an old lady standing.

He has a lot of fortitude—he'll stand for nearly anything but a woman on a train or a bus.

He hasn't stored up enough treasure in heaven to make the down payment on a harp.

He sheds tears, but they never reach his heart.

His motto is, "A tooth for a tooth"—but he expects yours to have gold in it.

He was engaged to a girl with a wooden leg. He got mad and broke it off.

He's so cold, he has to part his hair with an axe.

He's as hard-boiled as an Easter egg.

When his mother-in-law comes to visit, he buys her a jar of vanishing cream.

He's very friendly—he offers to take the postman out for a nice long walk on his day off.

He thinks everything is funny—so long as it happens to someone else.

He folds his newspaper so the guy next to him in the bus can read only half the headline.

On his employee's twenty-fifth year of loyal service he took back the watch he gave him fifteen years before, to have it overhauled.

He's a boss spelled backwards—double s.o.b.

His staff is quitting, not because of low wages, but because they're too tenderhearted to keep horses out of jobs.

As a boss, he believes hire should be lower.

He's so envious of others' possessions, he even sighed at his deceased friend's beautiful mausoleum, "That's living!"

He has a keen sense of humor—you can easily amuse him by slipping on an icy pavement, or on a banana peel.

The next time you'll meet anyone like him, it will have to be in a nightmare.

You couldn't warm up to him if you were cremated together.

Lots of people would enjoy working for him—if they were gravediggers.

Nudists

She grins and bares it.

He goes coatless and hatless with trousers to match.

She's never been accused of wrong undoing.

He sneaked his girl out of the nudist camp because he wanted to see what she looked like in a bathing suit.

From the time she joined the colony, every morning marked the dawn of a nude day.

She's wrapped up only in herself.

He joined the colony because he was anxious to see life in the raw.

He's the colony's Peeping Tom. He was caught looking through a knot hole at the girls passing by outside.

She's feuding with her boy friend—they're barely talking.

She's suffering from clothestrophobia.

He's the camp athlete. He runs 100 yards in nothing.

The police arrested her but they couldn't pin anything on her.

He was asked to grow a long beard so he could go to the village for supplies.

He was thrown out because he asked for dressing on his salad.

He was ostracized because his breath came in short pants.

She was expelled because she had a coat on her tongue.

When he drove into the camp for the first time, he even had to strip his gears.

Even her sewing machine is without a stitch.

They've asked her to leave. She demands panties on her lamb chops and jackets on her baked potatoes.

She broke off with her boy friend because they were seeing too much of each other.

You can't blame her for being the way she is—she was born that way.

Old Fogies

He's not the man he used to be—now his age is *really* showing.

His get-up-and-go has got-up-and-went.

That's not a gleam in his eye—it's just the sun hitting his bifocals.

There's spring in the air, but not in him.

All girls look alike to him.

Sunday night is the weak end of his weekend.

His thoughts have turned from passion to pension.

He's finding it tougher and tougher to make ends meet—such as his fingers and toes.

Now that he knows his way around, he doesn't feel like going.

He gets tired just wrestling with temptation.

His temper is getting shorter and his anecdotes longer.

He's buying moccasins so he won't have to lace his shoes.

When he has a choice of two temptations, he passes up the one that might keep him up late.

After a night on the town, he feels his oats—and his corns.

His daily dozen is followed by days of daily doesn't.

He has an off day after his day off.

He's done before the day is.

He propositions a girl—and hopes she says No.

He's more interested in "yes" from his banker than from a blonde.

When he turns out the lights, it's for economy instead of romance.

It's getting so even making a long-distance call tires him out.

Lately, he keeps saying "I remember when" instead of "What's new?"

His plan for getting ahead is to stay even.

He's given up trying for home runs; he's satisfied just not to be struck out.

He complains, "I've run out of gas," and his wife believes him.

His wife powders and he puffs.

He not only has rheumatism—he has reminiscences.

He feels like a cigarette lighter. The spirit is willing but the flash is weak.

He's got gold in his teeth, silver in his hair, and lead in his pants.

The only thing he grows in his garden is tired.

The hardest things for him to raise in his garden are his knees.

He putters around the garden and mutters around the house.

It's taking him longer to rest than to get tired.

He's done long before the day is.

He's chock-full of pep—for an hour or two a day.

He considers a 10 P.M. TV program the Late Late Show.

He feels like the day after the night before, and he hasn't been anywhere.

His feet hurt even before he gets out of bed.

His forehead is getting higher and his energy lower.

He's begun to have thoughts about women instead of feelings.

His head is making dates that his body can't keep.

He hears one voice counseling "Why not?" and another, "Why bother?"

He pays more attention to the dish on the menu than to the dish who brings it in.

He's a WOW—a Worn-Out-Wolf.

He chases women only if it's downhill.

He picks up a woman's handkerchief, but doesn't pick up the woman.

Optimists

He puts his shoes on when a speaker says, "Now, in conclusion. . . ."

He asks his wife to help him with the dishes.

If he fell from the sixtieth floor of a skyscraper, he'd say, "So far, so good" at the thirtieth floor.

When he goes fishing, he takes along a camera and a frying pan.

On $60 a week take-home pay, he's marrying a girl who longs to have six children.

He saves the illustrations in seed catalogues to compare with the flowers and vegetables he grows.

He goes looking for an apartment with a drum in one hand and a saxophone in the other.

He's as bald as a billiard ball, but he buys hair restorers that have combs with every bottle.

He married his secretary, thinking he'd continue to dictate to her.

He blames the dry cleaner for his shrunken pants-waistband.

He starts working on a crossword puzzle with a fountain pen.

He starts figuring the taxes on $75,000 and $100,000 when trying to decide whether to buy one or two sweepstakes tickets.

All his life he's been a sinner, but he's taking harp lessons.

He goes into a hotel without baggage, and asks to have a check cashed.

He goes into a restaurant without any money, expecting to pay for the meal with the pearl he'll find in an oyster.

He looks for eggs in a cuckoo clock.

He's marrying at seventy, and is looking for a home near a school.

When he buys anything, he sees only the initial payment.

She sows wild oats and hopes for a crop failure.

She thinks her bulge is a curve.

Pessimists

He goes through life with morose-colored glasses.

Given the choice of two calamities, he chooses both.

She lives on the fret of the land.

He's a mountain climber over molehills.

He wouldn't be content with his lot even if it was a corner one.

He's constantly keeping his bad breaks relined.

Give him an inch, and he measures it.

She's always pulling tomorrow's cloud over today's sunshine.

He manages to find a little bad in the best of things.

To him, O is the last letter in "Zero" instead of the first letter in "Opportunity."

He has an optimistic stomach and a pessimistic digestion.

He's always building dungeons in the air.

He's always blowing out the light to see how dark it is.

Tell him that life begins at forty, and he laments, "So does rheumatism."

He's suffering from skeptic poisoning.

His usual greeting is: "Good morning, probably."

He never builds castles in the air for fear they'll have mortgages on them.

She broadcasts over such a fretwork of wrinkles, she needs to get her faith lifted.

He never worries about tomorrow—he knows everything is going to turn out wrong.

He wears not only a belt, but suspenders as well.

Wherever there's an optimist who sees a light where there is none, he's sure to be around to blow it out.

First things she looks for on entering a department store are the complaint and exchange counters.

He fills up every time he sees a gas station.

Playboys

So long as a woman has curves, he has angles.

He can take one look at a girl and tell what kind of a past she's going to have.

His love is just a passion fancy.

He studied meteorology so he could look in a woman's eyes and tell whether.

He loves his neighbors—especially their wives.

If a girl has the time, he has the place.

In his opinion, there's nothing like good music, good wine, a good meal, and a bad girl.

He starts with orchids and ends with forget-me-notes.

He treats all women as sequels.

He's the time of your wife at a party.

He has a terrific literary reputation; he's in practically every diary in town.

Women think at the start that he can be their soul mate, but he turns out to be a heel.

Nobody is his equal at making a peach cordial—he buys her a drink.

He believes a woman's best measurements are thirty-sex, twenty-sex, thirty-sex.

He's the kind of guy with whom a woman should eat, drink, and be wary.

When he gives a girl a string of pearls, he makes sure there's a string attached to it.

His motto is: "Life, Liberty and the Happiness of Pursuit."

All he knows about women is what he picks up—and, boy does he pick 'em up!

He's real broad-minded—in fact, he thinks of nothing else.

He's a man of single purpose and double talk.

You can always find him at a woman's door—the bedroom door.

He believes in nothing risqué, nothing gained.

He has a good line; first he talks about the weather, and then about the whether.

He gives a girl sloe gin to make her fast.

Give him an inch, and he takes the whole 36-27-35.

He encourages a woman to tell him about her past. Before she's through, he's part of it.

He always gives up something fancy for something fancier.

As a lover, he's a passing fiancé.

He has given up big game hunting for big dame hunting.

He's always on the lookout for the unbelievable—a passionate girl who is inconceivable.

His life is a bed of ruses.

The only footprints he'll leave on the sands of time will be the marks of a heel.

All he asks of a woman are two keys—to her heart and her apartment.

He's a wolf in chic clothing.

One thing is sure—he knows all the ankles.

At college, he signed up for all the romance languages.

Life for him is just one continuous round of dame foolishness.

He's the friendly type—always inviting women up to his apartment for a Scotch and sofa.

He has two hobbies—collecting old masters and young mistresses.

So far as he's concerned, love is just a passing fanny.

He loves babes—especially those born eighteen to twenty-five years ago.

He goes around with more women than a revolving door.

He specializes in women who believe in romance, while he depends on his eye-cue.

He treats women to rum and coax.

He's a reprobate who counts on a reduction in the wages of sin.

When it comes to seduction, he's always ready, villain, and able.

He gives women the kind of look that could be poured on waffles.

He can read a woman like a book, but he always forgets his place.

He's a modern dry cleaner. He works fast and leaves no ring.

Lots of women may not recall his name, but his hands are familiar.

He has wandering hands that go from pat to worse.

He's tall, dark, and hands.

He has submarine hands. Girls never know where they'll turn up next.

When he kisses a girl, he wishes their hearts would stand still—and she wishes she could say the same about his hands.

The way he dances, it looks like the vertical expression of a horizontal idea.

He's an expert on love—it's remarkable how he grasps the subject.

Everyone calls him "Chestnut" because he's nuts about chests.

He tells women he wants to be a good friend when all he wants is to be good and friendly.

He's a master of the art of getting attention without intention.

He got beaten up fighting for a woman's honor. Seems she wanted to keep it.

He was a victim one time of an air disaster—her husband flew home instead of returning by train.

When the wages of sin are paid, he'll get time and a half for overtime.

He thinks that sleep is the best thing in the world—next to a woman.

He just can't play straight with a girl who's all curves.

He believes if a good girl can't be led into temptation, then what is she good for?

He frequents resort hotels where when the bell rings at 6 A.M. everybody has to get out of bed—and return to his own room.

He only goes out with girls who wear glasses—he breathes on the lenses so they can't see what he's doing.

Even as an infant, he grabbed for the nurse instead of the bottle.

He only goes out with women who don't "no" too much.

He made a perfect 36 on the golf course, but she dropped him when she found out he was married.

He acts as if he had just invented sex and can't wait to spread the idea around.

When a woman resists his advances, he holds her for further questioning.

He likes dumb girls because a dumb girl is a dope, a dope is a drug, doctors give drugs to relieve pain—so a dumb girl is just what the doctor ordered.

He always hangs around a woman with a past in the hope that history will repeat itself.

As a guy who knows his oats, he sure can talk a girl into a serial.

If he ever went to Honolulu to see native dancers, he'd take a lawn mower along.

He likes to see a broad smile—when she's smiling at him.

He spends summers in the Alps, winters in Miami, and springs at blondes.

He prefers well-formed women to well-informed ones.

He always harps on the weather—whether she will or she won't.

He's a gentleman who befurs blondes.

Last New Year's he made a solemn resolution to cut down on wine and women. It was the most miserable afternoon he ever spent.

He's fast going to the dogs, chasing chickens.

He invites women to his farm and gets lofty ideas in the barn.

Every time he goes out with a woman, either she's married or he is.

His approach to love and romance is soft music, soft breezes, soft lights, and soft soap.

He's a yes-man with no interest in a no-girl.

His motto is: "Strike while the eyein' is hot."

He was in trouble recently for holding up a train. It was a bride's train and it seems he held it too high.

He's a regular Cashanova.

He'd be in clover if it wasn't for his wild oats.

When he gives a check to a girl, it's liable to bounce back, marked "Insufficient Fun."

They call him "Sailor"—he likes a little port in every girl.

He's waiting for the right girl to come alone.

He whistles while he lurks.

He's the kind that men don't trust too far and women don't trust too near.

No sooner is he alone with a sweater girl than he tries to pull the wool over her eyes.

When he hears that a woman has a past he goes to work to brighten up her present.

He not only knows how to hold a girl tight—he knows how to get her that way.

The only time he likes to see a girl stick to her knitting is when she's in a wet bathing suit.

He can count only up to sex.

Take a good look at him and his shoes and you'll see three heels.

THE PLAYBOY BOSS

He never hires a stenographer unless she's thoroughly sexperienced.

He pinches and scrapes at the office—pinches his secretary's cheeks and scrapes the lipstick off his own.

As a husband he acts like a boss, and as a boss he acts like a husband.

He demands of his secretary a period after every sentence—a recreation period.

He fired his secretary because of lack of experience. All she knew was shorthand and typing.

He's real ungrammatical—when dictating to his secretary he always ends a sentence with a proposition.

He's a perfect gentleman. All his secretary has to do is slap his face once in awhile.

His female employees aren't so tired of punching the clock as of punching him.

He's very pleased—she's the best little secretary he ever got his hands on.

He's an efficiency expert. He can juggle every figure in the office—including his secretary's.

He's a stockbroker, but he's busier trying to corner his secretary than he is the market.

He's an architect. He hired a curvaceous blond secretary—he has great plans for her.

He takes a look at his attractive secretary, and starts nightdreaming.

His stenographers have to have a lot of experience handling shorthand—and long arms.

He never passes up a chance to miss business with pleasure.

He dictates to his cigar, and gets his stenographer lit.

He doesn't play around during office hours—he likes them naughty but nights.

IN THEIR SECOND WOLFHOOD

He may be old, but he's still in there pinching.

He's an over-sexy over-sixty.

He's a little roué of sunshine.

He thinks he's a thing of beauty and a boy forever.

He's still chasing women, but he can't remember why.

He's in his second Brigitte Bardotage.

Taken to the hospital recently, he took a turn for the nurse.

All he asks of life is a little peach and quiet.

Some day he may realize that time wounds old heels.

He should be paying more attention to soaking his wild corns than to sowing wild oats.

At his age, all women look the same—good.

The old rapscallion hands out minks to keep some young blondes warm, proving there's no fuel like an old fool.

He's taking dancing lessons to teach his old dogs new tricks.

He believes he's still as good at attracting women as he never was.

He's an antiquated sugar daddy who takes a girl buy-buy—then she goes bye-bye with a younger guy.

He's a real cave man—one hug-and-kiss and he caves in.

He's keeping a young mistress. He knows at his age it may be fatal, but he says he doesn't know a better way to die.

This frisky, flirtatious eighty-year-old fossil's greatest ambition is to be shot by a jealous husband at ninety.

The girls all love this old "bird" for all he's worth—after he passes the assets test.

The romantic antique has a lot of trouble opening the windows in his love nest. He now has them marked "His" and "Hernia."

The old reveler is going through that last-fling period when he isn't dangerous to anything except his reputation.

Playgirls

She has a Sunday-school face and Saturday-night ideas.

She's a capable girl—capable of anything.

She's a mere stripling—but how she can strip!

She may be a miss, but she doesn't miss much.

She's a girl that's game—everybody's.

The only time she says "Stop" is when she sends a telegram.

Her good times began when she had her no's fixed.

She's a lush blonde fast becoming a blond lush.

She looks like a little lamb, but she's really a wolf in she's clothing.

She's the proverbial good time that was had by all.

She knows the right answers, which is why she is often asked things out of the question.

Between her "No" and her "Yes" you couldn't stick a pin.

The best years of her life are figured in man hours.

She's like a flower—she grows wild in the woods.

She has a mink coat but she's still paying nightly installments on it.

There's a rumor she's pregnant—it's a miss-conception.

She's insulted when you offer her a drink, but she swallows the insult.

The only thing that can ever make her blush is the corner drugstore.

She never whispers sweet nothing-doings in fellows' ears.

She's been around more than a carousel.

She has a sunny disposition and a shady past.

She believes in affair play.

Offer her a Scotch and sofa and she's sure to recline.

It's a safe bet that she writes her diary in invisible ink.

She keeps her hair light and her past dark.

She has been tried and found wanton.

In the summer, you'll always find her at the beach in her baiting suit.

She's the demure, shy type—the kind you have to whistle at twice.

She knows how to say things with her torso that other girls waste a lot of time putting into words.

Her wink can give you a whether signal.

She's a cutie on the q.t.

She's preparing for a European tour—she's learning how to say "yes" in five languages.

She never hesitates when torn between vice and versa.

She has a sylphlike figure and doesn't keep it to her *sylph*.

Ask her if she's free for some night and she answers, "No, but I'll be reasonable."

She can give you a beau-by-beau account of her affairs.

She has a heart like the Army—open to all men between eighteen and forty-five.

She drinks sloe gin and is made fast.

She'd rather have beauty and curves than brains—she knows that the average man can see better than he can think.

Her theory is that girls who do right get left.

It's a lovely fur coat. She's not saying how much she played for it.

For a girl without principle, she draws considerable interest.

She's a public relations girl. Her biggest job is keeping her relations from becoming public.

She has a line that makes her popular—the line of least resistance.

She can't swim a stroke but she knows every dive in town.

Anyone can get her number—it's on the walls of phone booths all over town.

The way she flips her hips and tosses her torso, she has to be sin to be appreciated.

She's been on more laps than a napkin.

She can make five laps during a short party.

She's like a six-day bike rider—she finds it easy to make laps.

She says, "Who needs brains? Fellows don't whistle at a girl's brains."

When a fellow gets fresh, she counts to ten—thousand.

She claims she got her fur coat for a mere song, but more likely it was an overture.

She doesn't mind if her date is a cad, so long as his convertible is too.

She's leading a date-to-date existence.

She has hidden charms and she thinks it's silly to hide them.

She has shapely legs and she's proclaiming it from the hose-tops.

Tight clothing is said to stop circulation, but so far as she's concerned, the tighter her clothing the more she's in circulation.

She's popular on account of her tight sweaters and loose habits.

She doesn't make a practice of necking. It's been years since she needed any practice.

She always obeys the boyological urge.

She won't go anywhere without her mother, and her mother will go anywhere.

She knows where bad little girls go—everywhere.

She's not a beauty—but is she a cutie!

She's an expert at keeping men hip-notized.

Marriage isn't important to her. She's willing to mate a man half way.

She has seen more of life in the raw than a night watchman in a nudist camp.

She moves in the best triangles.

There's an old saying, "You can never tell about a woman." In her case, it's charitable not to.

She doesn't know any four-letter words—like can't, won't, stop, and don't.

She's a *petite* girl—but she'd rather pet than eat.

She makes good impressions on the boys—with her lipstick.

She's the type who likes to be taken with a grain of assault.

Her father sells real estate and she gives lots away.

She lets her boy friend's conscience be her guile.

She advances pulses by not repulsing advances.

She knows that men make passes at girls who drain glasses.

She's like an automobile radiator—she'll freeze up on you if you don't fill her with alcohol.

The way she crawls away from temptation it invariably overtakes her.

She recently met a man in the strangest way—they were introduced.

She's the type who isn't picked out but picked up.

At seventeen, her voice started changing—from no to yes.

She'll scream at a mouse but will get into a convertible with a wolf.

The fellows think she's from the South, the way she says "You-all may."

She goes with men who prefer women who know what men prefer.

She started out as a schoolteacher, but she never had any principal.

She's a postman's daughter and she's certainly fast with the males.

She's a parson's daughter and she sure has her following.

She's a shoemaker's daughter and she sure gives the boys her all.

She's a dressmaker's daughter and she's always making a slip.

She's a gardener's daughter and she knows all the rakes.

THOSE OFFICE CUTIES

Under "Experience" on the application blank, she wrote, "Oh, boy!"

She got the job when she wrote on the application blank: "No bad habits—willing to learn."

She failed the typing test but passed the physical.

She was hired on the basis of glamour—not grammar.

She can't add, but she certainly can distract.

She was three laps ahead of the nearest competition.

She's never been positionless because she's always inhibitionless.

She lost her last job because of illness—the boss's wife got sick of her.

Her salary goes up as her neckline goes down.

She's dangerous to have around the office—too many moving parts.

She's very efficient—never gets lipstick on the boss's collar.

She's very efficient—always manages to be out of the office when the boss's wife visits him.

She likes her job—lots of opportunities for advances.

She doesn't punch the time clock because she doesn't punch the boss.

She's the main squeeze in the office.

She looks for "bankruptcy" under the r's. She knows how to spell "bank"—she's looking for "ruptcy."

She has a remarkable brain. It starts working the moment she gets up in the morning, and doesn't stop—until she gets to the office.

She's the latest thing in secretaries—always an hour late.

She can't type so well, but she can erase 60 words a minute.

She has a great future. She's really going places—with the boss.

She's the perfect secretary—types fast and runs slow.

Her boss told her he'd pay her $85 a week with pleasure, but she said with pleasure she wanted $125.

She's a thoroughly sexperienced secretary.

She recently changed her position—the boss's wife made an unexpected appearance.

She makes an excellent deceptionist.

Her typing and spelling are improving—she may soon give up those tight sweaters.

The last two months of the year, she starts working her fingers to the bonus.

She always stops to think—trouble is, she forgets to start again.

When the little bell on her typewriter rings, she thinks it means a coffee break.

She's wearing low-cut dresses since the firm has been thinking of installing automation.

She says to her amorous lawyer-boss: "Stop, and/or I'll slap your face."

She shifts her typewriter into neutral and lets her tongue idle on.

She's tickled pink when she gets a job and she's tickled pink when she goes in for dictation.

She's been run around more desks in the office than a vacuum cleaner.

She's earning every cent of her salary. Her boss is so bowlegged, she's always falling through his lap.

She won't be around the office much longer because she's expecting too much—she's getting too big for her job.

Political Acrobats

He's full of promises that go in one year and out the other.

He stands for what he thinks people will fall for.

Honesty is his policy. When he's bought, he stays bought.

He has three hats: one to cover his head; one that he tosses in the ring; and the one he talks through.

He'll do anything for the worker but become one.

He approaches every question with an open mouth.

To him, politics is a game with two sides and a fence.

He always studies both sides of an issue so that he can get around it.

He never keeps his fences so high that he can't straddle them.

He's very acrobatic—he can straddle a fence while keeping his ear to the ground.

He has a straightforward way—of dodging issues.

He shakes your hand before election and your confidence after.

For him, the path of glory leads but to the gravy.

There's no doubt he's doing something about hidden taxes—he hides them better.

He's always trying to save both his faces.

He's sure to leave pussyfoot prints on the sands of time.

He refuses to answer any questions on the ground that it will eliminate him.

"Economy" is his slogan, provided it's not in his own district.

His political plums didn't grow from seed—they're the result of clever grafting.

His favorite menu is applesauce served with pork.

Around election time, he always announces his views, from his hedgequarters.

At the start of a campaign, he comes out shooting from the lip.

He fills the air with speeches, and vice versa.

He's standing on his record—to keep the voters from taking a good look at it.

He's skilled in the art of talking in circles while standing on "four-square."

No one can call him a cheap politician. Look how much he's costing the taxpayers.

He claims to be self-made, but he's really machine-made.

He's moving to an election district where the population is dense—from the neck up.

When he asks you to vote for him and for good government, he's asking you to vote twice.

He's running for office, but if they ever look up his record, he'll be running for the first plane to Rio de Janeiro.

He divides his time between running for office and running for cover.

He gets campaign contributions from the rich and votes from the poor on the pretense that he's protecting each from the other.

He finds out which way the crowd is going, then jumps in front and waves his banner.

He's mastered the art of appearing unenvious when he accuses his opponent of flimflamming the public.

His campaign slogan is: "I'm a simple man of the community." You can go still further and say he's the simplest man in the community.

You can count on him to lay down your life for his country.

He got himself elected by passing both the buck and the doe.

He's like the earth—he was flattened at the polls.

He tried to straddle an issue by staying in the middle, and he got hit from both sides of the fence.

Defeated at the polls, he can't decide whether he handed out too much baloney, or not enough.

His defeat is a real news story—a case of the bull throwing the politician.

Sad Sacks

If it rained soup, he'd have a fork instead of a spoon.

If he started out on a shoestring, everyone would start wearing loafers.

If he invested in an automobile stock, wagon trains would start making a comeback.

He's the kind of guy who falls on his back and breaks his nose.

He runs into accidents that started out to happen to someone else.

He married a girl for her money, and her dad went bankrupt the following week.

His ship finally came in, and sure enough there was a dock strike.

He has a wife and a cigarette lighter—neither one works.

He waited years for Dame Fortune to knock on his door, but it was her daughter, Miss Fortune, who showed up.

He bought a big house with lots of doors for Opportunity to knock on, but only his relatives did.

He's had the seven-year itch for eight years.

If he went into the men's pants business, men would start wearing kilts.

177

He started to fool with the market, but it was the market that did the fooling.

Just as his turn came for a check from the TV show "The Millionaire," the show went off the air.

He finally figured a way to make ends meet, but someone moved the ends.

He spent years developing skill as a second-story man, and along came ranch houses.

He worked two years on his boss's signature; then the perfectly forged check came back, marked "Insufficient Funds."

He's had bad luck with two wives. The first one left him and the second won't.

A couple of times he was crossed in love; then he got married and was double-crossed.

He picked a horse that he was sure would win in a walk, but the other horses ran.

He goes through life as handicapped as a cornet player with loose teeth.

His suit is so shiny, if it tears he'll have seven years' hard luck.

He went bankrupt three times and didn't make a cent once.

Just as a breeze blows a girl's dress up, it blows a cinder in his eye.

He has more ups and down than a theatregoer in an aisle seat.

He wound up in jail for making big money—it was a quarter of an inch too big.

He's always in as tight a spot as a cork.

He's a yes-man, but he's working for a boss who always says No.

He worked a long time perfecting a bourbon toothpaste; when he had it just right, he no longer had any teeth.

He's a two-handicap golfer—he has a boss who won't let him off early and a wife who keeps him home weekends.

He was once shipwrecked on a desert island with his own wife.

He got a divorce and got custody of his wife's parents.

He was once a tree surgeon, but he kept falling out of his patients.

His bank account is his shrinking fund.

He made money as a men's pants manufacturer. Then he lost it on one skirt.

He followed the dictionary on buying stocks, where "invest" comes before "investigate."

He's had to give up his new home—it was on the outskirts of his income.

He's all set for a rainy day, with a pair of dry socks, rubbers an umbrella, and a bottle of cold tablets.

Screwballs

His mother saw something in him that no one else saw—she saw that he was nuts.

He's getting a jacket for his birthday—the strait kind.

He's psychoceramic—a crackpot.

He has such a split personality, his psychiatrist had to buy a sectional couch for him.

He has such a split personality, his towels are marked "His" and "His."

He has such a split personality, his psychiatrist charges $50 each per visit.

I'm a-Freud he isn't all there.

Has he told you about his aberration?

He listens to his psychiatrist, and then draws his own confusions.

When he was born, no bells were rung—a pot was cracked.

He's as happy as if he were in his right mind.

His wife married him because she can't resist anything that's 50 per cent off.

They're thinking of putting him in the nut-house—for no reason at all.

His future position looks very secure—they're planning to put him in a strait jacket.

He reminds you of Whistler's mother standing up—he's off his rocker.

He has a one-crack mind.

In appreciation of his many years of service to the firm, they presented him with a gift certificate for two years' psychoanalysis.

He always eats in restaurants where they serve soup to nuts.

One look at him and you know why he's so self-conscious in the presence of monkeys.

He's as nutty as a fruit cake—as gone as a gone goose.

He carries a compass so he'll know whether he's coming or going.

His ideas are sure to be honeys—he has bees in his bonnet.

Maybe he's not nutty, but why does he stuff tobacco in his ears and ask for a light?

He's as sane as a lunatic's dream.

They call him "the Trainman"—he's plain loco and no motive.

They call him "Chocolate Bar"—he's half nuts.

They call him "the Liberty Bell"—he's half-cracked.

They call him "Bottletop"—he has a cork top and he's screwy.

He's stopped visiting his psychiatrist. He's an actor and he won't talk without a TelePrompTer.

Poor guy! He was in jail one time, and when they put him in charge of cooking the soup he went stir-crazy.

His psychiatrist is so expensive, all he gets for $25 is a get-well card.

His psychiatrist is so strict, he makes him stand up if he comes late.

He has an Irish psychiatrist—he uses a Murphy bed instead of a couch.

His psychiatrist asks him a lot of questions for a fat fee that his wife asks him for nothing.

He's learning how to stand on his feet while reclining on a couch.

He has a problem. If he doesn't pay his psychiatrists' bills, they'll let him go crazy, and if he pays their bills he'll certainly go crazy.

He goes to a psychiatrist who advertises this way: "Four couches—no waiting."

His psychiatrist has a new type of shock treatment—he sends his bills in advance.

Every year-end he gets a card from his psychiatrist reading, "Happy Neurosis!"

Sharpies

He always goes through a revolving door on someone else's push.

He's like French bread—not much dough, but lots of crust.

If he murdered his parents, he'd ask for mercy on the ground that he's an orphan.

He'd steal the teeth out of your mouth, and then come back for your gums.

He thinks he can substitute brass for brains.

He wouldn't hesitate to drive up to the gate of heaven and honk.

He picks up a girl on another fellow's whistle.

He'd ask for a coffee break if he worked for a tea company.

He picks up your chick instead of the check.

With his gall, he can hand back a letter for a third retyping to a steno he's playing around with.

As an executive, he delegates all the authority, shifts all the blame, and takes all the credit.

He got a bill with a notation on it: "This bill is one year old." He returned it with his own notation: "Happy birthday!"

He has nerve enough to flirt with a woman standing in a bus while he's sitting.

He's brazen enough to take a taxi to bankruptcy court and then ask the driver in as another creditor.

He sold two milking machines to a farmer with one cow, and then took the cow as a down payment.

He's always nice to waitresses—he plays them for big steaks.

He's a sly fox. He always manages to get what a wolf is after.

He can convince his wife she looks fat in a fur coat.

He can tell you to go to hell so persuasively, you actually look forward to the trip.

A woman tried to talk him into buying her a dress, and he talked her out of the one she was wearing.

He bought his wife some fine china so she wouldn't trust him to wash the dishes.

He can change a subject faster than a dictionary.

He sells cigar butts to midgets as king-sized Havanas.

He pins badges on frankfurters and sells them as police dogs.

He was a bellboy once in a swank hotel. Called for a deck of cards, he came up fifty-two times.

He keeps his wife on a pedestal so she can't put her foot down.

He's as cautious as two porcupines making love.

The last two months of the year he starts working his fingers to the bonus.

He hasn't let a woman pin anything on him since he was a baby.

He's looking for a rich girl who's too proud to have her husband work.

He's a man with coffee nerves. He has the nerve to take more than two coffee breaks.

Show-oafs

He thinks he's the life of the party. Actually, he's the laugh of the party—and the laugh's all on him.

He has one of those fun-track minds.

His idea of fun is throwing an egg into an electric fan.

At a party, he's the guy that always starts the bull rolling.

He makes you wonder why all the clowns you see around aren't in the circus.

He should have his jocular vein cut.

He's a comedian of the first water—a big drip.

He has a brother in prison who is also very popular—the lifer of the party.

The only place he has hair is on his jest.

He's a real vocalamity.

He sure has a good line. Too bad he doesn't hang himself with it.

He's snappy on the comebacks—like his checks.

Everyone takes his remarks with a grain of epsom salts.

He'll ask a question, answer it himself, and then tells you what's wrong with it.

He's the kind of show-off who's showed up in a showdown.

He blows his horn the loudest, but that's because he's in the biggest fog.

He thinks he knows it all, and keeps proving he doesn't.

He always manages to open something by mistake—his mouth.

As a cut-up, he missed his vocation. He should have been a barber.

Everyone calls him "Paul Revere" because he's always horsing around.

He's the life of the party, until it comes to picking up the check.

He looks like an owl and behaves like a jackass.

He's a real party live-wire—not only on his toes but on everyone else's.

His wife always begs him, "Now, if it's a dull party, just leave it that way."

He thinks he's a gay young buck—he isn't even two bits.

He's as popular as a mouse at a women's club meeting.

He needs only two glasses to make a spectacle of himself.

He thinks he's amusing, but he couldn't even entertain a doubt.

He's been nicknamed the "Surgeon"—he's a real cutup.

She's the belle of every party—everyone wants to wring her neck.

He has a repertoire of three jokes all told—and told and told.

He thinks he electrifies a party, but he merely gasses it.

He's as loud as a Christmas tie and just about as welcome.

He graduated from college magna cum loudest.

He's the kind of braggart with whom it is no sooner done than said.

She's a real clamor girl.

He's always offering "sound advice"—99 per cent sound and 1 per cent advice.

He could never be a janitor. He's always putting out an over-supply of hot air.

If you took the air out of that big wheel, all that would be left of him would be a flat tire.

He has a voice like a buzz saw striking a rusty nail.

She thinks she's a siren, but she only sounds like one.

She's always mistaking the right of free speech for free screech.

Every time he opens his mouth he puts his feats in.

He's such a show-off, he even boasts that he's losing his mind.

She has a gum-chewer's mouth—it goes without saying.

At every party he's the M.C.—Mental Case.

They call him "Asthma"—he's so full of old wheezes.

At a party, he's loudmouthed, egotistical, and obnoxious, but in spite of all that, there's something about him that repels everyone.

Someone once told him to be himself. He couldn't have been given worse advice.

Snobs

She should go to a plastic surgeon to have her nose lowered.

He claims he dines with the upper set—he uses his lowers too.

They hired an upstairs maid—and they live in a ranch house.

He's one of the Bore Hundred.

They've just bought a statusfying home.

They're only flakes off the upper crust.

He's such a blue blood, he never uses a fountain pen when he writes. He just cuts his finger.

The way she acts, you'd think it was her duty to be snooty.

Their old butler is serving their third degeneration.

She's one of those women who snoop and snub.

They belong to the upper crust—a lot of crumbs sticking together.

He looks like something that's been stuffed by a good taxidermist.

She's as stuck-up as a billboard.

He's proof that an empty head and a stuffed shirt can go together.

188

He's trying to go from the cash register to the social register.

They belong to the kind of country club where the men are stuffed shirts and the women are stuffed shorts.

She was born with her face lifted.

She has so many jewels, she's getting too big for her brooches.

She returns from her tours brag and baggage.

They're always talking about their inferiors, but no one has ever been able to find them.

She has the kind of look that hangs a price tag on every object in the room.

She struts around as if she were balancing her family tree on her nose.

He's so ritzy, he wears a riding habit just to pitch horseshoes.

She's so fashionable, if she decided to shoot her husband, she'd wear a hunting outfit.

Her head is so uplifted, she has a double chin on the back of her neck.

She even wallpapers the insides of the medicine chest and the refrigerator.

He claims he dines with the brass—which is quite understandable. They wouldn't trust him with the silver.

He may be listed in Who's Who, but he doesn't know what's what.

She belongs to the uppish classes.

He's as snooty as a clerk in a swank shop ringing up "No Sale" on a $25 purchase.

Her nose is so upturned, everytime she sneezes she blows her hat off.

She's as overbearing as a woman giving birth to quadruplets.

What a snob!—he must be inclined as the prig was bent.

The only thing he ever did for a living was inherit.

He'd feel snubbed if an epidemic overlooked him.

He claims his ancestors came over on the Mayflower—the immigration laws are much stricter now.

He paid a big fee to have his genealogy looked up, and now he's paying a bigger one to have it hushed up.

His family tree was started by grafting.

His family tree could stand a lot of trimming.

He boasts about his family tree—he comes from the shady side.

He claims his ancestors spring from a long line of peers—three of them sprang off the docks.

The best part of his family tree is underground.

He should be less concerned with what he's descended from and more concerned with what he's descended to.

He wants to be one of the Four Hundred; the way he's getting his money to achieve it, he's liable to wind up as Number 400.

She's studying geometry to learn how to move in the best circles.

They had their baby kidnapped so they could get their pictures in the papers.

They have wall-to-wall carpeting, wall-to-wall windows and back-to-the-wall financing.

They're going into debt trying to keep up with people who already are in debt.

They have an exquisite Morris chair in their living room, but Morris is taking it back.

They buy lovely period furniture—it's only a short period before the installment people take it back.

They claim they belong to the early settlers but you'd hardly think so judging by the bill collectors on their front steps.

They have holes in their sleeves trying to rub shoulders with the society crowd.

Even when they're finally buried underground, they'll try to keep up with the mausoleum crowd.

Their idea of social prominence is to have their names found everywhere—except in the phone book.

They forget that God created the world in a round shape so that no one could be first in a circle.

They're getting an awful inferiority complex—they've just met someone as good as they are.

Speakers

He gives you in length what he lacks in depth.

He's a dry talker who is usually all wet.

He covers indefinite ideas with infinite words.

His speeches are like the horns of a steer—a point here, a point there and a lot of bull in between.

When he finally finishes his speech, there is a great awakening.

His speeches go over like a pregnant woman trying to pole-vault.

He can usually rise to an occasion, but he doesn't know when to sit down.

He appeals to the emotions by beating the eardrums.

He's a sound speaker—oh, those sounds!

Only one man applauded; he was slapping his head to keep awake.

He speaks straight from the shoulder. Too bad his remarks don't start from higher up.

He claims to be speaking for posterity; if he isn't quick about it, they'll be along to hear it.

He doesn't put enough fire into his speeches. It would be better if he put his speeches into the fire.

All he needs to get his second wind is to say, "And now, in conclusion. . . ."

As a speaker, he's like a ship. He toots loudest when in a fog.

He gave a moving speech—long before he finished, his audience had moved out into the hall.

He uses a lot of verbiage to say little about nothing.

His audiences never drink coffee before his after-dinner speeches —it might keep them awake.

He can dive deeper into a topic than anyone else, remain down longer, and come up drier.

He needs no introduction—what he needs is a conclusion.

He can make you feel numb on one end and dumb on the other.

His speech is like a bad tooth—the longer it takes to draw it out, the more it pains.

His audiences not only keep looking at their watches, they shake them.

The fault with many speakers is that you can't hear what they're saying. The trouble with him is that you can.

He hasn't a watch with him to time his talks. He should look at the calendar on the wall behind him.

Listening to his speeches, you can't help wondering who writes his immaterial.

He doesn't strike oil even in an hour, but he keeps boring.

His speech is like a wheel—the longer the spoke, the greater the tire.

His chairmen never say, "Our speaker needs no introduction." He needs all the introduction he can get.

Toastmasters can introduce him, but they can't guarantee him.

If all the people who have to sit through his speeches were lined up three feet apart, they would stretch.

He has his tongue in your ear and his faith in your patience.

In biblical days, it was considered a miracle when an ass spoke. Listening to him, you can't help but realize how times have changed.

Arrangement committees never see the need to supply him with a filled pitcher—you can't run windmills with water.

He never learned to leave his audience before his audience leaves him.

His speeches should be like a woman's skirt—just long enough to cover the subject, and short enough to create interest.

Tactless Boors

He has the manners of a gentleman. Obviously, they don't belong to him.

He's a rarely well-mannered person—very rarely.

We've all heard soup gargled and siphoned, but he yodels it.

The way he drank his soup in a nightclub, ten couples got up and danced.

He eats with his fingers and talks with his fork.

He has a nose that is not only seen but heard.

He's as refined as a cabbage.

He's as at home in refined company as a pig in a parlor.

The greatest points of interest in his life are 7 and 11.

He's such a lowbrow that when he gets a headache, he puts the aspirin in his shoe.

The only way he can live up to his ideal of himself is from a hole in the ground.

When he drops cigar ashes on a host's rug, he spills his Scotch and soda on it to prevent a fire.

As a tourist, his slogan is: "Stop, Look, and Litter."

He's a contact man—all con and no tact.

He would walk into an antique shop and ask; "What's new?"

He's tactless enough to tell a woman that something is as plain as her face.

The only high thing he's ever concerned with is the cost of living.

He's completely bald, but that still doesn't make him a highbrow or a polished individual.

He can talk louder than a TV commercial.

He's a real gentleman—he'll never strike a woman with his hat on.

He's lower than a horse's hoof or a baboon's forehead.

He's disappeared from his usual hangouts and hasn't been obscene since.

He thinks he's refined because he knows which fingers to put in his mouth when he whistles for the waiter.

He has dirty fingernails, and a mind to match.

He's never troubled by improper thoughts—in fact, he enjoys them.

He has one of those mighty minds—mighty dirty.

He's a fast eater. He starts on his dessert before the echo of his soup has died away.

He has an approach like a dentist's drill.

He smokes the kind of cigars that hold you smellbound.

He is very class-conscious. He has no class and everyone is conscious of it.

He has a laugh like the screech of a rusty door.

He dances like a cattle stampede.

He's as shallow as a pie pan.

He has a one-track mind—a dirt track.

The only way he's ever tidy is when he drinks his whiskey neat.

His neighbors call his TV set the "Astronaut" because it has conquered the air.

He's a fellow of a few, ill-chosen words.

His hair must be loaded with electricity with all those shocking things on his mind.

The only uplifted thing about her is her bust.

Her escort wouldn't mind her eating so much when he takes her nightclubbing, if he could only hear the orchestra.

She has foot-in-the-mouth disease.

The only person he's ever treated with kid gloves is a fingerprint expert.

Tightwads

He thinks the world owes him a giving.

He got his money the hoard way.

He drinks with impunity—in fact, with anyone who'll buy.

The only time he picks up a check is when it's made out to him.

He's so tight, when he winks his kneecaps move.

He has low pockets and short arms.

When it comes to picking up a dinner check, he has an awful impediment in his reach.

He does his Christmas shopping surly.

Someday a check is going to reach out and grab him.

He gave his wife a ring that once belonged to a millionaire—Woolworth.

He wouldn't even buy happiness if he had to pay a luxury tax on it.

It's an art the way he avoids picking up a check. You have to hand it to him.

You can get anything from him for the asking—and, boy! the eyes, arms, and legs he's asking.

198

He takes his wife window-wishing regularly every week.

He's such a bargain-hunter, he married a half-wit because she was 50 per cent off.

When he goes on a week's vacation, all he spends is seven days.

He has never taken up hunting because he can't find a store that sells used bullets.

He believes charity begins at home—and should stay there.

He's a lady-killer—when he takes out a girl he starves her to death.

He talks through his nose to save wear and tear on his teeth.

He's the first to put his hand in his pocket—and keep it there.

He's so cheap he never takes anything but a sponge bath.

When his old mother visits him, he takes possession of her false teeth so she won't eat between meals.

He hasn't ever cut much ice because he's a real cheapskate.

His motto is: "Money doesn't grow on sprees."

He always has his nose in a book. He's too stingy to use a handkerchief.

He insists two drinks are enough for anyone—especially if he's paying for the third.

After the doctor gives him a blood test, he demands his blood sample back.

He got his parents a fifty-piece dinner set for their golden anniversary—a box of fifty toothpicks.

He's so small, if he ever sat on a dollar, ninety-five cents would show.

He tosses quarter tips around like manhole covers.

He's so stingy, he won't even tip his hat.

He orders asparagus and leaves the waiter the tips.

When he says it's not the money but the principle of the thing, you can be sure it's the money.

He's heard that you can't take it with you, but he says if he can't take it with him he won't go.

The way he nurses a Scotch and soda you'd think it was an hourglass.

He's an I.W.W. filling station customer. He stops only for Information, Wind, and Water.

If he drank poison, he'd try to get the deposit back on the bottle before passing away.

You know it's really summer when he throws out his Christmas tree.

He never paws a girl. His hands are too busy hanging on to his wallet.

He takes a girl to a drive-in restaurant, and then won't open the window.

He's always living within his relatives' means.

He has a greater love for specie than the species.

The only thing he ever gave away was a secret.

When it comes to doing some good he gives the Lord credit. Too bad he doesn't give some cash too.

He clasps his hands so tight in church during prayers that he can't get them open when the collection box comes around.

He takes a keen interest in the sermon, but only a passing interest in the collection.

He throws money around like a man without arms.

He goes out with his girl Dutch treat—they dance check to check.

When the brakes of his car give way, he tries to hit something cheap.

The way he reaches for a check, he must have inspired the inventor of slow-motion movies.

He'd skin a flea for its hide and tallow.

He's so grudging, when everyone else gives three cheers he gives two.

He'll sit through three showings of a lousy movie to get his money's worth.

Money flows from him like drops of blood.

He'd give you the sleeve out of his vest.

He tears the December page off the calendar during the Christmas season to fool his children.

He's so closefisted, he only gives you one finger when he shakes hands.

When he pays you a compliment, he asks for a receipt.

His pockets always outlast the rest of his suit.

He's so niggardly, he takes his kids' glasses off when they're not looking at anything.

He's always trying to get something for nothing, and then complains about the quality of the service.

If he ever found a box of corn plasters, he'd start wearing tight shoes.

He so stingy, when he lets out a breath of air, it's practically a vacuum.

He's the kind of guy who drinks on an empty pocket.

He's a cheerful giver—cheerful because he gets away with giving as little as possible.

His wife expected roses on their anniversary, so he came home with Four Roses—on his breath.

He had a brass band at his wedding—he put it on his bride's finger.

He's taking up singing lessons because the scale begins and ends with "do."

He won't buy rattles for his kids. He lets them grab his nose and he shakes his head.

Anyone can borrow his lawn mower. It has a coin slot on it.

He can drink for hours—but that's before he gets to his own booze.

He's so tight, he even refuses to perspire freely.

He puts boric acid on his grapefruit in order to get a free eyewash.

Money is the last thing he thinks of—just before going to bed.

He's suffering from costrophobia—the fear of parting with a buck.

He's so close, he won't even let you borrow trouble.

He's a nodding acquaintance. Ask him for a loan and he says, "Nodding doing."

He keeps ten-dollar bills folded so long, Hamilton gets ingrown whiskers.

On their 40th wedding anniversary, he sent his parents forty pieces of silver—forty dimes.

He figured out a good way to save money on his honeymoon—he went on it alone.

Before spending a buck, he considers carefully how it will affect his favorite hobby—hoarding money.

His standard apology for not lending a friend any money is that it's all tied up in currency.

He drinks a glass of soda—then he tickles a mule to get a kick out of it.

He went to a swank seashore resort and got a suntan. When he got the bill, he turned white again.

His friends have an apt nickname for him "the Dough-nut."

He'll lend you an umbrella, and then takes it back when it starts to rain.

You can easily spot him in a nightclub. He's the one who's sitting with his back to the check.

His tailor has a problem—how to make a suit for him with one-way pockets.

He uses the same calendar year after year.

You can always find him where his best friend is—his bankroll.

He wouldn't ever get into a fight—not unless it was a free-for-all.

He's still single. Every time he was ready to get married, the price of rice went up.

He pays as he goes, except when he goes with somebody—and he always goes with somebody.

He's satisfied to let the rest of the world go buy.

Un-Altar-able Beaus

When a girl asks him for a diamond ring, he turns stone-deaf.

Women are always trying to drive him to the altar, but they can't make him link.

He adores women, but he doesn't let the feeling become nuptial.

He wants only one single thing in life—himself.

His wallet is full of pictures of near Mrs.

He avoids bride-eyed women.

In the land of the free and the home of the brave, he would rather be free than brave.

He avoids entanglements with women who would rather knot.

He never takes yes for an answer.

When he speaks of "tying one on," he doesn't mean an apron.

He believes in the guarantee of life, liberty, and the happiness of pursuit.

He's a fellow of un-altar-able views.

No one is more miss-informed than he is; he can only be miss-led so far.

He does right and fears no man; he doesn't write and fears no woman.

He has no children—to speak of.

He's a gay dog and no woman has ever been able to get him spousebroken.

His life is a bed of ruses.

One time he was crazy to get married, but he says that fortunately he realized it in time.

He's skilled at one-handed driving without skidding into a church.

He has been seen everywhere with a woman—except at the altar.

When he chases a woman, he makes sure not to catch her.

He hasn't got a thing against marriage—and he wants to keep it that way.

He sees no point in buying a cow when milk is so cheap.

He has yet to meet a woman whom he couldn't live without.

His motto is: "What God has put asunder, let no man join together."

The minute a girl starts asking her mother for recipes, he does a fast fade-out.

Just because he falls in love with a dimple, he sees no reason to marry the whole girl.

There's one gift he never gives a girlfriend—an electric blanket with dual controls.

His married men friends may have better halves, but he prefers his better quarters.

The only woman who ever pinned anything on him was his mother, when he was a baby.

He has a leaning toward women, but he never falls.

He always looks before he lips.

He believes in wine, women, and so-long.

All his romances have been carried off without a hitch.

He's always foot-loose and fiancée free.

His only objection to love is that it can become parsonified.

In his estimation, even once in a wifetime is too much.

He believes that being marriage-minded is a mental condition —when the mind is out of condition.

The only months in which he'd consider getting married are those that have a "w" in them.

To him, marriage is just a lot of dame foolishness.

Every morning he arrives at his office from a different direction.

He's a man of double purpose but single thought.

Wives

THE BALL AND CHAIN

She's sticking to him through all the trouble he never would have had if he hadn't married her in the first place.

He remembers when and where he got married, but what escapes him is *why.*

He takes his daytime problems to bed with him—she's opposed to separate bedrooms.

When he first married her, he could have eaten her alive. Now he's sorry he didn't.

He believed in dreams—until he married her.

He calls her the salt of the earth—he's been trying to shake her for years.

Asked how long he's been married, he says forlornly, "Every minute of the day and night."

He's just been given two months to live—that's how long she'll be away on vacation.

He blames his troubles on Adam for not having been adam-ant.

What he likes about her is that she drives him out to seek his happiness elsewhere.

A jeweler urges him to smother her with diamonds, but he's got a cheaper way in mind.

A friend told him, "My wife is an angel." "You're lucky," he commented, "Mine's still living."

She's so suspicious, if she finds no blond, black, or red hairs on his jacket, she accuses him of running around with bald women.

He should have known how jealous she is—she had male bridesmaids.

She left him once; then she came back again—she couldn't bear his having such a good time.

She swore she wouldn't talk to him for a month and he's unhappy about it—the month is almost up.

She has no minor voices.

This is his second marriage. He's been unlucky in both—his first wife left him and this one won't.

He insists Early American customs haven't changed—the Indian is not the only one who sleeps with a battle-axe by his side.

He shot a guy who planned to run off with her—the fellow changed his mind.

When he first announced that he had half a mind to marry her, he didn't realize that's all it required.

He never knew what happiness was until he married her—now it's too late.

He's the third man she's led to the halter.

Her towels are labeled His, Hers, and Next.

He should have been warned when he read the inscription on her last husband's tombstone: "Rest in Peace—Until We Meet Again."

He's bequeathing everything to her, provided she remarries within six months after his death. He wants someone to feel sorry he died.

He's leaving her because of another woman—his mother-in-law.

He's trying real hard to drown his troubles, but he can't get his wife and mother-in-law near the water.

He offers to send her mother to Africa at his expense to teach the Mau-Maus how to fight dirty.

He's a big success, and in back of him stand his wife and her mother—telling him how stupid he is.

BABBLERS

He has given her the best ears of his life.

She's an angel—always up in the air and harping on something.

The only chance he has of getting her to listen to him is to talk in his sleep.

He had laryngitis for three weeks, and didn't know it.

They're always having words, but they're always hers.

Every time he argues with her, words flail him.

He speaks six languages, she speaks two—just the right handicap.

They both wear pants, but it's not difficult to tell them apart —he's the one that's listening.

He can read her like a book, but he can't shut her up like one.

He's overweight. He became that way because eating gave him a chance to open his mouth.

She's wrecking the matrimonial bark with her matrimonial barking.

He carries pictures of the children—and a sound track of her.

He should have picked her with his ears instead of his eyes.

She's easily entertained—all he has to do is listen to her.

He has two mouths to heed—hers and her mother's.

Their marriage is a partnership—he's the silent partner.

He spends a good deal of his time by a babbling brook, because he can't brook her babbling.

When they first met, she looked like a siren. Now she talks like one.

He's happy when she's in bed, safe and soundless.

He has several mouths to feed, and one big one to listen to.

She hasn't spoken to him for a week. He's wondering what to give her to show his appreciation.

She's so tired at the end of the day, she can hardly keep her mouth open.

Their marriage is the walkie-talkie type. She's all talkie, which makes him go for a walkie.

If he wants to get in a word with her, he has to sit sidewise.

He's a good listener. He can't break in because she won't break off.

She not only has the last word when he argues with her—she has the last two thousand.

He went to a New Year's Eve party without noisemakers—but he had her along.

She believes in free speech. She's certainly free enough with hers.

They have words, but he never gets to use his.

He got rid of the noise in the back of the car—he made her sit up front.

He's in favor of safety-belts. She's a back-seat driver, and he'd love to give her a belt.

He doesn't know what she thinks of his new dentures—he never gets a chance to open his mouth.

She's already had four dentures. She wears them out with her tongue.

He calls her "Echo" because she always has the last word.

He wishes he had married a stutterer so he could get a word in now and then.

She had laryngitis once and it was like having the phone discontinued.

She chatters so much on the phone, he's asked the telephone company to come and remove her.

Talkative?—she was married to her first husband five years before she discovered he was deaf and dumb.

He has just drawn his last will and testament. The first line reads: "At last I have a chance to open my mouth."

HOUSEKEEPERS

When she put her finger through the wedding ring, it was the last thing she did by hand.

She thinks her work was done when she swept down the aisle.

She's not bothered when her husband reads the papers at breakfast—she never gets up for breakfast.

Before they were married, she promised she'd keep her kitchen immaculate. She's kept her promise—they eat out.

She'll put on almost anything for dinner, except an apron.

The only exercise she gets is running up bills and jumping to conclusions.

She's dissatisfied with their house because the household appliances aren't automatic—she has to turn on a switch.

The only reason her hair looks like a mop is that she doesn't know what a mop looks like.

She's one of those modern wives who believes in love, honor, and disarray.

Her closet would be messy even if she lived in a nudist camp.

As a housekeeper, she sweeps the room with a glance.

Her husband is very persevering. He can get to the bottom of most anything, except her pocketbook.

The only time she looks just right to him is on Halloween.

Her house is such a mess, when the phone rings she can't find it.

They're celebrating their tin wedding anniversary—five years of eating out of tin cans.

She can dish it out, but she can't cook it.

It takes her an hour to cook Minute rice.

She dresses to kill, and cooks the same way.

He brings home the bacon and she burns it.

They don't have pot roast—they have roast pot.

She must be very religious and a very loving wife. Every night at dinner time she places burnt offerings before him.

When their apartment burned down, it was the first time the food was hot there.

He takes one look at her burnt offering and exclaims, "What in cremation is it?"

He can always tell when they're having salad for dinner—he doesn't smell anything burning.

Life for him is one canned thing after another.

First thing he asks when he gets home at night is, "What's thawing?"

You never thaw such meals as she serves.

She was amazed when a neighbor told her you don't open an egg with a can-opener.

Her husband is a real gentleman. He never tells the true reason why the family prays before each meal.

She's kept her schoolgirl complexion, but you can't say that she's done much for his schoolboy digestion.

HIS GETTER-HALF

They're a balanced couple. He makes the money and she spends it.

She couldn't stand his ways, but she married him for his means.

She cares not one bit for him, but she lives on his account.

He thought she was going to make him a home, but she just made him.

She vowed at the wedding "to love and to cherish until debt do us part."

He's handsome. When she wants money, he has to hand some.

All the period things she buys are keeping him baroque.

He married her 125 checkbooks ago.

She made him a millionaire. Before she married him he was a multi-millionaire.

She gets expensive rocks from him, but she's otherwise stone-deaf.

He thinks nothing is too good for her—and so does she.

She's very gifted—he has the bills to prove it.

She's a human dynamo—she charges everything.

She can bring more bills into the house than a congressman.

Her upkeep will be his downfall.

She married him because he looked like a good support.

She cries a lot—not so much to get things out of her system as out of his.

She can get a mink coat out of him without half crying.

Her clothes make her, and break him.

He'll soon be destitute because she's dresstitute.

She has positively, absolutely nothing to wear—and four closets to keep it in.

She's sticking to him because he has a will of his own—and it's made out in her favor.

They were having their pictures taken, and the photographer told her to look natural—so she posed with her hand in his pocket.

She had four only requirements for a dutiful, loving husband —cash, stocks, bonds, and real estate.

The way she can spend money, he should become a counterfeiter.

Watching her purchases, he's constantly amazed to see all the things she'd rather have than money.

He's giving her the best expense-account years of his life.

When she goes shopping, she comes back with everything but money.

She can't cook or clean, but she can lick her weight in trading stamps.

The food she serves is not only high in calories but high in trading stamps.

She's less interested in her cookbook than in his checkbook.

They have a joint checking account. He puts in the money and she draws it out.

When he reproaches her for buying things as if there was no tomorrow, she says, "Name me one other extravagance."

She's a woman who's five years ahead of her time. In 1963, for instance, she had already spent his salary for 1968.

She won't mend his socks because he won't buy her a new mink coat. If he doesn't give a wrap, she doesn't give a darn.

He never realized how much she would want whc he promised her before marriage that she would never want for anything.

She's a human gimme-pig.

What a woman! Without her, he'd never be what he is today —broke.

STRAYERS

She's more interested in spice than spouse.

She's a home-loving wife. When her husband is away, she's home loving another guy.

A couple of times he was crossed in love; then he married her, and was double-crossed.

His absence makes her heart go wander.

Her bathroom towels read, "His," "Hers," and "To Whom It May Concern."

She's getting indifferent—in different men's arms.

Every once in awhile, she feels like a new man.

While on vacation, she sent him a card reading: "Having wonderful time. Wish you were he."

He's interested in her happiness. In fact, he's so interested, he hired a detective to find out who was responsible for it.

He thought she was the salt of the earth until she started going with fellows with more pepper.

When he accused her of infidelity, she shouted indignantly, "That's an insult. I've been faithful to you dozens of times!"

He didn't mind her enjoying crackers in bed until he came home and discovered a crumb in the closet.

One night a week he goes out with the boys—on the other nights she goes out with them.

He's supposed to be brilliant, but he not only doesn't know everything, he doesn't even suspect anything.

When he travels, he doesn't understand that the XX's at the bottom of her letters means she's double-crossing.

She's leaving him for a crazy reason—she's crazy about another guy.

Woolgatherers

He wound up the cat, put out his wife, and got into bed with the clock.

He poured ketchup on his shoelaces and tied knots in his spaghetti.

He wears a wrist compass so he can tell whether he's coming or going.

He held an egg in his hand and boiled his watch three minutes.

He sent his wife to the bank, and kissed his money good-bye.

He picked up a snake and hit a stick.

He spent seven years studying why people are absent-minded. He finally came up with the answer—and promptly forgot it.

He rolled under the dresser and waited for his collar-button to find him.

He kissed his horse good-bye and hitched his wife to the plow.

He stood in front of a mirror for a half-hour trying to remember where he had seen himself before.

He took his wife out to dinner instead of his secretary.

Three months behind with his payments, he parked his car in front of the finance company's office.

217

He took a memory course and memorized one hundred phone numbers. Now he can't remember the names that go with them.

He slammed his wife and kissed the door.

He read an erroneous account of his death in the obituaries, and sent his wife a condolence card.

He dictated to his cigar and got his secretary lit.

He put the typewriter on his lap and started to unfasten the ribbon.

He fell overboard and forgot he could swim.

At her wedding, she told her corsage how lovely it looked, and threw her bridesmaid down the stairs.

Nicknames

They call her ALICE: her German parents took one look at her and said, *"Das ist Alles!"*

They call her AMAZON: she's so big at the mouth.

They call her APPENDIX: the fellows take her out once—that's enough.

They call him ARCH: he always needs support.

They call him ARCHITECT: when he meets a girl he's full of plans for her.

They call him ARCHEOLOGIST: his career lies in ruins.

They call him ARTIE: they hope he chokes.

They call her A.T. & T: she's always talking and talking.

They call him AUCTIONEER: he always looks forbidding.

They call him AVIATOR: he's a real high-flyer.

They call him BAKER: his career is one big loaf.

They call him BALDY: he's real smooth.

They call him BANANA: he's always getting skinned.

They call her BANJO: she's easy pickings.

They call him BARBER: he trims everyone he can.

219

They call him BUTCHER: he's a real cut-up.

They call her BASEBALL GIRL: she was thrown out at home.

They call her BEAN: anyone can string her.

They call him BLACKSMITH: he shoos his daughter's boy friends—out of the house.

They call her BOTTLER: when she goes for a fling no one can stopper.

They call him BOTTLETOP: he has a cork top and he's screwy.

They call him BOWLER: he builds himself up by knocking everyone down.

They call her BROWN SUGAR: she's so sweet and unrefined.

They call him BUTCHER: he's always giving everyone lots of tongue.

They call him BUTCHER: he's always scrimping to make both ends meat.

They call him BUTCHER: he's taking short cuts to wealth.

They call him BUS DRIVER: he tells everyone where to get off.

They call him CALVERT: he's so reserved.

They call her CARNIVAL QUEEN: she makes a lot of concessions.

They call him CARPENTER: he knows every vise in the book.

They call him CEMETERY: he's so grave.

They call her CHECKERS: she jumps when the boys make a wrong move.

They call him CHIROPODIST: he's always starting off on the wrong foot.

They call him CHIROPODIST: he's always down at the heels.

They call him CHIROPODIST: give him an inch and he takes the whole foot.

They call him CHOCOLATE BAR: he's half nuts.

They call her CINDERELLA: you have to slipper ten, slipper twenty.

They call him COLISEUM: he's a monumental ruin.

They call her COMMUNIST: all the fellows get their share.

They call him COMPOSITOR: he has such set ways.

They call him CONTRACEPTIVE: he's always evading the issue.

They call her CONTORTIONIST: she's always patting herself on the back.

They call him CORK: his head is always at the mouth of a bottle.

They call her CREAM OF WHEAT: she's so mushy.

They call her CUCUMBER: he's usually pickled.

They call him DENTIST: he bores everyone to tears.

They call him DENTIST: he lives from hand to mouth.

They call him DENTIST: he always looks down in the mouth.

They call him DENTIST: he works largely on nerve.

They call him DENTIST: he gets along on pull.

They call her DICTIONARY: she always has the last word.

They call her DINER: she likes to eat men's hearts out.

They call her DRAFTSMAN: she draws the lines on fellow's plans.

They call her DRESSMAKER: she's always making a slip.

They call her DRESSMAKER: she keeps the boys on pins and needles.

They call her DRESSMAKER: she knows the seamy side of life.

They call him DRUGGIST: he's a real pill.

They call him DRY CLEANER: he gets everyone all steamed up.

They call her DUSTY: she's been on the shelf so long.

They call her EASTER EGG: she's painted on the outside and hard-boiled inside.

They call her ECHO: she always has the last word.

They call her ELECTRICITY: she sure shocks 'em.

They call him ELEVATOR OPERATOR: he's always running people down.

They call her ESKIMO MAID: she always gives you the deep-freeze.

They call him FIREMAN: everyone tells him to go to blazes.

They call him FIREMAN: he never takes his eyes off the girls' hose.

They call him FLANNEL: he sure shrinks from washing.

They call her FLO: she talks in a steady stream.

They call her FLO: she has water on the knee and a creak in her back.

They call him FLORIST: he's going to seed.

They call her FLORIST: she's always showing her stems.

They call her FLORIST: she has Four Roses on her breath.

They call her FLOUR: she's been through the mill.

They call him FOOTBALL: everyone kicks him around.

They call him FOOTBALL: he's such a windbag.

They call her GARDENER: she knows all the rakes.

They call him HARPIST: he pulls strings to get ahead.

They call her HONEY: she has the hives.

They call him HOSPITAL ORDERLY: he's a real panhandler.

They call him JIGSAW: when faced with a problem he goes to pieces.

They call him JUNKMAN: he's always picking scraps.

They call him KING-KONG: he's always monkeying around.

They call her KITTY: she's dyed nine times.

They call him LAUNDRYMAN: he'll take the shirt off your back.

They call him LIBERTY BELL: he's half-cracked.

They call her LILY: she always goes out with dead ones.

They call him MAGICIAN: he walks down the street and turns into a saloon.

They call him MAGICIAN: he goes out fit as a fiddle and comes back tight as a drum.

They call her MAPLE SYRUP: she's such a sap.

They call him MASSEUR: he's always rubbing it in.

They call him MATZO: he's not well-bred.

They call him METEOROLOGIST: he can look at a girl and tell whether.

They call him MICROSCOPE: he magnifies everything.

They call her MINER: she makes the most of her natural resources.

They call her MOON: she's out all night.

They call him MOON: he becomes brighter the fuller he gets.

They call him MORTICIAN: life to him is a grave undertaking.

They call her MOTH: she's always chewing the rag.

They call him MUSICIAN: he's a playboy who's always making overtures.

They call him NERO: he's always fiddling around.

They call him NUDIST: you can never pin anything on him.

They call him NURSERYMAN: he's a professional grafter.

They call him OPTICIAN: two glasses and he makes a spectacle of himself.

They call him PARATROOPER: he falls down on the job.

They call him PAROLE: he interrupts you in the middle of a sentence.

They call him PAUL REVERE: he's always horsing around.

They call him PAWNBROKER: he makes advances.

They call him PHOTOGRAPHER: he sure can accentuate the negative.

They call him PILGRIM: he makes progress with women.

They call her POISON IVY: she's an awful thing to have on your hands.

They call her POSTMISTRESS: she's had lots of experience picking up males.

They call him PRESCRIPTION: he's always getting filled.

They call him PRETZEL MAKER: he makes crooked dough.

They call her PRINTER: she's real choosy, the way she picks her type.

They call him PSYCHIATRIST: he's always trying to get a girl on a couch.

They call him REALTOR: he has lots on his mind.

They call her ROBOT: she was made by a scientist.

They call him RUBBER BAND: he has an elastic conscience.

They call him QUITS: when he was born his parents decided to call it quits.

They call him SAILOR: he likes a little port in every girl.

They call her SANKA: there's no active ingredient in the bean.

They call him SANTA CLAUS: you should see the bags he runs around with.

They call him SANTA CLAUS: he won't leave women's stockings alone.

They call him SARDINE: he always lands in the can.

They call him SCULPTOR: he's some chiseler.

They call her SECONDHAND DEALER: she won't allow much on a sofa.

They call him SERUTAN: he's so backward.

They call her SEVEN-ELEVEN: she's so thin, when she walks you can hear her bones rattle.

They call him SHOEMAKER: he thinks he knows all.

They call him SHOWBOAT: he's been up the river so many times.

They call her SHOW GIRL: she's more show than girl.

They call her 6-DAY BIKE-RIDER: she finds it easy to make laps.

They call him SLIVER: he gets under everyone's skin.

They call him SNUFF MAKER: he puts his business in other people's noses.

They call him SPONGE: he's so flabby.

They call her STRETCH: she has an elastic conscience and a rubber neck.

They call him SUBWAY: he's a big bore.

They call him SURGEON: he's a real cut-up.

They call him SURRENDER: you take one look at him and give up.

They call him SYNCOPATION: his movements are irregular —from bar to bar.

They call him TAILOR: his policy is one of needles and threats.

They call him THEOPHILUS: he's theophilus-looking guy you ever met.

They call him TONSILITIS: he's a pain in the neck.

They call him TRAINMAN: he's plain loco and no motive.

They call him TROMBONIST: he's always blowing his own horn.

They call him UNDERTAKER: he has no use for anyone living.

They call her VILLAGE BELLE: everyone wants to wring her neck.

They call him WATCHMAN: both his eyes keep watching his nose.

They call him WEBSTER: words can't describe him.

They call him WHAT'S-IT: his father took one look at him when he was born, and yelled "What is it?"

They call her WILD-WEST GIRL: she comes into a room shooting from the lip.

They call her WINDOW DRESSER: she never pulls down the shade while dressing.

Squelches

I don't know what makes you tick, but I hope it's a time bomb.

I couldn't warm up to you if we were cremated together.

I don't know what I'd do without you, but I'd rather.

I can't think what I'll do without you, but it's worth a try.

The more I see of you, the worse I like you.

Don't you ever get tired of having yourself around?

Have a drink on me—a Mickey Finn.

Next time you pass my house, I'll appreciate it.

Why don't you get yourself X-rayed to see what people see in you?

You've got a fat chance to get me sore—and a head to match.

You're snappy on the comeback—like your checks.

Why don't you go on a diet, and quit eating my heart out?

Let's play horse. I'll be the front end—you just be yourself.

Why don't you take a long walk on a short pier?

I like you better the more I see you less.

The last time I met you was in a nightmare.

There's a biblical quotation, "Judas went out and hanged himself." And there's another: "Go thou and do likewise."

Why don't you blow your brains out? You've got nothing to lose.

Why don't you send your wits out to be sharpened?

Do me a favor—on your way home, please don't forget to jaywalk.

Let's play house. You be the door and I'll slam you.

Let's play Puss-in-the-corner. You stand in the corner and I'll kick you in the puss.

Please don't insist on telling me who you are. Let me detest you incognito.

If I've said anything to insult you, believe me, I've tried my best.

You have the manners of a gentleman. Tell me, to whom do they belong?

I can't remember your name, but your nasty manners are familiar.

I admit you're a distant relative. Trouble is you're not distant enough.

The sooner I never see you again, the better it'll be for both of us when we meet.

Let's go some place where we can each be alone.

I never forget a face, but in your case I'm willing to make an exception.

I'll swear eternal friendship for anyone who dislikes you as much as I do.

Don't go away—I want to forget you exactly as you are.

For a minute I didn't recognize you. It was the most enjoyable minute I ever spent.

I need a bookmark more than I need you. So step in front of a steamroller on your way out.

Stick around while I have a few drinks. It will make you so witty.

Stay with me—I want to be alone.

According to the theory of evolution, we're descended from either birds or monkeys. I don't see any feathers on you.

What's on your mind?—if you'll please excuse the exaggeration.

I'm sure you'll be all right—after the marijuana wears off.

Didn't I meet you in Las Vegas the day you blew your brains out?

Until you came along, I never saw a prune that exceeded six inches in diameter.

I understand you throw yourself into everything you undertake. Please go and dig a deep well.

I'm told you were down with a virus. I'm surprised it had a chance.

Your manners aren't half bad—they're all bad.

I'll be glad to have you over to my swimming pool—for a drowning lesson.

You know, you make me believe that man's descent from the ape hasn't started yet.

Look, there's a train pulling out shortly—get under it.

I hear you're taking lessons in deportment. Two more weeks and you'll be deported.

You look like the kind of person who throws himself into everything. I live over a lake—come and see me sometime.

You may be a social lion to your friends, but you're just an animal cracker to me.

You think you're such a great wit. Give me a couple of minutes to go out and check my brains—then we'll start even.

Don't tell me—I know who you are. You're the reason for birth control.

Just keep on talking, so I'll know what you're not thinking.

You're every other inch a gentleman

Why don't you sue your brains for nonsupport?

Take some friendly advice—send your wits out to be sharpened.

You have a wonderful head on your shoulders—whose is it?

If they ever put a price on your head, take it.

Folks, he's a cousin of mine once removed. I only wish someone would remove him still further.

I'll bet your name is Webster. Words can't describe you.

I've got two minutes to kill, so tell me all you know.

I'm getting awfully cold—there's a breeze here stirred by a windbag.

Let's talk about your mind. On second thought, no matter.

You could make a good living hiring yourself out to haunt houses.

I recall your name all right, but I just can't force myself to think of your face.

You have a very striking face. How many times were you struck there?

You were given a nose to breath through so that you could keep your mouth shut.

You're not really two-faced. If you had two, why would you be wearing that one?

If you want to save face, keep the lower half shut.

If I had your face, I'd pay a pickpocket to lift it.

What happened? Did an undertaker do an incomplete job on you?

Just remember—the mosquito that buzzes the loudest gets swatted first.

Years pass on, but you don't—more's the pity.

You have a nice head on your shoulders—too bad it's not on your neck.

Why don't you leave and let live?

2000 More Insults

Introduction

Like its predecessor, *2000 Insults for All Occasions*, this volume is a compilation of capsule caricatures, rapid-fire repartee and roguish ribs for all those who can view human shortcomings, vagaries, and pretensions with a keen sense of humor.

The comic insult is far from being of contemporary origin. It has always been in vogue in this funny and strange world full of funny and strange people doing funny and strange things for funny and strange reasons. From ancient times it has been in high favor with knowing wits for sizzling squelches and on-the-spot ammunition to dissolve deserving targets in acid retorts.

Said the French philosopher and satirist Voltaire, "You can't tell the truth without singeing someone's beard." Flattery itself might well be defined as insult wrapped as a gift. As soft soap (90 per cent of which is lye), it plays upon a person's vanity and susceptibility with its insincere excessiveness of praise. Inversely, the so-called insult gag has the virtue of calling a spade a spade. It offers everyone with a perceptive eye and a sensitive recording ear a comical but nonetheless commonsensical view of people's characteristics, actions, speech, and peculiarities of dress and appearance.

As in *2000 Insults for All Occasions*, I have sprinkled the pages of this book generously with virtually every form of sardonic wit and humor. The alert reader will recognize such specimens as paradoxes, comic similes, puns, reversible meanings, hyperboles, spoonerisms, boners, ironics, and firecracker repartee, and to seize upon many of them for his own nefarious use in conversation, speech, and writing.

As with the earlier volume, this sequel is designed to put the right retort in the right head at the right time. It is tailor-made for those who observe human foibles with ironical amusement, and who only need a handy thesaurus of bons mots, wisecracks, and pot shots for the fullest expression of their critical faculties.

Human nature being what it is, the insult gag is most popular when it is directed at someone else, since no one other than its hapless target ever identifies himself with it. Used, however, good-humoredly and without malice, to characterize mankind's failings collectively, it is certain to be most effective as a well-enjoyed laugh-getter. It can also be used in reverse for rewarding effect by the simple expedient of switching from the third-person personal pronoun to the first.

It is to be hoped that this compilation will enjoy its predecessor's gratifying popularity as a handy "goadbook," and as a laugh-package of rib-tickling reading.

LOUIS A. SAFIAN

Bamboozlers

His mind is a real scheme engine.

He gets along fine; he's living off the fatheads of the land.

It's been so long since he's been upright, his shadow is crooked.

He's always up and doing—up to trickery and doing everybody.

His friends don't know what to give him for Christmas. What do you give a guy who's had everybody?

He'll go down in history as the leading exponent of the age of chiselry.

He belongs in Hollywood as a character actor. When he shows any character, he's acting.

If he offers you a deal, see your lawyer—and if your lawyer approves, see another lawyer.

You're safer trusting a rabbit to deliver a leaf of lettuce than to trust him.

He's so crooked, he can hide in the shadow of a corkscrew.

He's so crooked, when he dies they'll have to screw him into the ground.

Help him when he's in trouble, and he'll never forget you—especially the next time he's in trouble.

He never worries ahead of time. He's sure he can always double-cross a bridge when he comes to it.

When he's in a department store, the clerks all shake his hand —to keep it out of the cash register.

He comes from a family of writers. His brother writes novels, his sister writes songs, his mother writes poetry. He writes bum checks.

He's very superstitious. In a fight, he always keeps a horseshoe in his glove.

He never lets a day go by without doing someone good.

He's managing his life on the cafeteria plan—self-service only.

Don't take his checks if you're allergic to the smell of burning rubber.

He not only wants to eat his cake—he also wishes for some other fellow's cookie.

He's hoping for a lucky stroke—his rich uncle's.

With him as your financial adviser, you can run your fortune into a shoestring.

He's the kind of guy who can take it or leave it—mostly he takes it.

When he borrows money, it's not only against his principle to pay interest, but also against his interest to pay the principal.

He's willing to do an honest day's work—only he wants a week's pay for it.

He has a sure-fire method for saving money. He forgets whom he borrowed it from.

He has always paid his taxes with a smile—the Internal Revenue Service is now after him for the cash.

It may be that all the people can't be fooled all the time, but he sure is trying.

In his present job as treasurer, it's been found that he banked five times his salary in two years. The company is investigating—to see what took him so long.

When you lend him money, he's telling the truth when he says, "I'll be everlastingly indebted to you."

He never puts off till tomorrow what he can put over today.

It doesn't take long to notice that his character is like a decayed walnut—it's not what it's cracked up to be.

He's so two-faced, he stands up in both the top and bottom halves of the seventh inning of a ball game.

He pretends to be burying the hatchet when he's only digging up the dirt.

The way he discharges an obligation, you can hear the report miles away.

He's sure to leave pussyfoot prints on the sands of time.

The only time he isn't himself is on Sundays in church.

A wealthy widow has been paying his expenses on a vacation in Paris—he's a real *Paris-ite*.

He's the type who'll sell himself to the highest biddy.

He fell in love with a woman at second sight. The first time he saw her he didn't know she was rich.

He denies that he married her because her dad left her a fortune. He insists he would have married her no matter who left it to her.

He's the type who can soft-soap you so that you can't see for the suds.

His flattery makes you feel like a pancake that's just had the syrup poured on it.

He's one of those professional reformers who manage to get the pie out of piety.

At a dinner party, he's the guy who's sure to eat all the celery.

He can convince you that you're going places when he's really taking you.

He's a guy that's really going far—always one step ahead of his creditors.

Lend him money and you'll learn the difference between capital and labor. The money you lend him represents capital—getting it back represents labor.

His success is the result of two things—luck and pluck. Luck in finding someone to pluck.

He's a real success story. He started out with $1,000; now he owes $100,000.

He's so crooked, he has to screw his socks on.

He's so sneaky, he could steal second base with his foot on first.

He's the most highly suspected person in the community.

He's one of those self-effacing, sweet, unpresuming persons—a real phony.

If all the breath he expends on his phony claims could be converted into power, it would supplant atomic energy.

He's a first-class kibitzer—always willing to bet your shirt on someone else's hand.

He claims he does his duty as he sees it—boy, does he need an optometrist!

To get 10 per cent out of him, you've got to be at least his 50-50 partner.

In his footprints on the sands of time he'll leave only the heel marks.

He doesn't do as well at bowling or at the races as he does at poker. That's because he can't shuffle an alley or keep a horse up his sleeve.

He always has a lot of trouble with those fluffy, thick hotel towels—he can hardly close his suitcase.

His wallet is always full of big bills—all unpaid.

He claimed a tax exemption for his mother who's been dead five years. His explanation: "Mother's still very much alive in my heart."

He's making a good living selling burial suits with two pair of pants to people who believe in the hereafter.

He can sell a double-breasted suit to a chap with a Phi Beta Kappa key.

He not only gets a girl up to his apartment to see his etchings, he even sells her a few of them.

Once he hit a man and knocked him six feet in the air; then he sued him for leaving the scene of the accident.

Looking at the high prices on the restaurant menu, he says to his date, "What'll you have, my plump doll?"

When he slaps you on the back. it's only to make sure that you'll swallow what he's told you.

He's making money bottling ashes from a crematorium and selling them to cannibals as Instant People.

You wouldn't even put it past him to pin badges on frankfurters and sell them as police dogs.

He spends a lot of time shining up to the boss instead of polishing off some work.

He not only expects to get something for nothing; he also wants it gift-wrapped.

He recently advertised: "Man with income tax blank would like to meet lady with income."

He has more crust than a pie factory.

He's just a little boy, after all—after all he can get.

If he ever fell over his own bluff, that would really be his downfall!

He's always dating his checks ahead. If he should die, say, on May 15, his tombstone inscription will undoubtedly read: HE DIED MAY 15TH, AS OF JUNE 1ST.

Birthdaze

She claims she's just turned thirty—it must have been a U turn.

Her youth has changed from the present tense to pretense.

She says she's just reached 32. Everyone is curious to know what detained her.

You really can't raise an eyebrow when she says she's only 29. Anybody who sticks to the same story for ten years has to be telling the truth.

She never really lies about her age. She simply says she's as old as her husband—and then she lies about his age.

She's 42, going on indefinitely.

She claims she's approaching 35. Everybody wonders from which direction.

No more candles for her on her birthday cake. On her last birthday the candles looked like a prairie fire.

Now that she's reached 40, it's like launching a rocket—she's started her countdown.

Once on the witness stand she was instructed by a gallant judge: "Madam, state your age—then take the oath to tell the truth."

If you ask her her age, she tells you it's her business—and she's been in business quite a long time.

She claims that she feels like a young colt, but she looks more like an old 45.

She'll never live to be 50. Not at the rate she's been overstaying at 40.

She's a very decisive person. By the time she reached 45, she had definitely decided what she wanted to be—36.

You can tell her age like you do a used car's. The paint job may conceal the age, but the lines show the years.

She claims that when she was eighteen the President of the United States gave her a beauty prize. It's hard to believe that Woodrow Wilson had time for that silly stuff.

There's a woman who really knows how to keep her age—as a matter of fact, she hasn't changed it in seven years.

She says she's around 30, and in a way she's right—nearly the second time around.

The only thing she'll admit about her age is that she's pushing 40. She's not pushing it—she's dragging it.

She's not lying when she claims she just turned 23—she's 32.

On her last birthday she baked the cake herself and inserted the candles—one for every year. She had every reason to be prouder of the design than of her arithmetic.

On her last birthday there were enough candles in the cake to give everyone there a suntan.

The guests tried to count the candles on her cake, but the heat drove them back.

You can't call her a "fast woman." Although 35, she hasn't reached 29 yet.

She was born in the year God only knows when.

It's not that she's shy or demure when she doesn't tell her right age—she dishonestly can't remember.

She's so old, she can get winded at a run in her stockings.

She knew Madame Butterfly when she was a caterpillar.

Boozers

He's not one to do things in halves—he does them in fifths.

When he returns from lunch, he's so loaded they make him use the freight elevator.

The way he's drinking, liquor mortis is sure to set in.

One of these days he'll be killed by a flask of lightning.

He's been frequenting a new night club. It has the nicest tables he's ever been under.

In college he had the reputation for being the highest student in the class, and was voted the man most likely to dissolve.

It's not true that he does nothing but drink—he also hiccups.

He has his doctor worried—he has too little blood in his alcohol stream.

So far as he's concerned. "Sweet Adeline" is the Bottle Hymn of the Republic.

The skeleton in his closet is in the shape of a whiskey bottle.

When he gets a cold, he buys a bottle of whiskey, and in no time it's gone. Not the cold—the whiskey.

There's been a marked difference in his drinking since he's been going to a psychiatrist. Now he drinks on the couch.

There's hardly a morning when he doesn't get up with a toot-ache.

Once he went to a party incognito—stone sober.

He's the nicest chap on two feet, if he could only stay there.

In taverns all over town he's regarded as one of their unsteadiest customers.

He's been expelled from Alcoholics Anonymous. He wasn't anonymous enough to suit them.

The cocktails on his expense account run into a staggering figure.

He's a very friendly drinker. He's always shaking hands—even when no one else is around.

He's been hiccupping a lot lately—just messages from departed spirits.

He gets very indignant when told that he drinks too much—particularly when he can't stand up to dispute it.

An orthopedist is immobilizing his elbow. He drinks so much, everytime he bends it, his mouth snaps open.

If it wasn't for the pretzels, he'd be entirely on a liquid diet.

He can sit for hours in a tavern, where he pays as he glows.

He spends so much time in bars, he's developing rheumatism from picking up wet change.

A woman drove him to drink. He's remembering her in his will as an expression of his gratitude.

He has never cultivated the fine art of nixing drinks.

He frequents so many bars, his suits aren't dry-cleaned—they're distilled.

He's been drinking Bloody Marys mixed with carrot juice. They haven't sobered him any, but he sees better.

If there's a nip in the air, he even tries to drink that.

An entomologist would be interested in him—he's a rare specimen of a barfly.

When you say he's "soused," you can mean it in the "full" sense of the word.

The only thing his health means to him is something to drink to.

He's a man with a lot of liquid assets.

He's having his elbows furrowed so they won't slip off wet bars.

The only exercise he ever gets is hiccupping.

On his last birthday, with just one breath he lit all the candles on his birthday cake.

When the boss asks him to work overtime, he demands time and a fifth.

They have an apt name for him—Jack the Pint Killer.

He's half Scotch—and half shot most of the time.

In a saloon his conversation always buds in the nip.

He's been warned that liquor is a slow poison, but he says he doesn't mind—he's in no hurry.

He's a very public-spirited individual—he always drinks spirits in public.

It takes only one drink to make him drunk, but he's not sure whether it's the ninth or the tenth.

There are times he gets so lit up you can read by him during a blackout.

At the rate he consumes liquor, you can hear the pretzels splash as he eats them.

No wonder they call him "Truck"—he always has a load on.

He's an alcoholic intellectual—a fried egghead.

He's been unsteadily employed at the same job for the past ten years.

He believes in a balanced diet—a highball in each hand.

He's handsome after a fashion—after a couple of old-fashioneds.

At a party he never plays Spin-the-Bottle. He won't let go of it.

At bedtime he drinks a pint of whiskey for his bad case of insomnia. He hasn't cured it, but it's making it a pleasure to stay awake.

Bartenders all over town warn him not to stand up while the room is in motion.

He's a man of settled habits—he's settled down to a continuous round of drinking.

He's a kiss-and-tell, tippling lover. All his loves are brandied about.

Several times he's been held up on his way home; in fact, it's the only way he could have gotten home.

You have to take his drinks apart to see what makes him hic.

Once, in the hospital, he kept asking for water, and everyone knew without a doubt that he was delirious.

His eyes and nose are so red, the Communist Party has sent him a membership card.

He deducts his liquor bills as a medical expense. His customers and he always drink to each other's health.

He's an outstanding candidate for the Alcohol of Fame.

The way liquor makes him fly, bartenders are asking him to land some other place.

A judge told him: "It's alcohol, and alcohol alone, that's responsible for your condition." He answered: "You've made me very happy, judge. Everyone else tells me it's all my fault."

He's been getting so high, he'll have to drink soon with a net under him.

He'd go on the wagon anytime—if he could find one with a bar.

He sure knows how to carry his liquor. When he opens a bottle he gets carried away.

He often goes on a crying jag when he's in a state of melancholism.

He was recently a judge in a beauty contest. The competition wasn't very stiff—but he was.

When he donates blood to the Red Cross, there's so much alcohol in it, they use it to sterilize the instruments.

He's playing a better round of golf lately. He can go around now in a little less than a quart and a half.

He enjoys an energizing workout when he gets up, so he has his own parallel bars—one for rye and one for bourbon.

The way he's flying blind, he'd better sober up real soon for a landing.

The distance between his office and his favorite bar is four blocks going and five blocks coming. He walks straighter going than coming.

It's called for a tremendous amount of will power on his part, but he's finally succeeded in giving up trying to give up drinking.

He's been on the new Drinking Man's Diet, and now he's a thin lush.

He's been using a bourbon-flavored toothpaste. It hasn't helped cut down on his cavities, but "Who cares?" he says.

Recently he fell downstairs with a quart of whiskey, but he didn't spill a drop—he kept his mouth shut.

He's one guy that wasn't just born—he was mixed!

It isn't the *ein* or the *zwei*, but the *drei* martini that gets him lit.

He drinks to soothe and steady his nerves. The trouble is he gets so steady he can't even move.

He hates the very sight of liquor. That's why he drinks so much—to get it out of sight quickly.

He's been practicing yoga as a cure. It hasn't exactly cured him, but now he can get soused standing on his head too.

He talks with more claret than clarity.

It's his ambition to join the Diplomatic Corps. If he ever gets there, he'll live on protocol, alcohol, and Geritol.

He'll never get married. His girl won't marry him when he's stewed, and he won't marry her when he's sober.

Chatterboxes

She's a constant source of earitation.

He's a great talker—one of the best you can ever hope to escape from.

She has a voice that's very hard to extinguish over the telephone.

She can talk 50 per cent faster than anyone can listen.

When she talks you can't even get in a word sledgewise.

He's the type that holds everyone spielbound.

Why, it even takes him two hours to tell you that he's a man of few words.

The smaller his ideas, the more words he uses to express them.

It's not accurate to say that she always has the last word—she never gets to it.

She has a very disconsolate parrot. He's never had a chance.

There are any number of things in life that go without saying —her tongue more than anything else.

She must have been raised on tongue sandwiches.

Her husband can bend a horseshoe with his bare hands, but she can tie up twenty miles of telephone wire with her chin.

He has a picture of her that he took with a highspeed camera —her mouth was closed for a split-second.

It's easy to understand why she talks twice as much as most women—she has a double chin.

She even talks to herself—to be sure of getting in the last word.

Her mouth is so big, it takes her fifteen minutes to get her lipstick on.

She could even have the last word with an echo.

His idea of an ideal conversation is one part you and nine parts me.

He's had ten sets of dentures. He doesn't lose them—he wears them out as a nonstop talker.

You get a gliberal education listening to him.

You like him a lot when you first meet him, but he soon talks you out of it.

No one is his equal at using more words to say less about nothing.

It's just too much to hope that one day he may come forth with a few brilliant flashes of silence.

His lodge brothers are far safer taking their fingers out of a dike than letting him take the floor at a meeting.

He regards free speech not as a right but as a continuous obligation.

He has never made a mistake—and for a good reason. He's never stopped talking long enough to do anything.

He's bought a dozen books on "How to Speak in Public." What he really needs is one on how to shut up.

He thinks by the inch and talks by the yard, until you feel like removing him by the foot.

They call him "the Westerner," because he comes into a room shooting from the lip.

He's a specialist in monopologues.

He makes you wish you were wearing a hearing aid so you could shut him off.

She has a gift for conversation, and everybody would be happy to give her another one to stop talking.

She's the type who's always babbling over with enthusiasm.

It's simply amazing how—with only one tongue and two eyes —she can say more than she sees.

Where she's concerned, one word leads to another 10,000.

You can count on her to respond to any wordy cause.

She's just returned from the seashore with a sunburned tongue.

With her, you can't think twice before you speak—not if you want to get a word in.

She claims that she travels to broaden her mind, but it only seems to lengthen her conversation.

With operations too common these days to talk about, she's hoping for a real serious one so that she can work it into a conversation.

She's the kind of woman who would be enormously improved by laryngitis.

She's sure to be an old maid. She'll never quit talking long enough for any man to kiss her.

Her feelings get terribly hurt when you talk while she's interrupting.

He's as gabby as a barber.

On the witness stand, she swore to tell the truth and the whole truth—but not to stop there.

She's like a clothes moth—always chewing the rag.

He says the Constitution of the United States permits him to talk as much as he likes. The trouble is, the United States has a stronger constitution than his listeners.

His father was an auctioneer and his mother was a woman—thus he comes by his talkativeness naturally.

You can be sure of one thing. He wouldn't listen to you talk if he didn't know it was his turn next.

He regards even a minute's pause in conversation as a social indiscretion. It's his signal to go right back into verbal high gear.

As a conversationalist he's inimitable—and illimitable.

He always has too much conversation left over at the end of his ideas.

He can speak for an hour without a note—and without a point.

His expenditure of words is too great for his income of ideas.

He says the only trouble with his speaking is that he doesn't know what to do with his hands. He should hold them over his mouth.

As a speaker and conversationalist he reminds you of that famous Chinese philosopher, On Too Long.

On the golf course his trap is more annoying than any of the others on the course.

No wonder he's always leading with his chin—his mouth is wide open.

Cranks

One thing an alarm clock never arouses is his better nature.

He has such a long face, barbers charge him double for shaving it.

The idea for whiskey sours must have come from a look at his face.

He's a chip off the old glacier.

He doesn't get ulcers—he gives them.

He has a perfect way of ending office conferences. He says: "All those opposed to my plan say 'I resign.'"

He arrives at the office promptly at 9:00 A.M. in a huff, and departs in it at 5:00 P.M.

There are so many yes men working for him, his firm is called "the Land of Nod."

When he finishes dining, waiters always ask him, "Sir, was anything all right?"

He should have been an undertaker—he has no use for anyone living.

He can cut you dead faster than a coroner performing an autopsy.

One time he was sick in bed for a week, and his secretary sent a sympathy card to his wife.

The last time he was in a hospital, he got get-well cards from all the nurses.

He's always willing to face the music—so long as he can call the tune.

He can become very unpleasant once you get to NO him.

Someone should tell him to idle his motor when he feels like stripping his gears.

He likes people who arrive at firm convictions—after they know what *he* thinks.

His liver is out of order, and his opinions are the same.

The thing he finds hardest to give is in.

His new glasses have helped his vision without changing his prejudiced point of view.

It would be interesting to know on what he biases his opinions.

He really should see a psychiatrist about his infuriating complex.

He hates know-it-alls—those who insist he's wrong.

His favorite expression is: "My mind is already made up, so don't confuse me with the facts."

There are times when he smiles when things go wrong—he has just thought of someone he can blame it on.

His one-track mind wouldn't be so bad if he was ever on the right track.

It's as easy to convince him as to get the hump off a camel's back.

He's so opinionated, his wife said to him one Sunday, "Tomorrow will be Monday, *if it's all right with you.*"

To him life is a mirror and he's always looking for a crack in it.

He's very quick on the flaw.

If he ever gets to heaven, he'll tell the angels, "I don't believe in the heretofore."

As a first-nighter at the theatre, he's always ready to stone the first cast.

He looks for faults as if they were buried treasure.

Give him something for free, and he'll gripe that it wasn't gift-wrapped.

He can make more cutting remarks than a surgeon.

Everything looks yellow to his jaundiced eye.

He hasn't been himself lately. Everyone hopes he'll stay that way.

He got where he is by the sweat of his browbeating.

Someone should tell him it takes only 15 facial muscles to smile and 65 facial muscles to frown, so he should stop overworking himself.

He's as glum as a tongue-tied parrot.

You can always depend on him to contribute more heat than light to a discussion.

His staff meetings are called "listening-things-over sessions"—nobody else expresses an opinion.

He writes all his office memos on "rapping" paper.

The only time he's pleasant is when his staff puts in a good week's work in a day.

You can't help admiring him if you work for him. If you don't, you're fired

The bone of contention in most of his arguments is above his ears.

There may be some rare moment during the day when he isn't disgruntled, but he's certainly far from being gruntled.

What a loser he is! He may be gripping the winner's hand, but he's glaring at his throat.

When he praises you, it's like having the hangman praise your pretty throat.

He'd better keep his words soft and sweet—one of these days he may have to eat them.

He wins all his arguments—but no friends.

He has a chip on his shoulder. It's easy to understand—there's wood higher up.

Cream puffs

He never has to worry about his station in life. Everyone is always telling him where to get off.

They have an apt nickname for him—Old Man Quiver.

When a fight starts, he always does his best—100 yards in 10 seconds.

He got into an argument once and could have licked his opponent with one hand—only he couldn't get him to fight with one hand.

He's as jumpy and fidgety as a long-tailed cat in a room full of rocking chairs.

He's more nervous than a turkey in November.

At the first sign of trouble, he thinks with his legs.

He's such a lightweight, he could tap-dance on a chocolate éclair.

If he goes into an auto showroom just to use the phone, he buys a new car because he hasn't the nerve to walk out without buying something.

He even says "Thank you" when an automatic door opens for him.

He has a sure-fire way of handling temptation—he yields to it.

He's a man of firm convictions. It manifests itself as soon as he knows what anyone else thinks on a given subject.

When he goes to a dentist, he needs an anesthetic just to sit in the waiting room.

Late TV horror pictures don't scare him. When they're over, he just crawls out from under his chair and makes a beeline for his bed.

On his way from home to the airport he even buys insurance for the limousine ride.

He bites his nails so much, his stomach needs a manicure.

He'd commit suicide if he could do it without killing himself.

He's the type of person who can make coffee nervous.

In his spinal column, all the bone is in a lump at the top.

They call him "the Caterpillar"—he keeps his job only by crawling.

You can break him easier than a biscuit.

He's always burying his head in the sand like an ostrich—that's why he's such a tempting target.

He crumbles up like an old ruin under responsibility.

His motto is: "It isn't who you know but who you yes."

His big trouble is that he never NO's his own mind.

He's the kind of guy who falls for everything and stands for nothing.

When faced with danger and threatening disaster, he sets his teeth, assesses the situation in the twinkling of an eye—and then runs faster than a jack rabbit who hears the howl of a wolf.

Since playing the stock market, he's stopped riding in elevators. He can't stand hearing the operator say, "Going down, going down!"

He has such a low, inferior opinion of himself, he wouldn't join any organization that would take him in as a member.

Maybe he doesn't exactly retreat in a fight, but he sure manages to back up enough for a good running start.

He's thankful that he lives in a free country where a man could say what he thinks, if he wasn't afraid of his wife, his boss, and his neighbors.

He'll never get over the embarrassment of having been born in bed with a woman.

She's so nervous she can thread the needle of a sewing machine while the machine is running.

She's never been the same since she opened the refrigerator and saw a Russian dressing.

He wouldn't say boo to a goose.

He's the sort of namby-pamby who gets lost in a crowd of two.

He's as spineless as spaghetti.

He's a willing minion to mass opinion.

In any emergency, he's as helpless as the owner of a sick goldfish.

It's not true that he kisses his boss's feet every day. His boss doesn't come to the office every day.

He has overcome his fear of flying. Pretty soon he may be fearless enough to open his eyes and watch the movies.

He's the kind of mollycoddle who asks permission to ask permission.

The only time he ever walks around with his head high and erect is when he has a stiff neck.

In a recent fight he had his opponent really worried. The guy thought he had killed him.

The average number of times he says "no" to temptation is once weakly.

Do-nothings

He's well known as a miracle worker—it's a miracle when he works.

You can tell he isn't afraid of work. Look at the way he fights it.

As a youngster, he swallowed a teaspoon and hasn't stirred since.

His boss is giving him a raise. His snoring keeps the rest of the employees awake.

He's so lazy, he sticks his nose outside, so the wind can blow it.

There's only one job he's interested in—as a tester in a mattress factory.

He's so lazy his feet hurt before he gets out of bed.

He's taking trombone lessons because it's the only instrument on which you can get anywhere by letting things slide.

His prayers are printed and pasted on the wall. At bedtime, he points to them and says, "Lord, please read them."

He's a real steady worker. If he gets any steadier, he'll be motionless.

Money doesn't grow on trees—even if it did he wouldn't shake a limb to get it.

There's one thing you can say for him. He puts in a good day's work—in a week.

He works eight hours and sleeps eight hours. His boss is firing him because they're the same eight hours.

His boss said to him recently, "I'd like to compliment you on your work—*when are you going to start?*"

He has a standard excuse for loafing. He says, "A body is a machine, and I'm no mechanic."

Generous Nature has provided him with a big cushion to sit around on.

Doctors have diagnosed his case as one of lazyosis, in an advanced stage of idleingytis, with acute symptoms of workophobia, and fearemia of activity.

Asked whether he has any romantic notions, his wife says sadly, "Maybe he has notions, but no motions."

His boss and his wife are demanding to see his birth certificate for proof that he's alive.

His wife is buying him an appropriate gift—something timely and striking—an alarm clock.

The only reason he gets up from bed in the morning is because he can't carry it with him during the day.

He has found a great way to start the day. He goes back to bed.

He's so lazy he won't even exercise discretion.

It's too much of an effort for him to make coffee, so he puts coffee beans in his mustache and sips hot water.

He gets his exercise watching TV horror movies and letting his flesh creep.

During an earthquake alert, he sat up waiting for the shock to shake down his folding bed.

He stands with a cocktail shaker in his hand, waiting for an earthquake.

It's lucky for him that beer cans have been made easier to open —until then he didn't have any exercise at all.

To give you an idea of how lazy he is, he wouldn't even help move his mother-in-law out of his house.

He's one person not likely to walk through a screen door— he's too careful not to strain himself.

He can fall asleep even while running for a bus.

He's made a career out of collecting unemployment insurance.

He's known as the N.Y.U. man—New York Unemployed.

Talk about occupational hazards! He had a narrow escape—he was offered a job when he reported to pick up his unemployment check.

Asked once, "What did you do for a living?" he replied, "I don't know. I've been out of work so long, I forget."

Advised to get a job, invest his salary, and accumulate capital so in time he wouldn't have to work anymore, he replied, "Why do I have to go through all that? I'm not working now."

He's one of those clock-eyed individuals who can't see opportunities.

He's suffering from overwork—overworking his alibi for why he isn't working.

The only exercise he gets is pulling balky ice trays from the refrigerator.

When he got married he proudly told his wife—a successful career woman—that marriage and a career don't mix. Since then he's never worked.

He's a person with his feet definitely on the ground—the trouble is, he doesn't keep them moving.

He joins as many unions as he can, so as to be sure he'll be frequently out on strike.

December is the only month of the year when he works his fingers to the bonus.

Dressed and undressed

She dresses like a lady—Lady Godiva.

She shows a lot of style, and the style shows a lot of woman.

The only thing holding up her dress is a city ordinance.

She wears such tight dresses, the fellows in her office can hardly breathe.

That's a very cute dress she almost has on.

She wears clothes not only to look slim, but to make men look 'round.

Don't try to judge her by her clothes—there isn't enough evidence.

She calls her latest purchase a "going away" dress. It looks like the best part of it left long ago.

When complimented on a dress she wears, she says modestly, "Oh, it's really nothing!" How true.

Tight clothes don't stop her circulation. The tighter her clothes, the more she circulates.

If a moth ever got into her gown, it would die of starvation.

She's switched her style—from off-the-shoulder blouses to off-the-body gowns.

With that dress, it's hard to tell whether she's trying to catch a man or a cold.

A doctor went crazy trying to vaccinate her in a place where it wouldn't show.

She dreamed that she was strolling down the street with nothing on but a hat, and she was terribly embarrassed. It was last year's hat.

Her neckline is pretty near where her waistline ought to be.

She never has to worry about getting into a strip poker game —she has practically nothing to lose.

That dress of hers should be called Opportunity—there's lots of room at the top.

There's one sure reaction to her clothes—low and behold!

It isn't easy to tell whether her dress has a low neckline or a high hem.

She's excited about her new low-cut dress—in fact, she can hardly contain herself.

She wears her clothes so tight, she must like to squeeze out the last ounce of value.

She's a gal with a lot of hidden talent—and she wears clothes that reveal it.

Her slacks are so tight that if she had a coin in her pocket, anyone could tell if it's heads or tails.

She wouldn't be wearing slacks if she had as much hindsight as foresight.

It looks as if her stretch pants had been put on her with a spray gun.

It can truly be said that she wears those low-cut gowns for ample reasons.

She goes out wearing less than her mother wore in bed.

Just as she's given up hope of getting a perfect fitting dress, she luckily finds one that's two sizes too small.

At the year-end, all her friends wish her a Happy Nude Year.

She's one gal who gets along with the bare necessities of life.

Her friends are urging her to run for office, as the only candidate with nothing to hide.

With that strapless gown, it's obvious she's not interested in shouldering any responsibility.

She's very partial to one of her dresses. She wears it when she wants to look halfway decent—but not completely.

Her clothes go to extremes—never to extremities.

As she was leaving the house for a party, she suddenly decided she didn't feel like going, so she put on something and went to bed.

She doesn't find it difficult to meet men—she exposes herself in the right places.

When her friends saw her in that topless bathing suit, it was quite a letdown.

The last night club she went to had a minimum—she was wearing it.

She wears gowns that bring out the bust in her.

One of these days she'll have an accident—catching her foot in her neckline.

She wears sweaters to accentuate the positive, and girdles to eliminate the negative.

Nobody can squeeze more out of a bikini than she can.

She once read the saying, "Man wants but little here below." Maybe that's why her dresses are getting shorter and shorter.

She claims that her new dress is the latest model from Paris. That's not a model—it's a terrible example.

She's worn that dress so many years, it's been in style five times.

Her hat is becoming—becoming worn-out.

She wears a hat with delirium trimmins.

Nobody asks her to remove her hat at a movie—it's funnier than the movie.

With those clothes she wears, her friends have dubbed her "Mrs. Rummage Sale of 1960."

That dress she's wearing will never go out of style—it will look just as ridiculous year after year.

Dumbbells

She has a pretty little head. For a head, it's pretty little.

No one can accuse him of being scatterbrained. He hasn't any brains to scatter.

He has a strange growth on his neck—his head.

She's so dumb, mind readers only charge her half-price.

He's recovering from an unusual accident—a thought recently struck him.

Everyone is rooting for him to get ahead. They don't like the one he has.

She's like yesterday's coffee—a little weak in the bean.

Wisdom often comes with age, but with him age came alone.

He's undoubtedly older than he looks. He never could have gotten so fatheaded so quickly.

No one can drive him out of his mind. At most it would be only a putt.

Any time he gets an idea into his head, he has the whole thing in a nutshell.

He has a chip on his shoulder. It's a splinter from the wood above it.

He says he has a mind of his own. He's welcome to it. Who else would want it?

They call her "Plymouth Rock." She has a shape like a Plymouth and a head like a rock.

He has one of those mighty minds—mighty empty.

He's the world's greatest proof of reincarnation. Nobody could get that dumb in just one lifetime.

An intelligent thought dies quickly in his head—it can't stand solitary confinement.

He should study to be a bone specialist. He has the head for it.

He's always putting off decisions—he's waiting for a brainy day.

They're inventing a new kind of coffin that fits right over the head. It's for guys like him—dead from the neck up.

There's a good reason why he always has that stupid grin on his face—he's *stupid.*

He even wrinkles his brow while reading the comics.

They put better heads than his on umbrellas.

She has a soft heart, and she's let it go to her head.

He has a one-track mind, and the traffic on it is very light.

It's a waste of time to ask him "You know what?" Of course he doesn't.

She doesn't know her own mind—and she hasn't missed much at that.

You can't help feeling sorry for that poor little mind—all alone in that great big head.

It's stretching the imagination a lot to picture him as the end product of millions of years of evolution.

Many doctors have examined his head—but they can't find anything.

The only way she can make up her mind is to powder her forehead.

An idea recently went through his head. That's not surprising —there was nothing there to stop it.

A book has just been written about him—*How to Be Happy Though Stupid.*

He keeps his head when everyone about him is losing his. No wonder—he's just too dumb to understand the situation.

He can safely go into wild country inhabited by head-hunters. They'd have no interest in his.

He's one guy that must have a sixth sense. There's no evidence of the other five.

If it wasn't for the changes in weather, she'd never be able to start a conversation.

She's like Venus de Milo—beautiful, but not all there.

He must be even smarter than Einstein was. Twelve people were said to have understood Einstein. *Him* nobody understands.

If your doctor suggests that you exercise with dumbbells, ask him to join you for a walk.

His train of thought is just a string of empties.

All his life he's worked his head to the bone.

She has a skin of ivory—and so is her head.

He paid $500 to have his family tree searched, and found he was the sap.

Every once in awhile she stops to think; then she forgets to start again.

She has a baby face—and a brain to match.

Be careful how you exchange ideas with him. The result is sure to be a blank for your mind.

They've named a Chinese restaurant after him—Low I. Queue.

In life's battle for success, he doesn't have a secret weapon—like a head.

He was in a fight once, and was knocked conscious.

There are times when he does have something on his mind—he wears a hat occasionally.

He should be careful not to let his mind wander. It's too weak to be allowed out alone.

When he was promoted from the fifth to the sixth grade, he was so thrilled he could hardly shave without cutting himself.

In school he got 100 in the exams—25 in Geography, 25 in Science, 25 in Arithmetic, and 25 in History.

Everyone called him "Corn" in school, because he was always at the foot of the class.

His parents always signed his report card with an X, so the teacher wouldn't know that anyone who could read and write had a son like that.

If ignorance is really bliss, he's the world's happiest guy.

He was born April second—one day too late.

The average man has 12 million brain cells; 11 million 990 thousand of his are unemployed.

If you traded on the stock market with his brains, you'd be wiped out fast.

The most underdeveloped territory in the world has just been discovered—it's under his hat.

His neck reminds you of a typewriter—Underwood.

If he ever talked about what he understood, the silence would be unbearable.

He'll never be too old to learn new ways to be stupid.

He's so dumb, he waters his garden with whiskey to grow stewed tomatoes.

He's hard at work on an invention—color radio.

He's crossing a piece of lead with a rabbit to get a repeating pencil.

He's feeding his hens racing forms so they can lay odds.

He's developing a new health food made of yeast and shoe polish. It's for people who want to rise and shine.

He's crossing a cow with a mule so he can get milk with a kick in it.

He's crossing asparagus with mustard to get hot tips at the racetracks.

He's working on a new invention—a bridge that goes halfway across a river, then turns and comes back again—for people who change their minds.

The only time he thinks is in a poolroom, where he can rack his brains.

He guards against being chilled to the bone—he always wears a hat.

He's not just an ordinary moron—he's the morons' moron.

Everything you say to her goes in one ear and out the other. There's nothing to block traffic.

It would take a surgical operation to get an idea into his head.

He should exercise his head more—to work off some of the fat between his ears.

The story of his life could be titled: *A Sap's Fables.*

Judging by the old saying "what you don't know won't hurt you," he's practically invulnerable.

He has to stand on his head to turn things over in his mind.

He could easily lose ten pounds of surplus fat—if they cut off his head.

He's getting a B.A. degree. He's finally mastered the first two letters of the alphabet—and backwards at that.

He's halfway between a low-grade intellect and high-class numskullery.

He's in real trouble. The electronic brain in the office broke down—now the boss expects him to think.

If you want to get the real dope about anything, go to the real dope—HIM.

He parts his hair in the middle because his head isn't well balanced.

He won't buy a concrete swimming pool. He says he doesn't like to swim in concrete.

He heard about a movie in which a hunter shot an elephant in his pajamas. He says it's silly—what would an elephant be doing in pajamas?

A traffic court judge asked him, "Have you ever been up before me?" He said, "I don't know, judge. What time do you get up?"

A lifeguard told him, "I've just resuscitated your daughter." He roared, "Then, by God, you'll marry her!"

Asked if any big men had ever been born in his town, he replied, "No, only little babies."

He's applying for an insurance policy so that if he should bump his head, they'll pay him a lump sum.

Told by an insurance agent that his company paid over $5 million for broken arms and legs, he asked, "What do they do with all of them?"

He bought a topless bathing suit for his half sister.

Once he saw an old woman fall down, but didn't pick her up. His mother had warned him not to have anything to do with fallen women.

When the librarian asked him if he wanted a heavy book or a light one, he answered, "It doesn't matter—I have my car outside."

He bought a million 1960 calendars for one cent apiece. He figures if 1960 ever comes back again, he'll make a fortune.

He had to see his doctor in the morning for a blood test, so he stayed up all night studying for it.

He shot his wife while buying a house, because the contract read: "Execute all three copies together with your wife."

He admits he's unfamiliar with the works of Sigmund Freud, but says he knows his brother, French.

He's never bought Christmas seals; says he wouldn't know what to feed them.

She was invited to a bridal shower, so she brought the soap.

Asked what she thought about the Common Market, she answered, "I really wouldn't know—my cook does all the shopping."

Following a honeymoon trip to the Twin Cities she had twins. On a later visit to Three Rivers, Ontario, she had triplets. Now she refuses to go with her husband to the Thousand Islands.

He stopped a guy from beating his donkey—a real case of brotherly love.

She won't go to a beauty parlor for a fingerwave. She says, "Who wants wavy fingers?"

She often serves her guests in the nude—whenever the cookbook says "Serve without dressing."

After reading *Les Misérables*, he still can't figure out which of the characters was "Les."

When she goes to a meeting, she never accepts tickets for a door prize. She says she has no use for a door.

A life insurance agent asked him, "Do you want a straight life?" He answered, "Well, I'd like to step out and fool around once in awhile."

The boss told her if her work didn't improve she'd find a pink slip in her envelope. She said, "How nice! Make it a size 36."

He made love to his wife in a jeep over a bumpy road so they'd have a bouncing baby.

He carried a double-barreled gun to the ball game because he heard the Lions were playing the Tigers.

He was asked for a contribution to help the Old Ladies' Home. His question was: "What are the old ladies doing out on a night like this?"

She yanked her daughter out of the co-ed school when she learned that boys and girls matriculated together and were required to engage in extracurricular activities.

She was horrified when her daughter returned from college saying that she weighed 118 pounds stripped for gym. "Who in blazes is Jim?" she wanted to know.

Tell him that since you last saw him a lot of water has gone under the bridge, and he'll be sure to ask, "What bridge?"

He's afraid to take his boots off for fear he'll hurt his feet when he kicks the bucket.

She keeps her baby in a high crib on an uncarpeted floor, so she can hear him if he falls out.

She lies in the sun for hours at the beach so she can be the toast of the town.

She was asked if she cared for Dickens, Shakespeare, and Keats, and she whispered, "Please keep your voice down; my husband has a terribly jealous disposition."

She was asked if she liked codfish balls. "I don't know," she said, "I never went to one."

He went to an oculist to have a tooth pulled. He knew it was an eye tooth.

He bought his girl a pair of stockings with a run in each one; he wanted to get a run for his money.

In the last election, voters were urged to vote bright and early. He voted early.

A real estate man asked him, "How would you like to see a model home?" He answered, "Swell! What time does she quit work?"

His doctor tells him that exercise will kill germs. He says it's silly—how can you get germs to exercise?

He didn't go to the movies to see *Dr. Jekyll and Mr. Hyde.* He doesn't like double-features.

A doctor told her she had acute appendicitis and she snapped indignantly, "Look, Doc, I came here to be examined, not flattered."

He's the kind of lunkhead who would buy the sleeping pills concession in a Niagara Falls hotel.

Where an employment questionnaire requested "Length of residence in home town," his answer was: "About 40 feet."

Asked whether she was in the arms of Morpheus last night, she answered indignantly, "I don't even know the man."

He denies the charge that he's illiterate. He says he can prove his parents were married.

There's no point in telling him a joke with a double meaning. He won't get either one of them.

He always begins a mystery novel in the middle, so he won't only have to wonder how it will end, but also how it began.

Peeking through a hole in the fence of a nudist colony, he was asked, "Are there men or women in there?" He said, "I dunno—none of them's got any clothes on."

He jumped off a bus backward when he heard a man say, "Let's grab his seat when he gets off."

About to extract his tooth, the dentist told the wife, "I'm giving him an anesthetic so he won't know anything." She said, "Don't bother—he doesn't know anything now."

She told her boss, "I'm fed up with the way you criticize my steno work. How do you spell 'quit'?"

Asked, after a late snack in a fellow's apartment, "Now, how about a little demitasse?" she snapped, "I should have known there was a string attached to the invitation."

As a plump tourist in Italy, she was curious to know what makes the Tower of Pisa lean, so she could take some too.

Her husband's name is Otto, and she still can't spell it backwards.

Statistics always confuse him. He heard that every minute a woman gives birth to a baby, and he thinks she should be stopped.

He read that a man gets hit by an automobile every twenty minutes. He says, "What a glutton for punishment that guy is!"

He called it quits when his fourth child was born, because he read that every fifth child born in the world is Chinese.

He wants to live to be 103. He figures he'll have it made then, because few people die after that age.

He took his daughter out of college when he learned that graduates of women's colleges have 1.8 babies.

He heard that more people die in bed than anywhere else, so he doesn't sleep in a bed.

He says if it hadn't been for Thomas Edison we'd all be watching TV by candlelight.

He's too scared to get married. Every time he's about to, some insurance man asks him to take out life insurance.

Asked whether he knows Poe's *Raven*, he replied, "No, what's he mad about?"

She can't find a thing to buy in antique shops. She claims they're not making antiques nowadays like they used to.

He won't let his daughter go to college because he heard that female students have to show their male professors their thesis.

The first time he heard about the Boston Tea Party, he asked who the caterer was.

He went to a fortuneteller to find out where he was going to die, so he can stay away from the place.

She's only had her present job for four days, and already she's two weeks behind in her work.

A fellow asked her if she was a somnambulist. She didn't know what it meant, so she slapped him just to be on the safe side.

He goes to a fortuneteller who charges $10 to read brilliant minds, and $5 for average minds. For him it's only 50 cents.

He keeps jumping up and down after taking his medicine— he forgets to shake the bottle.

She wonders why everyone thinks she has a crazy cat—they keep telling her she has a silly puss.

When a beggar asked him, "Can you give me a quarter for a sandwich?" he said, "Let's see the sandwich."

She came to the office in a bathing suit because the boss had promised to let her get in the office pool.

Sick as he was, he didn't go into the doctor's office because the sign read "9 to 1," and he wanted better odds than that.

He lost his dog, but he won't put an ad in the paper. He says it's no use—his dog can't read.

He was told to try nude painting as a hobby—now he's caught a cold.

She was ruined before she discovered that what her doctor had ordered was not—as she misunderstood—three hearty males a day.

Worried about her poor reflexes, her doctor asked her, "Do you ever wake up with a jerk?" She replied, "I'll have you know I'm pretty choosy about my boyfriends!"

He still hasn't bought an electric toothbrush. He doesn't know if his teeth are AC or DC.

Asked "How do you like bathing beauties?" he answered, "I don't know. I never bathed any."

When the new mayor announced that he was getting rid of some unnecessary bureaus, she wrote him that she was furnishing a new apartment, and could use some of them.

You can't trip him up. Asked to spell Mississippi, he'll come right back and ask whether you mean the river or the state.

He's never slept with his wife. He says it isn't honorable to sleep with a married woman.

She asked her clergyman whether there was any possibility of his sermons being published, and he answered, "Perhaps posthumously." Replied she: "Oh, how nice! And the sooner the better!"

Asked by his psychiatrist whether he had any pet hostilities, he demurred, "Oh, no. I just love animals."

He's fathering a fifth child after four daughters in a row, because the doctor keeps telling him he needs a little sun and air.

She told the bank teller, "I want to make this withdrawal from my husband's half of our joint account."

He's so dumb he thinks that the English Channel is a British TV station . . . that a naturalist is a crapshooter who throws sevens . . . that the Kentucky Derby is a hat . . . that *sic transit* is being sick on an ocean voyage . . . that syntax is the money the church collects from sinners . . . that the St. Louis Cardinals are appointed by the Pope . . . that a cortege is what you buy for your wife on her anniversary.

Entertainers

His audience couldn't have been colder if he had performed in the morgue.

What an actress! Even if she were cast as Lady Godiva, the horse would steal the show.

His performance is most refreshing. The audience always feels good when they wake up.

He went on right after the monkey act and everyone thought it was an encore.

The audience would have loved her voice except for two things —their ears.

As a musician, he should have kept his dissonance.

Ever since he's been on the air, people are tempted to stop breathing it.

He sang one of his numbers during a thunderstorm. To the audience, it sounded like hail.

He claims he took his piano lessons through a correspondence course. He must have lost a lot of lessons in the mail.

He plays just like Van Cliburn—he uses both hands.

If anyone ever belonged at the top of the ladder in the theatre, it's he—helping the stage hands hang a curtain.

After her performance, they gave her the off-key to the city.

He was egged on to acting by ambition and egged off by the audience.

After that performance, if he had any enemies in the audience, he got even with them.

People wait in line at every one of his performances—to get out.

His most recent tour was a big success—he outran every audience.

He could be more successful if he were given the right vehicle —a truck.

As an M.C., he's an outstanding Massacre of Ceremonies.

As an entertainer, he's half comedian and half wit.

He claims his performance was unprepared and unrehearsed. He might have added that it was also uncalled-for.

His performance was up to his usual substandard.

He gave a soon-to-be-forgotten performance.

He's one of those highstrung actors who should be strung even higher.

If Nero played the fiddle the way this fellow does, no wonder they burned Rome.

He thinks he has a finished act. There's no doubt about it— his act is really finished.

He was flattered when a man in the audience applauded—but the guy was only slapping his head to keep awake.

He used to be an architect, and he's still drawing poor houses.

Some actors can stop a show—he's good at slowing it up.

After his performance, the audience clamored for him to come back, but he didn't dare.

As a comedian, he has a repertoire of six jokes all told—and oh! told and told.

The curtain rose on his performance at 8:30. The audience rose at 8:40.

Last night's performance proved beyond doubt that he's going to go far—the audience chased him five miles.

He's such a ham, he'd feel at home between two slices of bread.

He may be a tenor, but he's overpaid if he gets more than a fiver.

She claims she sings by ear. Unfortunately, that's the way her audience listens.

She's a singer who's destined to go far—and the sooner the better.

Her act goes over like a pregnant woman doing a pole-vault.

The way she carries a tune she seems to be staggering under the load.

Such a voice! She couldn't carry a tune if it had handles.

The trouble with her solo is that it's so high.

She's had a very expensive musical education—her father was sued by five neighbors.

She has a wide range—from a high C to a low V.

She has a large repertoire—and that tight dress she wears sure shows it off.

She gives a soap opera performance that's real corn on the sob.

His audiences always look more like posses or juries.

He gave a down-to-earth performance, and the critics buried it.

He could make a lot of stage, TV, and film stars take back seats—if he drove a cab.

She gives· a very moving performance. Long before she's finished, half the audience has already moved out to the lobby.

She sang a very sad number. In fact, the way she sang it, it was pitiful.

His name should always be up on a marquee in bright lights—so that theatregoers can avoid the shows he's in.

Movies and TV programs would be greatly improved if they shot fewer films and more actors like him.

His performance might have gone over better if the seats in the theatre weren't so bad. They faced the stage.

Egotists

If he should ever change his faith, it'll be because he no longer thinks he's God.

If he could ever get anyone to love him as much as he loves himself, it would be history's greatest romance.

She thinks she's a siren, but she looks more like a false alarm.

He always wants to be the center of attraction. Whenever he goes to a funeral, he's sorry he isn't the corpse.

He has an alarm clock and a phone that don't ring—they applaud.

He'll never get married. He can't find a woman who will love him as much as he does.

Someone should tell him the difference between pulling his weight and throwing it around.

He doesn't read books, look at TV, or listen to the radio—they take his mind off himself.

The hardest secret she's ever had to keep is her opinion of herself.

Her body has gone to her head.

He's too puffed up to remember that Napoleon is now a cake and Bismarck is a herring.

Success is going to his head, but it's bound to be a short visit.

He brags that he's sitting on top of the world. Someone should remind him that it turns every twenty-four hours.

He stands high in his own mind, but he's still a long way from the top.

Success turned his head, and it left him facing in the wrong direction.

He's one of those big-shot executives who has to have two desks—one for each foot.

All he needs to boost his ego is a swivel chair.

He likes well-informed employees—those whose views coincide with his own.

He knows when an idea is good—when it's one of his.

One of these days he'll fracture his pride in a fall over his own bluff.

He's the type who talks big and performs small.

Her head is like a weather vane on top of a house. It's easily turned by the slightest wind.

The only time she won't look in a mirror is when she's pulling out of a parking space.

Money has brought him everything except sense and humility.

He thinks he's worth a lot of money just because he has it.

He's never been known to say an unkind thing about anyone —that's because he only talks about himself.

Just get into a conversation with him, and the night will have a thousand I's.

Success hasn't changed him one bit. He's the same stinker he always was.

He's looking for a woman who will look up to him as smart and handsome. What he needs is a nearsighted midget.

He'll never install machines that can do employees' jobs. When he talks, they couldn't listen and nod.

He can pat himself on the back better than a contortionist.

When he brags that he's a self-made man you can't help wondering who interrupted him.

He claims that he's self-made. Too bad he left out the working parts.

If he's *really* self-made, he has no one to blame but himself.

He boasts that he's a self-educated man. There's no question at all about his being his own toot-er.

If he tells you he's a self-made man, just accept his apology and let it go at that.

He keeps reminding everyone that he came upstairs in the world as a self-made man. He must have been born in a cellar.

When it comes to seeing his own faults, he's blinder than an earthworm in a London fog.

He's an eel who thinks he's a whale.

He's going through life with his horn stuck.

Success has not only gone to his head, but to his mouth as well.

His big bankroll is only matched by his big head and his big stomach.

Because this is the machine age, he thinks he has to be the big wheel.

He's a bachelor. He thinks the only justified marriage on record was the one that produced him.

He could take a great weight off his mind—by discarding that halo.

No wonder he suffers from migraine—his halo is on too tight.

He's so egotistical he even signs his name to anonymous letters.

One thing he'll never be in danger of—delusions of humility.

It's a good thing he doesn't have to pay taxes on what he thinks he's worth.

He has a mirror on the bathroom ceiling so he can watch himself gargle.

He can get up in the air faster than a rocket with his inflated ego.

His conceit is in inverse ration to his lack of ability.

He's always singing his own praise, but it's an unaccompanied solo.

His bragging is simply the loud patter of little feats.

He gets carried away with his own importance. The trouble is, not far enough.

He always hires people who like what he likes—him.

If you've never heard a good word about him, it's only because you haven't heard him talking about himself.

He's such a big gun in the office they're planning to fire him.

He's master of the art of making deep noises from the chest sound like important messages from the brain.

His greatest admirer is his wife's husband.

He's sure if he hadn't been born, the world would wonder why.

If you're not talking about him, he's not listening.

He overrates his value to his firm. Even a pair of shoe trees can fill his shoes.

He always envies his new acquaintances—imagine meeting someone great like him!

He needs two private offices—one for his head.

He's the type who swells in prosperity and shrinks in adversity.

He's a big problem to his psychiatrist—he's too big for the couch.

He denies he's conceited. He just happens to have a high opinion of people with ability, good looks, and personality.

He thinks he's cooking with gas. The trouble is, he inhales some of it.

He's never taken a hot shower. It clouds the mirror.

Failures

He has just made the list of the nation's Ten Best Nobodies.

He never made Who's Who, but he's sure to be in "Who's Through."

During the short time he's been on the job, he has displaced genuine ability.

He works his gums talking himself into a job, and gums the works afterward.

Maybe he had the right aim in life, but he's sure run out of ammunition.

He's money-mad. He's never had any money—and that makes him mad.

He's so seedy, he trembles every time he passes a canary.

His boss would gladly pay him what he's worth—but it's against the Minimum Wage Law.

He was voted by his graduation class as the man most likely to go to seed.

Not even the Missing Persons Bureau could help him find himself. He has that certain nothing.

He always takes his salary to the bank. It's too little to go by itself.

He's selling furniture for a living—his own.

He's been up against the wall so much, the handwriting is on him.

His aptitude test shows that his only aptitude is for taking aptitude tests.

He's always sounding off about capital and labor, but he's never had any capital and never did any labor.

His boss keeps telling him, "Your salary raise will become effective just as soon as you do.

He hatches a lot of ideas—the trouble is, he doesn't hitch them.

He sat around so long dreaming of when his ship would come in, his salary got docked.

His boss was disturbed when he told him he was quitting next week—he'd hoped it was this week.

He stayed awake nights figuring how to succeed. It would have been better if he had stayed awake days.

He left his last job because he was told to do something he didn't like—look for another job.

He has always itched for success, but he's never been willing to scratch for it.

There's lots less to him than meets the eye.

He can't tell the difference between working up steam and generating a fog.

He has always watched the clock, so he's still only one of the hands.

He's always been one jump ahead of the other fellow—the trouble is, he's never been headed in the right direction.

He's going steady now with a girl who's different from other girls—she's the only girl who'll go with him.

He's one guy who has ulcers without being a success.

The only thing that keeping his ear to the ground has ever done for him is to limit his vision.

He's *really* in debt! He has more attachments on him than a vacuum cleaner.

He often tells his boss how to run his business. Then his boss leaves in his chauffeured Cadillac, and he takes the subway home.

He's always suggesting campaigns for the future. A few more ideas like those and he won't have any future.

His motto is "All things come to him who waits." The trouble is, he doesn't know what he's waiting for.

A pickpocket once tried to snatch some money from his pocket, but all he got was practice.

He has five keen senses—sight, smell, taste, touch, and hearing. All he lacks is *horse* and *common*.

He worked his head off, and finally got to the top of the ladder —only to find that he'd leaned it against the wrong wall.

He knows that it's not whether you win or lose but how you play the game that counts. Now all he has to find out is: How do you get into the game?

Nobody can call him a quitter—he's always been fired from every job he's had.

He has so many irons in the fire, no wonder the fire is out.

He's making as much headway as a snake making love to a buggy whip.

He's like a fence—just runs around a lot without getting anywhere.

The easiest thing he ever ran into was debt.

Half-doing has been his undoing.

He had an itch to succeed—and got loused up just thinking about it.

His efforts count for as much as the speed of a runaway horse.

He can at least be thankful that his job is too crummy for any self-respecting electronic machine to take it away from him.

If his life's story is ever written, it will be about the Man Who Started at the Bottom—and *stayed* there.

Whenever opportunity knocks, instead of getting off his feet to open the door, he complains about the noise.

Watching an opulent-looking man stepping into his chauffeured Cadillac, he sighed, "There but for me go I."

He has a positive genius for taking a bankroll and running it into a shoestring.

Sending him out to do a man's job is like sending a tadpole to tackle a whale.

He had the world by the tail—too bad he couldn't swing it.

Anytime you find him with his ear to the ground it's just because he's looking for a contact lens.

He's always dropping the ball and then complaining about the way the ball bounces.

He's been waiting for something to turn up. He should have started long ago with his own shirtsleeves.

At least you have to hand it to him for imagination. He thinks he can run the business better than the boss.

He's waited so long for his ship to come in, his pier has collapsed.

His last satisfactory letter of reference read: "—— worked for us for one month. He is no longer working for us. We are satisfied."

He took an aptitude test to find what he was best suited for. It showed the thing he was best suited for was retirement.

At 20 he knew nothing; at 40 he's done nothing; at 60 he'll have nothing.

Here's one guy who never has ups and downs—he always goes around in circles.

He was cut out to be a genius. Too bad someone didn't take the trouble to put the pieces together.

As an infant, his mother paid nursemaids ready cash to push him around in his buggy—and he's been pushed for ready cash ever since.

He'll never be a financial success. He's always coming up with ideas for items that are high-priced, non-habit-forming or non-tax-deductible.

He wanted to be a lawyer badly, and he realized his ambition— he became a bad lawyer.

Fallen angels

She came to the big city as just a slip of a girl, and she's been slipping ever since.

She had a sylphlike figure. Too bad she didn't keep it to her sylph.

She agreed to be a guy's intended. Too bad she didn't know what he intended.

A fellow made improper advances to her in a plane, and she didn't say "Stop or I'll chute!"

She went out with a sailor, not knowing he was a wolf in ship's clothing. Then she dated a G.I.—and didn't call a halt.

She has very little will power, and even less won't power.

A chap told her he was bringing her home to Maw, but he brought her home to paw.

Her boy friend said, "Let's get married or something." Too bad she didn't say, "Let's get married or nothing."

She could speak five languages, but couldn't say "no" in any one of them.

A fellow once fought for her honor. Too bad she didn't.

The boys tell her she's the salt of the earth, and they pepper her with propositions.

She was a well-bred girl—all the fellows buttered her up.

She was just the village belle who wasn't tolled, so she went from good to bed.

She closed her eyes one night when a fellow kissed her—she should have closed his.

Someone should have told her that lots of things have been started by kisses—especially *little things*.

She summers in the Adirondacks, winters in Palm Beach, and falls everywhere.

That fur coat does a lot for her—but then, she did a lot for it.

She skated on thin ice, and ended up in hot water.

They told her that if there was a cherry in it, it wasn't intoxicating.

She went out with chaps who were strict gentlemen from the word stop. Too bad she never learned the word.

She was just a little lamb who didn't give a fellow the cold shoulder, so she came home at 4:00 A.M. with a sheepish grin.

She could hardly wait until she got married—in fact, she didn't.

When a man bought her champagne and got her high as a kite, she didn't suspect there was a string attached to it.

A guy's overtures to her in his convertible drove her to distraction—too bad she didn't walk back.

A fellow said, "I look into your eyes, and I want to teach them the language of love." He found them very willing pupils.

She struggled for years to get a mink coat. Then she stopped struggling—and got it.

A chap gave her candy, and it meant he was thinking about her. He gave her flowers, and it meant he was smitten by her. Then he gave her some fine lingerie, and it meant business.

298 : : FALLEN ANGELS

She was a good girl until she stopped whispering those sweet nothing-doings in fellows' ears.

She went out on a date with a boy friend who took a camera along—she sure was a snap.

She permits fellows liberties only within certain limits—city and state.

The only thing she ever gives is in.

She went on a picnic with a boyfriend, but didn't go with certain provisions.

She was as green as grass, and it didn't take the fellows long to weed out her objections.

She went out with a guy who was a magician, and he turned into a shady lane.

All the boys have to do is put two and two together, and they have her number.

She runs the gamut of emotions—from yes to yes.

When the average girl says "no," she means it—but she's not average.

She claims if her parents had told her about the birds and the bees she wouldn't have got stung.

She went out with a fellow who said he could read her like a book. She didn't realize he liked to read in bed.

A fellow asked her to be his mistress, and she reclined to do so.

She was just a local girl who everybody made good.

She was an inexperienced secretary who didn't know how to keep her boss from ending a sentence with a proposition.

There's nothing complex about her—anyone can grasp her.

She started her sex education with a book titled *What Every Girl Should Know*. It wasn't too long before she was reading *The Care and Feeding of Infants*.

Whenever she was being seduced, she tried hard to remember her mother's warning about men, but she couldn't seem to recoil at the moment.

Features

He's the kind of fellow that girls dream of every night—it's better than seeing him in the light.

She looks good after a fashion—after a couple of Old-Fashioneds.

Looks aren't everything; in her case, they aren't anything.

When she goes down to the waterfront, even the tugboats stop whistling.

He has a very sympathetic face. It has everyone's sympathy.

There's only one trouble with his face—it shows.

She's on the 144th day of a 14-day beauty plan.

When she comes out of a beauty parlor, she looks as though she believes it.

What a face! He has to sneak up on the mirror to shave.

She had a coming-out party, but they made her go back again.

He looks much better without your glasses.

He's always concerned about losing face. He shouldn't be—it would be a decided improvement.

When he was born, folks came from miles around to look at him—they didn't know what he was.

He looks even worse than his passport photograph.

He was missing once, but his wife didn't go to the Missing Persons Bureau—they wouldn't believe it!

He looks like Grant. General—not Cary.

He was a war baby. His folks took just one look at him, and they started fighting.

He's smarter than he looks. *That* at least is reassuring.

He should only go out on Halloween—it's the only time he can pass as normal.

He should join the Ku Klux Klan—he would look a lot better with a hood over his head.

A photographer took his picture, but never developed it. He was afraid to be alone with it in the darkroom.

He looks like a canceled five-cent stamp.

His features don't seem to know the importance of teamwork.

A man's best weapons for attracting women are his physical charms. He should be arrested for carrying concealed weapons.

She appeared recently in a beauty contest, and got several offers—from plastic surgeons.

She smears so much cold cream and oil all over her body that she *slides* out of bed.

She's tried to get a man—but without avail. Maybe she'd better wear one.

At a holiday party, they hung her and kissed the mistletoe.

She has to wait until winter to get a chap on her hands.

A fellow told a friend of his that he'd dig up a girl for him, and evidently he did—he brought her.

A fellow took her out once and announced to his friends: "Was that a girl! Was that a girl! *That's what everyone kept asking*— Was that a girl?"

When she goes into a cornfield, she scares the crows so badly that they bring back the corn they took the year before.

A Martian took one look at her with her thick cold cream, curlers, and hairnet, and exclaimed, "Lantzman!"

She's not exactly bad-looking. There's just a little blemish between her ears—her face.

If a woman's face is her fortune, she'll never have to pay income tax.

Some generous person should give her a kitten—she could use a new puss.

She' had scores of fellows at her feet. They look up at her face, and they're promptly at her feet again.

She's an identical twin, but fellows can tell them apart—her brother has a mole on his cheek.

She looks like a million—every year of it.

Maybe her makeup is an improvement over Mother Nature, but it sure isn't fooling Father Time.

She can easily protect herself from Peeping Toms—all she has to do is leave the shades up.

Everyone says she's an angel fallen from the skies. Too bad she happened to land on her face.

After half a day in a beauty parlor, she still hasn't been worked on—they're still busy giving her an estimate.

As a blind date, fellows look forward to meeting a vision. She's a vision all right—a sight.

She has a bleaches-and-cream complexion.

Her complexion can best be described as seasick green.

She's had her face lifted so many times, she talks through her nose.

She's as wrinkled as a last year's apple.

She's trying a cream that's advertised as able to remove wrinkles from a prune. It hasn't helped her face much, but she sure has some smooth prunes.

She had to have her face lifted—it was a case of drastic surgery.

Her face was lifted the other day, but the crook who took it is bringing it back.

She's had plastic surgery on her face, but it doesn't look any different than it did $1000 ago.

She's never had her face lifted. She was having it done once, but the derrick broke.

Time may be a great healer, but she'd do better with a plastic surgeon.

Every once in awhile she gets a mud pack. It improves her looks for a few days—then the mud falls off.

With all that makeup on, she doesn't look like an old woman anymore—she looks like an old man.

That can't be the face he was born with—it must be a retread.

He has a face like a flower—a cauliflower.

With a face like his, he should sue his parents for damages.

He must be using gunpowder on his face—it sure looks shot.

He has so many chins, he should be careful not to burp—it would start a ripple.

He has so many chins, you can't be sure which one he's going to talk out of next.

Even her double chin has a double chin. Her husband would tickle her under the chin—if he could decide which one.

People look at her and exclaim: "Ah, those eyes, those lips, those chin!"

She has two mink wraps—one for each chin.

You can't blame her for getting mad at people when they tell her to keep her best chin forward.

She needs bookmarks to find her chin.

Her mouth is so small, she has to use a shoehorn to take an aspirin.

He has such a big mouth, he can sing a duet all by himself.

His mouth is so big, when he yawns his ears disappear.

He has a nice head on his shoulders. But it would look better on a neck.

He's been offered a good price for his head, for the top of a totem pole.

Some of his features he got from his mother, and his ears from his father, but that nose could only have been his own idea.

He has a Roman nose—it roams all over his face.

He has a fine set of tooth.

His teeth are like the Ten Commandments—all broken.

He has Pullman teeth—one upper and one lower.

He goes to a dentist twice a year—once for each tooth.

He's a very resolute person—he keeps a stiff upper plate.

He bit into an apple and broke three teeth, but he isn't too concerned. He still has three left.

He has a heart of gold, and teeth to match.

His teeth are his own. He just made the last payment on them.

As a blonde, she's a brunette with a top secret.

Any resemblance between her and a blonde is purely peroxidental.

She uses fine rouges to bring out her cheekbones; good mascara to bring out her eyes; good lipsticks to bring out her lips—but when she gives a good sneeze, it brings out her teeth.

Her hair has been dyed so often, her dandruff is technicolored.

She's a suicide blonde—dyed by her own hand.

She has so many wrinkles on her forehead, she has to screw her hat on.

She's not exactly fading—she's dyeing.

If you put a stick on her hairdo, you could mop the floor with it.

He's so bald, you have to wear sunglasses to look at him in a bright light.

He has waving hair—it's waving goodbye.

He's not baldheaded—he just has flesh-colored hair.

His hair is departed in the middle.

He has a crew haircut. The only trouble is, the crew is bailing out.

From a short distance away, it looks like his neck is blowing bubblegum.

There's one proverb that really depresses him: "Hair today, gone tomorrow."

He was very ambitious, but the only thing about him that has come out on top is his hair.

Barbers don't charge him for cutting his hair—they charge him for searching for it.

He can swat flies with his ears.

From the front he looks like a loving cup.

Ears? When he stands in a restaurant waiting for a table, in no time five hats are hung on them.

The only time you can see a head like his is in a bag of oats.

He's so nearsighted, when he can't fall asleep he counts elephants.

He kisses the cat and puts his wife out.

He walks into a closet and says, "Down!"

In the office he never stops working for even a minute—he can't see when the boss is approaching.

He once picked up a snake to kill a stick.

He has to have contact lenses to find his spectacles.

He belongs to an organization of nearsighted men. They have a theme song: "I've Lost My Glasses—I Wonder Who's Kissing Her Now."

His eyes are so askew, he can watch a tennis match without moving his head.

Her right eye must be real fascinating—her left eye keeps looking at it all the time.

There may not be much character on his face, but what a face on that character!

A face like a bottle of warts . . . like a busted sofa . . . like a smoked herring . . . like a squeezed orange.

She says her face is her fortune. That woman is full of hard-luck stories.

Figures

HERS

She has a real faminine look.

All her sweater does for her is make her itch.

That sweater doesn't do her too much good. The way she looks in it, the wool looked better on the sheep.

She'll never be a bonnie lassie as long as she has that bony chassis.

She just doesn't have the backbone to join a nudist colony—not with *that* knobby spine.

When she drinks tomato juice, she looks like a thermometer.

A fellow with a skinny girl friend like her doesn't get around very much.

She resorts to all sorts of devices to fill out her figure—and it's a sham dame.

She's straight and marrow.

She admits she has a boyish figure—and that's straight from the shoulder.

There's enough cotton in her sweater to start a goodsized first-aid station.

If it wasn't for her Adam's apple, she wouldn't have any shape at all.

There's only one trouble with her figure. It comes out where it should go in, and where it comes out it stays right where it is.

She doesn't have to take a back seat to anyone—and she has the back seat to prove it.

Her girdle is the outstanding example of the difference between fact and figure.

She looks like a piano. If she weren't so upright, she'd be grand.

Now that her husband has enough money to buy her dresses for a fancy figure, she no longer has one.

Her little daughter was once asked, "What will you do, dear, when you're as big as your mother?" and she answered, "Diet."

She's a light eater. As soon as it gets light, she starts eating.

She's been on several diets. The only thing that got thin was her temper.

She eats like a bird—a peck at a time.

Those between-meal snacks are the pauses that reflesh her.

She's been on a coconut and banana diet. It hasn't reduced her, but you should see her climb trees.

She went through with that 14-day diet, but all she lost was two weeks.

Her problem isn't just taking off weight, but rearranging it.

She's much too big in the first place, and in the second place, too.

She's a well-reared female.

She's a real big-hearted woman—with hips to match.

What a nice figure she had!—fifty pounds ago.

With a figure like hers, she has a brilliant career ahead—as a model for slipcovers.

They say figures don't lie, but her girdles sure condense the truth.

She claims to be one of the "400," but she doesn't look a pound over 350.

She's a real Oomph gal—when she sits on a sofa, it goes oomph.

She'll never take your breath away unless she takes a lot of that breadth away.

She's really watching her weight—watching it go up.

Everytime she steps on a scale, she's reminded of one of President Roosevelt's famous phrase: A gain—and a gain—and a gain.

You really enjoy seeing her laughing—so much of her has a good time.

She doesn't realize that while some women may look attractive in slacks, that doesn't hold true for the bulk of them.

Once she did have an hourglass figure, but the sands of time ran down—to the bottom.

Her girdles and corsets give her an hourglass figure, but without them—Big Ben.

For the past two weeks, she's been doing a lot of horseback riding, and she's taken off ten pounds—from the horse.

She's very prominent in the best of society circles, and around the hips.

Whenever she sings, you wonder how a little aria can come out of such a big area.

Examining her, an absentminded doctor said, "Open your mouth and say moo."

She once had a million-dollar figure. Too bad inflation set in.

She's looking for a girdle to support her in the manner to which she's accustomed.

When she walked down the aisle with her groom, they had to walk single file.

She's putting on so much weight, she's running out of places to hide it.

Trying hard to get on a bus, she snapped to the man in back of her, "If you were half a man, you'd help me onto this." He answered, "If you were half a lady, you wouldn't need any help."

HIS

He has a military figure—some of it goes to the front.

He's a do-it-yourself man. He made a bay window with a knife and fork.

It's not the minutes he takes at the table that put all that weight on him—it's the seconds.

He's real unhappy because he has only one mouth.

His indigestion is due to his inability to adjust a square meal to a round stomach.

Prosperity has not only gone to his head, but to his stomach.

He has a stomach without a memory.

He has T.B.—Twin Bellies.

You can always depend on him. With his avoirdupois he'll never stoop to anything low.

He's a man who carries a lot of weight—in his stomach.

He can take a shower without getting his feet wet.

The President of the United States should appoint him chairman of the government's Physical Fatness program.

If he's not overweight, then he's certainly six inches too short.

He's scared of his own shadow—it's beginning to look like a mob.

He's one guy who doesn't need a build-up—he has enough as it is.

When he has his shoes shined, he has to take the bootblack's word for it.

There's one thing bigger than his stomach—his appetite.

He's stopped dancing. He can't find a concave woman for a partner.

He certainly cuts a wide swath among women.

He quit his job as a food taster—didn't get enough time off for lunch.

His posterior isn't just a seat—it's a whole county seat.

He got on a talk-your-weight scale, and the voice called out: "One at a time, please!"

Does he love to eat! His stomach always comes first—especially when going through a door.

He got on one of those scales that stamps the weight on a card. When the card came out, it read: "Please return later—*alone!*"

He can sit around a table all by himself.

He snapped to his wife: "Where is all the grocery money going?" And she said, "If you really want to know, stand sidewise and look in the mirror."

There are just two things he can't eat for dinner—breakfast and lunch.

He's not only a heavy but a fast eater. He's starting on his desert before the echo of his soup has died away.

He has an optimistic stomach and a pessimistic digestion.

He's on a garlic diet. He hasn't lost any weight, but quite a few friends.

Lots of people in town knew him when he had only one stomach and one chin.

He always has intimate little dinners for two. Trouble is, no one else eats them with him.

Lately he's tried tranquilizers to reduce. He hasn't lost any weight, but he *has* stopped worrying about being beefy and paunchy.

He must have grown up when meat was cheap.

He's tried many diets, but let's face it—he's a poor loser.

He has a big heart, and a stomach to match.

He's a man with an outstanding personality, and it's all in his bay window.

THE SHAPE HE'S IN

He looks like his dear departed brother—ten years after he departed.

Better bodies than his can be found in a used car lot.

You take one look at him, and wonder whether there were any other survivors.

He looks like he'd been sent for and couldn't come.

He loves nature, despite what nature did to him.

The only reason he doesn't beat his breast in time of trouble is that he can't find it.

He's one guy who'll never be a blood donor—in fact, he's not even a blood owner.

He must have gone to the blood bank and forgotten to say "when."

Following his physical, he asked the doctor, "How do I stand?" Replied the doctor, "I don't know—it's a miracle."

He's taken vitamins A, B, C, D, E, F, and G, and still looks like H.

As an insomniac, he takes yellow, green, blue, and red sleeping tablets before retiring. He still doesn't get much sleep, but at least when he does he dreams in Technicolor.

He looks like he gave his pallbearers the slip.

When he sneezes, it's really germ warfare.

On his wedding day, they didn't throw rice as he left the church—they threw vitamins.

His insurance man takes a look at him and turns pale.

He's the perfect picture of health. Unfortunately, the frame isn't.

Maybe he isn't quite ready yet to kick off, but his doctor doesn't think it'll do him any good to start a magazine serial.

He's seeking a new type of insurance company—the Black and Blue Cross.

A doctor told him he's "as sound as a dollar"—and he hasn't figured out yet that he's half dead.

One time a cop accosted his wife as she was out in the street with him, and inquired, "Lady, did you report this accident?"

His doctor has just advised him: "In your condition, you'll have to give up wine and women, but you can sing as much as you want to."

He's got a ringing in his ears like a bellhop.

As the doctor compared his latest X rays with last year's X rays, he asked, "No worse?" The doc took a good look and answered, "No man."

With that bad liver because he's a good liver he's likely to be a short liver.

Not for him are night clubs—he patronizes a spot called the Slipped Discotheque.

He claims he's taking a strength- and health-building correspondence school course. They must have forgotten to mail him the muscles.

He's so thin, it takes two of him to make a shadow.

They had to make room for him on a transcontinental flight—so they removed ten airmail letters.

When he takes his clothes off, it's like watching the unveiling of a golf stick.

He's been offered a job modeling for thermometers.

When he wears a black suit, he resembles a closed umbrella.

His wife says exactly the same about him as she does about astronauts and male movie stars. She looks at one of them and says, "This is a man!" And she looks at him and says, "This is a man?"

Flat tires

Her boy friends like her just the way she is—single.

A square like him they could build a town around.

She's one girl you like to bring home to Mother—her mother.

She can trace her ancestors back to the wallflower.

For years now, she's been planning a runaway marriage with her boyfriend—but every time they plan, he runs away.

She's a real "It" girl. People take one look at her and ask, "What is it?"

He goes out with very religious girls. They take a look at him and exclaim, "Oh, God!"

She swears she's never been kissed. She can hardly be blamed for swearing.

She prays every night, "Dear Lord, I don't ask a thing for myself. Just send my parents a son-in-law."

Her last boyfriend is wondering who's kissing her—and why.

Even at a charity ball, fellows don't ask her to dance.

She thinks she knows now when she's getting married. A fellow told her it will be a cold day in December when he marries her.

The boys don't call her attractive, nor do they call her homely —they just don't call her.

She's had a love seat for three years, and one half of it is still new.

She's willing to enter into the give-and-take of marriage. The trouble is, she can't find anyone who'll take what she has to give.

With those low-cut dresses it's obvious she's out to catch a man—but all she catches is a cold.

She has to change her seat four or five times in a movie theatre before she can get someone to annoy her.

She's never been able to train a guy's voice to have an engagement ring in it.

Every night when she climbs into bed, she sighs, "Ah-men!"

She was two-thirds married once. She was there, the minister was there, but the groom didn't show up.

She's in the prim of life.

She's such a prude, she blindfolds herself while taking a bath.

She won't even stay in the same room with a clock that's fast.

She won't even look at anything with a naked eye.

In school she refused to do improper fractions.

She even blindfolds the goldfish when she takes a bath.

Fellows only take her to the movies when they want to see the picture—and they sit in the orchestra.

A guy took her out recently—an outstanding member of the Humane Society.

She's just met a fellow who's unquestionably her type—he's alive and breathing.

She not only kisses a fellow to hold him, she has to hold him to kiss him.

She's not like some girls who rush into marriage—she's waiting for someone to ask her.

One time she was engaged and she and her boyfriend were half serious about getting married. She was and he wasn't.

Lately she's been hanging around draft boards waiting for rejects.

She's having a disagreement with her fiancé. She wants a big church wedding—and he doesn't want to get married.

She likes to be looked at and up to, and fails on both counts.

He's the answer to a maiden's prayer. No wonder so few girls are praying nowadays.

He has a leaning toward blondes—but they keep pushing him back.

When he sits on a couch with a girl and the lights go out, he spends the rest of the evening repairing the fuse.

If his girl friend puts out the light when they're sitting on the couch, he gets up and goes home—says he can take a hint.

With a bit more effort on his part, he could be a nonenity.

He's the type that has that certain nothing.

Any woman who goes out with him sure must love the simpler things in life.

He's gotten all his letters back from his latest girl friend, marked "4th Class Male."

He has as much passion as an exercise in calculus, and as much romance as a stockyard.

His father wanted a boy, his mother wanted a girl—and they're both satisfied.

He asked a girl for "just three little words that will make me walk on air." She obliged him—with "Go hang yourself."

So far as women are concerned, he's nonhabit-forming.

He claims that women are shorter than they used to be. No wonder—they shrink from his touch.

He says he can marry any girl he pleases. The trouble is, he doesn't please anybody.

He's the type who attracts raving beauties—escapees from the booby hatch.

For years he's been looking for a girl who's tall and willowy. Now he'll settle for one who's short and willing.

Goat-getters

He thinks he is the very apex of creation. Actually, he's the ex-ape.

Whoever first said "Love thy neighbor" never had one like him.

If Moses had known him, there would positively have been another commandment.

He's the type you'd like to run into sometime—when you're driving and he's walking.

Some people are born great, some become great—he just grates.

He has a dual personality—Dr. Heckle and Mr. Snide.

He's the kind who can really creep into your heart and creep into your mind. In fact, you'll never meet a bigger creep.

He's a square shooter—one of those squares you'd love to shoot.

Whoever made that pest should have kept the mold and thrown *him* away.

There's nothing wrong with him that a miracle couldn't cure.

Two women once fought a duel over him to decide who'd get him. One got him in the leg and the other in the arm.

One of these days he's sure to be arrested for impersonating a human being.

If he ever needs a friend, he'll have to get a dog.

The only way he'll ever avoid having enemies is to outlive them.

He's one person who'd make a perfect stranger.

He recently asked someone for a dime to call a friend. "Here's twenty cents," he was told. "Call *all* your friends!"

He'll never get sick—no germ could stand him.

There are no two people alike, and everyone who knows him is glad of it.

He hasn't been himself lately—everyone has noticed the improvement.

He's such a pain in everyone's neck, the aspirin people are considering giving him a royalty.

When he was born, they fired twenty-one guns. Too bad they missed.

He comes from a really brave family. They just didn't know the meaning of "quit" until he was born.

When the stork brought him, he flew around the zoo for a week before he had the nerve to drop him off at his parents' house.

His folks took one look at him when he was born, and hired a lawyer immediately to find a loophole in the birth certificate.

His father passed out from sheer fatigue—from throwing rocks at the stork. He should have kept the cigars and given *him* away.

People have watched him—man and boy—for many years, and they don't like him any better as a man than they did as a boy.

Everyone confuses him with a hockey player. They tell him, "You stink on ice."

The next time you'll meet anyone like him it will be during a siege of heebie-jeebies or delirium tremens.

The only time in his life that he was ever popular was as a kid in school. He gave all the kids measles just before exams.

He's in no danger of being kidnaped—he hasn't a friend who could be contacted for ransom arrangements.

He has only two faults—everything he says and everything he does.

When he calls you on the phone and says, "Guess who this is," you don't have to guess what he is.

He makes you wish his parents had never met.

People like him don't just grow on trees—they swing from them.

No one really knows what makes him so obnoxious, but whatever it is, it works.

He's nasty, repulsive, repugnant, disagreeable, offensive, belligerent, pugnacious, and antagonistic—and those are his good points.

He thinks he's out of this world—and everyone wishes he were.

He's one of Nature's disagreeable blunders.

He'll waste his time doing his Christmas shopping early. The odds are definitely against his having any friends left by Christmas.

There's no middle ground where he's concerned—you either hate or detest him.

A number of his acquaintances have named their first ulcers after him.

He has grown up to be the kind of a fellow his mother warned him not to associate with.

He's a man of many parts—and it's a lousy assembly job.

Bees are much too busy for birth control, which makes it understandable why there are so many sons of bees like him around.

His girl friend demanded a refund on the perfume she had purchased because all it attracted was *him*.

You really have to know him to depreciate him.

He's a real smellcbrity.

He's in the public cye all right—as a cinder.

He's made quite a name for himself, but his acquaintances are too gentlemanly to tell him what that name is.

He is one person who should speak well of his enemies—after all, he made them.

He's the kind of guy you'd rebuff even if you were bleeding to death and he had the only available tourniquet.

Scientists who have studied him go even further than Darwin did. They say people like him have already started on the return trip.

A newspaper erroneously printed a notice that he had died. Next day they announced: "We regret that the notice of his death was not true."

He's fond of travel. He's always going from city to city, greeting old enemies and making new.

If a revolution ever breaks out in this country, it will be everybody against him.

The chief trouble with human nature is that there are too many guys like him connected with it.

He's the outstanding justification for mercy killings.

He thinks everyone worships the ground he crawled out of.

"You remind me of the ocean," a girl told him. "Oh," he asked, "you mean wild, restless and romantic?" "No," she said, "you just make me sick."

With his money, he has just about everything a girl could want. The only trouble is, he goes with it.

He's the kind of guy who can give a headache to an aspirin.

When he dies, they'll bury him face down—so he'll see where he's going.

On his demise, a great many people will attend his funeral—to make absolutely sure he's dead.

His death notice is sure not to appear in the obituary columns, but under "Public Improvements."

Whoever eulogizes him will undoubtedly say, "He was a fine man, a good citizen, a great friend—provided he's really dead."

In psychoanalysis he finally found his real self—only to discover that he stood for everything he disliked.

He's the type you like better the more you see him less.

If he ever has his life to live over again, he shouldn't do it.

Gold diggers

She has a split personality. Whenever she meets a man with money, she's ready to split it with him.

She doesn't care especially for a man's company—unless he owns it.

She's a real athlete—always ready to play ball with a man with a bankroll.

She enjoyed swimming with a playboy banker. Now she can float a loan.

If you think postage rates are high now, you should see what she charges just to play Post Office.

When she strokes men's foreheads, little do they suspect it's their scalps she's after.

She's ready to put her trust in a man—if he'll put his money in trust for her.

Her specialty is promoting well-heeled playboys—thar's gold in them thar heels.

Green is the color that's most restful for her eyes—especially the long green.

She's a girl with a past, and the only way to figure in her future is with a present.

324

Her idea of a romantic setting is one that has a diamond in it.

She likes men who, when they look at her, make dollar signs run up and down her spine.

Her latest sugar daddy irks her—but after all, it's nice irk, if she can get it.

She doesn't mind if a man loves her and leaves her—if he leaves her enough.

It's not hard to meet her—just open your wallet, and there she is.

Any guy who's foolish enough to write her a love letter, might as well start it, "Darling, and Gentlemen of the Jury."

She likes men who go for stocks and bonds and put their stock in blondes.

She's going around with an eccentric rich guy who's really cracked; but she doesn't mind, so long as he isn't broke.

She drops in occasionally on her sugar daddy to take his wallet for a walk.

When she goes out with a man, she really thinks of his value —his cash surrender value.

No sooner does a fellow lose his capital than she loses her interest.

She has a peculiar idea of fair exchange. A boyfriend gave her an Oldsmobile and she gave him the Dodge.

She likes a four-letter man—whose four letters are enough to convince a jury.

She sure knows what to give a man who has everything—encouragement.

When a fellow goes out with her, his heart may be in the clouds, but her hand is in his pocket.

She knows how to get minks and sables. The same way minks get minks and sables get sables.

She got tired of trying to get a pearl out of an oyster, so she smarted up—and got a diamond out of an old crab.

She specializes in finding dopes who can be easily cleaned by soft soap.

She calls her latest boyfriend Louis, because he's the 14th whose bankroll she has taken.

Her head on a guy's shoulder accomplishes more than his does.

If you should exclaim, "Goodness, what a lovely fur coat," she'll admit that goodness had nothing to do with it.

She has the combination to open her paramour's safe—36-24-36.

She's not interested in every Tom, Dick, and Harry. She's out to get Jack.

With her, romance starts with sentiment and ends with a settlement.

The fellows all call her "the Baseball Girl"—she won't play without a diamond.

She doesn't talk all the time. Sometimes she listens—when money talks.

If you think women aren't explosive, just try dropping one.

Her current inamorato calls her "Resolution"—she's getting harder to keep.

She has no use for men who try to mess up the country's prosperity by living within their income.

When her latest lover broke off their engagement, she didn't take it to heart—she took it to court.

She resembles an insurance policy—both have cash surrender value.

She knows how to make a rich guy stop, look, and loosen.

She doesn't mind if a man doesn't have his name in the Social Register, so long as he has enough in the cash register.

In slang terms, her boyfriends may know their onions when it comes to tomatoes, but she knows her carats.

When friends ask her, "Where have you been keeping yourself?" she answers truthfully, "I haven't."

It doesn't take her long to snare a rich guy—just a little wile.

She was interested in do-re-me and went so-fa.

She's not the least bit interested in go-getters—she looks for already-gotters.

She enjoys being read to—from a bankbook.

When she tells a guy, "I'll never forget the loving things you wrote me," he'd better start looking for a good lawyer.

She's still a child at heart. She likes her sugar daddy to give her blocks to play with—48th to 52nd street.

She wears perfume that brings out the mink in a man without stirring up the wolf.

Her friends wonder who's the rich old geezer they've been seeing her outwit.

She scoffs at the idea of going to a psychiatrist. Why should she lie down on a man's couch, and then pay him?

When she told a man, "I can't learn to love you," he said, "But I have $100,000." Quickly she said, "Give me one more lesson."

She never got anywhere by putting her shoulder to the wheel, so now she puts her head on the shoulder of the man at the Cadillac wheel.

She has a real gift for love-making—usually it's a diamond.

She goes out with sentimental men—the very sight of her brings a lump to their wallets.

Since her latest boyfriend met her, he can't eat, he can't sleep, he can't drink. No wonder—he's broke.

She looks real nice in that new gown. She was not only just made for it, but for a fur coat, too.

She has a great sympathy for a lonely man—who needs someone to share a bank account with him.

Gossips

What she hears is never as exciting to her as what she overhears.

She takes people at their deface value.

Her favorite expression is: "I'm telling you this in confidence, because it was told to me in confidence."

You'll always find him at cocktail parties, where he drinks martinis, spears olives, stabs friends, and spills the beans.

You'll always find her in a beauty parlor, where she gets a faceful of mud and an earful of dirt.

She's never yet returned from the beach without a sunburned tongue.

She doesn't only engage in conversation—she syndicates it.

Tell most people something, and it goes in one ear and out the other. Tell her something, and it goes in both ears and out of her mouth.

She's very discriminating. She picks her friends—to pieces.

She knows how to guard a secret. She tells it to only one person at a time.

She weighs her friends' faults with her thumbs on the scale.

She's never happier than when she's taking someone for deride.

Sometimes she doesn't go into all the details. Her explanation is: "I've already told you more about it than I heard myself."

Time will never tell on her women friends as much as she does.

Recently she heard something about someone that she didn't repeat to anyone—*she didn't know it was a secret*.

The only two things that stop her from office-gossiping are the hands of the clock at 5:00 P.M.

She doesn't actually believe everything she hears—but that doesn't prevent her from repeating it.

She has gossip down to a fine art—she whispers it.

Her friends come to her parties with open throats and backs suitable for knifing.

One of these days she's going to get caught in her own mouth-trap.

His business is everybody's business.

He whitewashes himself by blackening others.

He never tells a lie—if the truth will do as much damage.

He must have goat glands—he's always butting in.

He'd have a few friends if he'd let opportunity do the knocking.

The only time he really gets interested in something is when he's sure it's none of his business.

His chief delight is giving you the low-down on the higher-ups.

Accustomed as he is to public peeking . . .

He's a professional athlete—of the tongue.

She was overheard breathlessly telling a friend: "I just must tell this before I find out that maybe it isn't true."

Her great fear is that if she doesn't gossip she'll have no friends to speak of.

She always listens to both sides of an argument—when it's by her next-door neighbors.

Watch out for her when she's in a train of thought—someone is about to get run down.

She's always flying around carrying her tale with her.

She has perfect gossip technique—she knows exactly how much to leave out of the conversation.

If she tended more to her knitting, she wouldn't get so tangled up in her yarns.

He should have been an elevator operator, the way he keeps running people down.

He can always be found at a cocktail party with a drink in one hand and a knife in the other.

In the business world he's known as the "meddle"-man.

He has the narrowest mind and the widest mouth.

It's easy to understand why he doesn't mind his own business —he doesn't have either a mind or a business.

He's been known to say: "And I can tell you all this without the slightest fear of verification."

He's the top man on the "quote-'em" pole.

He does all that knocking because he's never been able to ring the bell.

A bright eye may indicate curiosity; his black eye, too much.

She cultivates her friendships like a garden—with continuous little digs.

They call her "the Businesswoman." She's interested in business—everybody's.

Boy, can she turn an earful into a mouthful!

She's unhappy. She works in an office so big, it takes three days for one of her choice morsels of gossip to reach everybody.

One thing you've got to hand to her—she can put two and two together—whether they were or not.

With her a secret is either not worth keeping or "too good to keep."

Her gossip is enough to make everyone she-sick.

Her gossip is distilled wine from sour grapes.

Husbands

HENPECKED

He's underfed, undernourished, and over-wifed.

He wasn't born meek—he married her and got that way.

After all is said and done, it is she who has said it and he who has done it.

When they have an argument, they soon patch things up—his nose, his jaw, and his head.

They agree in their thinking—only she always has the first and deciding think.

The last time she said "yes" to him was when he proposed.

Before they were married, she promised to knit for him. Now she needles.

They once spent some time in a nudist camp; even there she told him what not to wear.

His big trouble is a superiority complex. The trouble is it belongs to her.

He really envies a bachelor who has to fix only one breakfast before he goes to work.

She has him on an allowance—fifty words a day.

333

He anticipated a peck of troubles when they were married, but not a hen-peck of troubles.

She's found a way to save on dishwashing time—she has him eating out of her hand.

In their home he puts his foot down—when she's through vacuuming under his chair.

She says she can read him like a book, but he wishes she didn't do it so loud.

Before they were married, he was an atheist and didn't believe in hell. However, she's now convinced him he was wrong.

He's a very efficient man-around-the-house. He knows the best time to take out the garbage—when she orders him to.

He bought a book, *How to Be the Boss in Your Own Home*, but she hasn't yet permitted him to read it.

He once asked a librarian, "Have you a book called *Man: the Master of the Home*?" She replied, "That must be in the Fiction Department, sir."

One thing is sure—any man would stay home with a wife like her. He'd have no choice—she has a double lock on the door.

When he proposed, he vowed he'd go through hell for her, and she's seeing to it that he keeps his promise.

He always takes her little hand in his—as she raises it to sock him.

When he isn't home she goes outdoors to insult the neighbors, just to keep in practice.

Once he decided to leave home, and he called up the zoo to find out whether they had an extra cage.

He walked out on her once, and she sneered: "You'll come back all right. How long do you imagine you'll be able to stand happiness?"

She keeps reminding him that when he proposed he vowed he'd die for her. All she wants to know now is how soon.

He's sorry now he put her on a pedestal. She can order him around better from that position.

He's so well trained, he feels in his pocket everytime he passes a mailbox.

He frequently has to phone her to say that he left his lunch money in his apron pocket.

He meets every matrimonial crisis with a firm hand—full of flowers and candy.

Marriage for him is like a railroad sign. When he first saw her, he stopped, then he looked—now he listens.

They have two cars, two TV sets, and two of many other things, but only one opinion—hers.

The only reason she promised at the altar to honor and obey him was that she didn't want to make a scene in front of all those nice wedding guests.

He should have suspected he was going to be henpecked when he hung the "Home, Sweet Home" plaque, and she snapped, "On the other wall, stupid!"

He should have known what he was in for when he carried her over the threshhold, and she commanded, "Wipe your shoes!"

He really should have been warned at the wedding reception when she tossed his bag of golf clubs from the top of the stairs.

He won her with soft soap; now he's washing the dishes.

Asked by the census taker what he did before he was married, he answered with a sigh, "Anything I wanted to."

His young son, studying geography, asked him, "What do you call those people who wear rings in their noses?" "Husbands," he replied.

When they were married, she promised to let him run the show, but forgot to add that she intended to write the script.

He's one husband who doesn't permit his wife to have her own way. She has it without his permission.

During their courtship he used to hold her hand and, ah! it was love. He's still doing it, but, oh! it's self-defense.

She doesn't always wear the pants in the family—sometimes she's satisfied with just a few cuffs.

When he asks her for a cup of hot chocolate, she gives him a chocolate candybar and a match.

She hires his office help. They're neither redheads nor blondes —they're bald and have mustaches.

Reincarnation really has him troubled. He's worried that if he comes back as a dog, she's sure to return as a flea.

In any argument with her, he's learned it's a bad idea to put his foot down—he's sure to get it stepped on.

He's satisfied to let her have the last word in an argument. Anything he says during one is the beginning of another argument.

Even when he hasn't said a word during one of her long tirades she's not satisfied—he has to wipe his opinion off his face.

He feels most at home at the race track, where it's nag, nag, nag.

His motto is: "A word to the wife is sufficient—just Yes."

After a poker session, he comes home and throws his arms right around her—before she can take a swing at him.

She's always glad to fix him a Bloody Mary—with *his* blood.

He's just been given three weeks to live—that's how long she's going to be away on vacation.

He's so henpecked, he'd have to ask her permission to kill himself.

He's the champion henpecked guy of all time. A year ago he got a Mexican divorce, and he still hasn't had the nerve to tell her.

THE BITTER HALF

There's only one thing that keeps her from being a happily married woman—*him*.

So far as she's concerned, he's one of the main reasons for twin beds.

She calls him "Hon"—Attila the "Hon."

Before they were married, he assured her that nothing was too good for her, and that's exactly what she's getting—nothing.

He's one guy who could make a wife a lucky widow.

When he proposed, he vowed their marriage would be for life. Now she wants to know why he doesn't show some.

She doesn't need a clock—she can tell the time by the length of his whiskers.

She keeps asking him to show her his birth certificate. She wants proof that he's alive.

She bought him an appropriate gift for their anniversary, something real timely and striking—an alarm clock.

He sleeps like such a dead one, she's already collected on his life insurance.

She was a career woman, and he told her at the start of their marriage that a career and marriage don't mix—so he's never worked.

She often tells him, "I do wish I'd known you when you were alive."

He likes to tinker around the house. In fact, she calls him the biggest tinker in town.

She's the power behind the drone.

He promised her a golden lyre when he proposed to her, and that's what she got—a golden liar.

She thought he was a bookworm, but soon learned that he was only a worm.

When the minister asked, "Is there anyone present who objects to this marriage?" she's sorry now she didn't say, "I do."

He vowed, when he proposed, that he would travel to the end of the world for her. Now she wishes he would, and that he'd stay there.

Ever since their wedding day she keeps asking, "When are you going to make me the happiest woman in the world—and leave me?"

She wishes she'd paid closer attention to the sign on the courthouse steps: "This way for marriage licenses. Watch your step."

Before their marriage, he told her he was unworthy of her. He should have kept it a secret—then it would have come as a complete surprise.

She has a bad case of matrimonial indigestion—something she married doesn't agree with her.

When he proposed, he asked her to say the words that would make her happy forever. Now she wishes she'd said, "Remain a bachelor."

He likes her in clinging dresses. The one she's wearing has been clinging to her for years.

She told him once she dreamed he had given her a mink coat. He generously said, "In your next dream wear it in good health."

She asked for a pearl necklace for her birthday, so he gave her a bushel of oysters and wished her luck.

She's money-mad. He never gives her any money—so she's mad.

She asked him for some money for a rainy day, so he gave her a rubber check.

He's hoping earnestly for a blessed event—her next raise in salary.

Right from the start he was determined to support her in the manner to which she was accustomed—letting her keep her job.

When they got married, he didn't expect her to give up her girlhood ways right away. He told her to go on taking an allowance from her father.

He always takes her to the best restaurants. Someday he may even take her inside.

She asked him for five dollars and he demanded: "What did you do with the five dollars I gave you yesterday—serial number B-6485291-F?"

She was his secretary and he married her because he didn't want to have to give her a raise.

She said she'd like to see the world, so he gave her a map.

When she complained that she'd had her fur coat for three years, he said, "That's not long—the animal had it for ten years."

He gets her all her jewelry from a famous millionaire—Woolworth.

She wears a diamond ring that reminds her of the capital of Arkansas—Little Rock.

He married her on $125 a week—she was earning it.

He got tired of hearing her complain that he never gave her anything, so he bought her a girdle and said, "Now, that should hold you."

She's had that fur coat so long, the Museum of Natural History is asking for it—they want to have it stuffed.

She says he's like a king to her—Henry the Eighth.

He tells her, "You're too extravagant. If anything happens to me, you'll probably have to beg." She says, "Oh, I'll get along —look at all the experience I've had."

She's wearing her wedding ring on the wrong finger—because she married the wrong man.

One of these days she's going to leave his bed—and bored.

She's sore at his family. When she told them he wanted to marry her, not one of them obpected.

He's a rarely faithful husband—very rarely.

He's surprised when anyone asks him if he cheats on his wife. "Who else?" he asks.

She's looking for a cook who can cook with one hand and hold him off with the other.

He's got a detective shadowing her. He wants to make sure he knows where she is when he's where he shouldn't be.

He never closes his eyes when he kisses—he has to be on the lookout for her.

She hasn't been speaking to him for quite a time—for quite a time he had with another woman.

They're carrying on a business together. She runs the business and he does the carrying on.

He's not worried about talking in his sleep. She and his girl friend have the same name.

He's really good at bringing home the bacon without spilling the beans.

It's been so long since he's made love to her, she wouldn't want him summoned if anything happened to her—he wouldn't be able to identify the body.

For him home is a place to go to, to raise a fuss because something went wrong at the office.

The only exercise he gets is being out seven nights running.

Drink makes him see double and feel single.

He's an indulgent husband—always indulging.

Too many bourbons on the rocks are putting their marriage there too.

He thinks home is where you go when all the bars close.

He leaves in the morning with a bundle of dough and comes home with a bun on.

When they met, she thought he'd make a good match. She didn't realize he'd always be lit.

In the morning, after one of his nights on the town, she asks: "How do you want your eggs—fried, scrambled, or intravenous?"

Asked if she cared to contribute something to the Home for Alcoholics, she said they could have him.

She's contemplating a divorce on the ground that he has alcoholic rheumatism—he gets stiff in every joint.

The way he tipsy-toes in late at night half shot, she's tempted to finish the job.

Just once she'd like to see him fix something around the house besides Manhattans and Martinis.

She keeps at a distance from him when she wears her leopard coat. With one deep 100-proof breath, he could change it right back to rabbit.

This is his third marriage—it seems he never loses an opportunity to make some woman miserable.

He tells her: "You don't deserve a man like me." She answers: "I don't deserve sinusitis either, but I've got it!"

Hypochondriacs

He's full of the joy of almost living.

His face is as long as a bankrupt undertaker's.

Her ailment is not so much chronic as chronicle.

She has a great talent for organ recitals—about those operations she's had.

Her life is a bed of neuroses.

He reads the obituary notices to cheer himself up.

She's constantly collecting ills and pills and getting chills.

He looks like a cheerleader for the morgue.

Being around him is like living in a pressure cooker with a stuck safety valve.

His usual greeting is "Good Moaning."

At the start of even a minor ailment she gets as hysterical as a tree full of chickens.

The way he groans and moans when he gets even a slight cold, you can't decide whether to call a doctor or a drama critic.

She has an indisposition that malingers on.

He's one of those rue-it-yourself experts.

Tell her how healthy she looks, and you've made a mortal enemy.

The inscription on his tombstone will undoubtedly read: *See!*

He not only expects the worst, but makes the worst of things when they happen.

She's one of those chronic invalids who have every ailment and disease described on television.

If an actor sneezes during a TV performance, she's sure she's caught cold.

He'll never shake anyone's hand if it's more than eighty degrees.

He's the kind of guy who goes to drive-in movies in an ambulance.

One of these days she's going to be *really* sick, and that will make her ecstatically happy.

She'll never feel better until the doctor tells her there's something wrong with her.

He must have been created for the benefit of doctors and psychiatrists.

No wonder he never has any rosy thoughts about the future—his mind is filled with the blues of the past and present.

He just quit his doctor. When he told him, "I have an awful pain every time I lift my arm," the doctor said, "So don't lift it."

He's very much against antibiotics since they've been found to cure some of his favorite diseases.

When nothing makes her sick, that's exactly what makes her sick.

One morning she woke up feeling real well, so she called the doctor to find out what was wrong with her.

He's one of those melancholy drinkers—every year is a good whine year.

When he has a sore throat he doesn't go to a doctor. He sits in front of his TV set with his mouth open so the actor playing the doctor's part can see his tonsils.

His wife says: "It's a damn shame the way he nurses a sham pain."

He doesn't look for pearls in oysters. Not he! He looks for ptomaine poisoning.

He's so high-strung, he should join the circus.

It's hard to tell, with all his complaints whether he's actually stricken or just chicken.

He's contemplating suicide, leaving a note reading: "I'm tired of being so damned happy."

Juvenile delinquents

The only sure cure for kids like him is birth control.

He's so tough, he's been turned down by every reform school in the country.

He's so tough, he makes his teacher stay after school.

The teacher asked him, "Who shot Lincoln?" and he snarled, "I don't squeal on nobody!"

He says he's a delinquent because he was repressed as a child. His parents punished him when he sawed the cat in half and gave his grandmother the hotfoot.

When he was eight years old, his parents pleaded with him to run away from home.

His parents almost lost him as a child. Unfortunately, they didn't take him far enough into the woods.

There's a kid who never fails to display his pest manners.

He's such a delinquent, he could go to reform school on a scholarship.

There's hardly a week when he doesn't come home from school with a note demanding a good excuse for his presence.

He hangs out in such a tough neighborhood that a cat with a tail is considered a tourist.

If he ever lives long enough to be an adult. it will be a remarkable tribute to his parents' and teachers' self-control.

He's given up one bad habit. He no longer smokes marijuanas during crap games.

His parents wish that birth control could be made retroactive.

It's too bad his parents didn't burn his britches behind him.

His parents don't give him all the allowance they can afford—they have to keep some back to bail him out.

He's 6 foot 3—until he gets a haircut; then he's 5 foot 7.

His folks spared the rod—and he's riding in it.

His parents were afraid to put their foot down, so now he steps on their toes.

He'd have been better off if his doting parents had been don't-ing parents.

His teachers have a good reason to spare the rod and spoil the child—they can't get the knife out of his hand.

The school psychologist advised the teacher: "You'll have to handle this boy carefully. Remember, you're dealing with a sensitive, high-strung little stinker."

He's real inventive. He took a fender from a Chevvy, the chrome from a Ford, the hubcaps from a Pontiac, and got—six months.

His parents gave him a motorcycle, hoping it would improve his behavior. All it did was to spread his meanness over a wider area.

Heredity is what makes parents of kids like him wonder about each other.

When he started off on the wrong track, his parents should have applied switching facilities.

Children can be a great comfort to parents in their old age—and this kid sure is helping his reach it faster.

Liars

You can tell when he's lying—if his lips are moving, he is.

On a recent safari, he encountered a bull and a tiger. He shot the tiger first. He figured he could shoot the bull anytime.

With him, truth is like a woman's girdle—it's made to be stretched.

They call her "Lilac"—she can lilac crazy.

He can never entirely murder the truth. He never gets close enough to it.

It's not so much that she exaggerates—she just remembers big.

She's almost truthful. She doesn't lie about anything except her age, her weight, and her husband's salary.

The way he handles the truth, he should work for the weather bureau.

He's the type who can make up his own bunk and then lie out of it.

Once he dislocated both shoulders describing the fish he caught.

Whether or not truth is stranger than fiction, in his case, in any event, it's scarcer.

He's the kind of fisherman who catches fish by the tale.

If he asks you to guess how much he made last year, you're safe in saying, "Half."

He says he enjoys a cold shower in the morning. He lies about other things too.

He's never been known to burn the candor at both ends.

His boss has received offers from four publishers for the fiction rights to his expense accounts.

You can believe half of what he tells you—the problem is, which half?

When his girl friend rejected him, he threatened to jump off a 300-foot cliff—but it was just a big bluff.

He's such a liar, when he has to feed his hogs, he has to get someone else to call them for him.

Testifying as a witness, he told a judge, "I have been wedded to the truth since infancy." Queried the judge: "Is the court to infer you are now a widower?"

When his conscience bothers him about something he's done to you, he'll come to you in a straightforward way—and lie about the whole thing.

He sadly, or badly, misuses the truth—which is the most charitable way of saying he's a liar.

He swears at himself after everything he says—he hates liars.

READING BETWEEN THE LYIN'S

I have to go to the mountains because of respiratory trouble. (*His creditors won't let him breathe.*)

I have hundreds of people under me. (*He's a watchman in a cemetery.*)

I dabble in oils. (*He's a gas station attendant.*)

My husband is a liver, brain, and lung specialist. (*He's a butcher.*)

I have a real big job. (*He washes elephants at the zoo.*)

The gowns I wear come from Paris. (*Paris, Kentucky.*)

My brother occupied a chair of applied electricity in a famous public institution. (*He went to the electric chair in Sing Sing.*)

My furniture goes back to Louis the 14th. (*It will, if Louis isn't paid before the 14th.*)

I got my fingers burned on Wall Street. (*He was picking up a lighted cigar from the sidewalk.*)

I have a big following. (*Five finance companies, 3 department stores, 4 landlords, and 7 collection agencies.*)

My ancestors go back as far as Columbus. (*Some of them even went as far as Chicago.*)

I hit the top in television. (*He fixes aerials.*)

I dine with the brass. (*No one would trust him with the silver.*)

No woman ever walks back when she goes for a ride with me. (*He drives a hearse.*)

My brother is a man of letters. (*He works in the Post Office.*)

Women are crazy about the way I kiss. (*They take one look at his face and exclaim, "What a kisser!"*)

I was a member of the underground. (*He was a conductor in the B.M.T.*)

I come from a family of standing. (*They're floorwalkers, elevator operators, and doormen.*)

I'm really clicking big around town. (*His dentures don't fit.*)

As a child, I was a musical prodigy. (*He played on the linoleum.*)

My father died before his time. (They hanged him at 11:45 instead of midnight, as scheduled.)

I'm doing settlement work. (His creditors have finally caught up with him.)

If I retired today, I'd have enough to live on for the rest of my life. (. . . if he died tomorrow.)

I had a hand recently in a big transportation deal. (He thumbed his way across the country.)

My dad was cleaned out in the 1929 stock market crash. (A broker jumped out of the window and landed on his pushcart.)

Losers

He's so fond of hard luck he runs halfway to meet it.

Just as he's about to make both ends meet, something breaks in the middle.

He had a fine job tramping on grapes to make wine—then he developed fallen arches.

He's the guy who always gets to the party after the liquor's run out.

He's as forlorn and neglected as Whistler's father.

He's one person who can buy artificial flowers and have them die on him.

His motto is: "Let a Smile Be Your Umbrella"—and he always gets a mouthful of rain.

He can always be counted on to do the right thing too late or the wrong thing too soon.

When he goes to the doctor to get a flu shot, it works real well—he gets the flu.

He's such a bumbler, when he gets to heaven he'll be sure to knock off one of the Pearly Gates.

He repaired his cuckoo clock; now it backs out and says, "What time is it?"

He bought a golf instruction book and followed its advice to keep his head down—and someone stole his golf cart.

No one is his equal at hitting the nail squarely on the thumb.

He even has to call in an interior decorator to change a typewriter ribbon.

He's standing on his own two feet—his car has been repossessed.

If he ever sold lighting fixtures, the sun wouldn't set.

Not only has he a hard row to hoe; he hasn't even got a hoe.

Lots of folks go through the School of Hard Knocks, but he's the one pupil who's sure to get hit on the head.

He was born with a silver spoon in his mouth. All the other kids had tongues.

He's the only person on record who used saccharine and got artificial diabetes.

He married a million-dollar baby, but after taxes she wasn't worth a dime.

In Las Vegas he even loses money on the stamp machine.

He plays cards and bets on the horses just for laughs. He's already laughed away his bank account and his car.

He bet on a horse that he was told would walk in. The only trouble was, the other horses ran.

He keeps putting bets on the horses' noses—he should bet on the legs.

When his bookie's place burned down, the only thing the firemen saved were his IOU's.

He bet on a sure-thing tip he got right from the horse's mouth —it turned out to be a horse laugh.

His life is like a razor—always in hot water or a scrape.

One thing has always kept him from making a fast buck—
a slow horse.

He comes up with a solution for every problem. It's always
practical, workable—and wrong.

Two business firms are fighting over his services—the loser
gets him.

He really has his ear to the ground—searching for his contact

He's a dependable person. You can always depend on him to
do the wrong thing.

He saved for years to buy an unbreakable, waterproof, shock-
proof watch—and lost it.

He bought a two-pants suit, and promptly burned a hole in
the jacket.

He's a real Don Juan with women—they *Don Juan* to have anything to do with him.

Not only is he not a Sir Galahad with women; he isn't even
a Sir Had-a-gal.

He dances as though he has two left feet—and also two right
ones.

All a girl has to do is agree to dance with him, and he's on
her feet in an instant.

When he trips the light fantastic, it may not be light, but it
sure is fantastic.

Lowbrows

He must be making a full-time career of coarseness and crudity. He couldn't be that good at it by accident.

His very presence holds you smell-bound.

He's a real baboon to society.

He says modestly that he's one of the common people. The fact is, you can't find anyone more common than he is.

Everyone has a real good word for him—they all whisper it.

He's such a lowbrow, his toupee is always slipping over his eyebrows.

He can't put his best foot forward without stepping on someone's toes.

He's the type who tells a woman her stockings are wrinkled—when she's not wearing any.

You can count on him to call a woman a cat instead of a kitten; a hen instead of a chicken; a goose instead of a duck; a sight instead of a vision.

If a woman asks him coyly if he can believe that she's 40, he's sure to say yes.

In the etiquette class he once attended, he was unanimously voted the student most likely to return.

He's real refined. He wears a T shirt to serve tea.

He likes to show off a picture of himself with a high-society friend. He's the one stepping on his cigarette so it won't burn his host's rug.

At every social event, he's the scent of attraction.

He's a stickler for etiquette. He knows which hand to use when tucking his napkin under his collar.

To show off his elegant manners, he holds a teacup with his pinkie sticking out—and the tea bag hanging from it.

Waiters are constantly offering to help him with the soup. From the sound, they think he might want to be dragged ashore.

It always did his dear mother's heart good to hear him eat.

You should see the sparks fly when he uses his knife and fork.

There's no denying that he has class—steerage.

He's an excellent illustration of the saying that age does not make a personage out of a person.

He's the type who keeps an elbow on each arm of his theatre seat.

He's as compatible with refined people as ham and matzohs.

If he ever finds himself out, he'll be the last one to do so.

He gets stabbing pains in his right eye every time he drinks tea. He should take the spoon out of the cup.

He never hurts anyone's feelings—unintentionally.

He's recently gone on a garlic diet. He lost a little weight and a lot of friends.

Once, studying some statistics, he said to his wife, "You know, every time I breathe, three Chinese die." She replied, "That doesn't surprise me."

He's the type who talks about rope to someone whose father was hanged.

He only opens his mouth to change feet.

He's a man with polish—on his shoes.

At his favorite night club, the tables are reserved. Too bad he isn't.

If he walked into a crematory he'd say, "What's cooking?"

He's a sportsman. When he spots an empty seat in a train or bus, he points it out to a lady—then he races her for it.

He prefers matches to a cigarette lighter. He can't pick his teeth with a lighter.

Years ago he was an amateur boxer, but he had to quit. He couldn't pick his teeth with the gloves on.

He's the economical type—he likes to save soap and water.

He recently said to his psychiatrist, "There's definitely something wrong with me—I keep getting this urge to take a bath."

He missed his vocation. He should be a garbage collector—he has that certain air about him.

That cheap aftershave stuff he uses stamps him as a guy with plenty of common scents.

He has a voice like a foghorn . . . like a buzz saw striking a rusty nail.

Never make the mistake of urging him to be himself—you couldn't give him worse advice.

Meanies

In any organization, he's the outstanding candidate for the Ways to Be Mean Committee.

He wouldn't dare eat his heart out—he'd break his teeth doing it.

Once a rattlesnake bit him. It was a terrible sight, watching it curl up and die.

He never hits a man when he's down—he kicks him.

He doesn't care what happens—so long as it happens to someone else.

He must have been raised on marble cake, brick ice cream, and rock candy.

Before firing an employee he gives him a raise, so he'll be losing a better job.

One night he dreamed he was dead—the heat woke him up.

He's the type who would steal the last fan from a fan dancer.

He once gave a blood transfusion to someone. The patient got double pneumonia from the shock of ice water in his veins.

When he visits a sick friend in the hospital he brings him some magazines, but advises: "If I were you, I wouldn't start any serials."

He always thinks twice before speaking, so he can come out with something really nasty.

There must be a lot of good left in him—none of it ever comes out.

He's the kind who'll borrow your pot and then cook your goose.

When it comes to helping someone, he stops at nothing.

There's nothing he wouldn't do for a friend, and he keeps it that way.

All his life he's followed the path of least assistance.

He rolls out the carpet for you one day, and pulls it out from under you the next.

So far as he's concerned, a friend in need is a friend to keep away from.

When you're in trouble, something is bound to turn up—his nose.

He'll never get dizzy from doing a good turn.

He's so cold-blooded, if a mosquito bit him it would die of pneumonia.

When he's finished with a mystery novel, he writes the name of the murderer on top of the first page before handing it on to his family.

He's never told his children that other families eat three meals a day.

He should buy fire instead of life insurance—there's no doubt where he's going.

His wife has to do her reading in the closet so his sleep won't be disturbed.

He's the type who can swim safely through shark-infested waters. He receives professional courtesy.

He once had a fight with a woman, and he would have won if she hadn't struck back with her crutches.

Muddleheads

He's so absent-minded, he went up to a horse at the race track and bet five dollars on a bookie.

He once fell down a flight of stairs. Landing at the bottom, he said, "I wonder what all that noise was about."

He keeps going around and around in a revolving door. He can't remember whether he's going in or coming out.

He kissed his wife good morning and said, "Take a letter, please."

He has three pairs of spectacles: one for near-sightedness, one for far-sightedness, and a third to look for the other two.

Once he attended a formal affair, properly attired in white tie and tails, and was the center of attraction. He should have worn pants too.

At a dinner party he was asked to pass his plate. He asked, "Which do you want—the upper or the lower?"

A nurse showed him the triplets his wife had just given birth to, and asked, "What do you think of them?" Absent-mindedly he said, "I'll take the one in the middle."

He bought a memory course, but never completed it. After the eighth lesson, he left the course in the subway.

He once left a note on his office door: "Back in an hour." When he got back he saw the sign, and sat down to wait.

When he told his doctor he couldn't remember things from one minute to the next, the doctor asked, "How long has this been going on?" He replied, "How long has what been going on?"

His wife asked him, "Do you remember me? I'm the woman you asked ten years ago to marry you." "Ah, yes," he answered, "and did you?"

He took up sculpture as a hobby, but had to give it up. Absentmindedly he kissed his model and chiseled on his wife.

An erroneous report of his death appeared in a newspaper, and he promptly sent himself a wreath.

Finding himself out in a pasture with a rope in his hand, he asked himself: "Now, have I found a rope or lost a horse?"

When a nurse informed him that he had just become the father of twins, he said, "Don't tell my wife. I want to surprise her."

He complained to a psychiatrist, "I'm always forgetting things. What shall I do?" The psychiatrist answered, "Pay me in advance."

He's so absent-minded, he kissed his wife goodbye and quarreled with his secretary when he got to his office.

At the Christmas office party he kissed his own wife.

Knowing how absent-minded he was, his family wired him a reminder while he was away from home: "Yom Kippur starts tomorrow." He wired back, "Put ten on the nose for me."

This guy is really absent-minded. He's a plumber—and when he answers a call he brings his tools with him.

Nudists

He's the camp's most absent-minded nudist. He went out one time with his clothes on.

There's a mutual attraction between her and a young man in the camp—they're in the nude for love.

She applied for the job as a guide in the camp—she enjoys showing visitors all over.

He's the camp's best golfer—he can go around the course in nothing.

He's the most handicapped fellow in the camp—he's near-sighted.

She joined the nudist colony because she's interested in the naked facts of life.

She's a fine specimen of the nuder gender.

He joined the colony because he wanted to join a back-to-the-form movement.

She's indignant because the police are always breaking in, trying to get the goods on her.

She has the biggest problem of all the women in the camp—she's a bleached blonde.

He enjoys the colony's theme song: "Stares and Strips Forever."

As soon as he checked into the camp he demanded a room with sudden exposure.

He was attracted to the camp because of its name—Bearskin Lodge.

He brought his wife with him so they could air their differences.

Even in the nudist camp his shrewish wife tells him what not to wear.

He's a lawyer, and ever since he joined the colony he hasn't had a suit.

He has his eye on the most attractive female in the camp—he only wishes he could see her in a sweater.

The only thing she wears are beads—of perspiration.

She met a chap in camp, and it was a case of love at first sight —she knew exactly what she was getting.

She realizes now that nudism is only a skin game that attracts thousands of followers—mosquitoes.

He was nearly expelled from the camp because of a social error. He didn't look the president's wife in the eye when she was talking to him.

He's in danger of expulsion from the colony. He's always putting on airs.

He's a real snob—he comes down in the evening wearing a tie.

He misses his favorite game now that he's joined a nudist colony—strip poker.

His daughter won't join the camp until the day of her wedding—she wants to be married in white.

He became a nudist because he wanted to spend days without seeing a human face.

She'll always remember her first day in camp. It's like learning to fly—you never forget the first take-off.

Perfect pairs

They're well matched. He's a past master and she's a past mistress.

He's a pill and she's a headache.

She drives from the back seat and he cooks from the dining-room table.

She's 45 going on 37; he's 49 going on pep pills.

He's paunchy and she's punchy.

She's a rag, a bone, and a hank of hair; he's a brag, a groan, and a tank of air.

They get breakfast together. She makes the toast and he scrapes it.

He compares the bread she bakes with his mother's, and she compares his roll with her father's.

He's a has-been and she's a been-had.

It's a beef-stew marriage. She's always beefing and he's always stewed.

It's a nip-and-tuck marriage. He takes a nip, and she tucks him in.

It's a 50-50 marriage. She signs the checks; he signs the receipts.

It's a musical marriage. She's second fiddle, and he's drumming new romances.

It's a 50-50 marriage. She spends $50 for a hat and he spends 50¢ for a shirt.

They're a sparkling, shining couple. She sparkles with diamonds; he shines in his seven-year-old suit.

They're a fastidious couple. She's fast and he's hideous.

They get along perfectly. He never finds her in, and she's never found him out.

He phones to say he'll be late for dinner, and she's already left a note saying it's in the refrigerator.

She annoys him all day with her chattering, and he annoys her all night with his snoring.

They're madly in love—he with himself and she with herself.

They've got an exciting marriage. She pretends she's his secretary, and he pretends he's a misunderstood husband.

There's nothing he wouldn't do for her, and nothing she wouldn't do for him; in fact, they're devoted to doing nothing for each other.

They have so little in common, they don't even hate the same people.

They're so incompatible, they have nothing in common to fight about.

The only thing they have in common is that both of them are.

They're really well mated. They're inseparable and insufferable.

They're very class-conscious. They have no class and their neighbors are conscious of it.

They're going blissfully through life together—two minds without a single thought.

Playboys

He may not be a leader of men, but he sure is a follower of women.

He thinks life is very unfair—so many women and so little time.

The first thing he notices about a girl's looks is whether she looks available.

He's the principal reason why hotels have house detectives.

He's always doing the town, but he doesn't do it any good.

Give him one kiss, and it develops into a one-man crime wave.

Life for him is a matter of profits and lasses.

He counts sheep all night because he counts calves all days.

He admits that girls are a problem—but it's problems like that he enjoys wrestling with.

The apple of his eye is a little peach with the prettiest pair.

When he meets a girl, he doesn't care about having a clear field—he's got a nice, cozy den.

His park is worse than his bite.

He can be fairly well behaved once a girl gets to "no" him.

He's always AWOL—After Women Or Liquor.

When he gives a girl a present, he's well on the way to giving her a past.

He doesn't want to take a girl out and do things—he'd rather take her in and undo things.

When he gives a girl a string of pearls, the clasp is sure to go with it.

He's always ready to go to bat for a girl, if she has the right kind of curves.

He prefers to eat in restaurants where the dishes they serve aren't delicious, but the dishes that serve them are luscious.

He's frank and earnest with women. In Cleveland he's Frank and in Los Angeles he's Ernest.

His favorite game is called Photography. The idea is to put out the lights and see what develops.

He has two requirements for a girl—her pantry must be stocked and she must be stacked.

He knows how to handle girls who like a good time—often!

He attended a co-ed college where the girls went in for facts and he went in for figures.

Girls go out with him by the dozens. They find it safer than going out with him alone.

He knows that love is blind, and he proves it by feeling his way around.

He's good at parlor tricks—especially slide of hand.

He's constantly in love instead of constant in love.

He prefers a girl who's sexy, not brainy. He says when he feels intellectual, there's always the public library.

He's tall, dark—and girls wish he were hands off.

He's a man of few words: Let's . . . Willya . . . Lemme.

He's a real playboy—he's constantly toying with sex.

He's gone around with more women than a revolving door in a supermarket.

When he pours a drink for a girl and says, "Say when!" he expects her to answer, "After this drink."

He doesn't believe a girl really understands a kiss until he has it from her own lips.

He's a guy who expects an "aye" for an eye.

So far as women are concerned, he's a perpetual-notion machine.

He's mastered the art of making a girl see the light when he has her in the dark.

He doesn't care at all about lengthening his days—he just likes to prolong his nights.

He's a man with no wife expectancy.

The only dates he's interested in are ones with no apron strings attached.

He has just one interest in life—himself.

He's a bachelor of arts. He's artful with women, yet has the art to stay a bachelor.

As a kid, he played Post Office. Now he plays Pony Express, because there's more horsing around.

One game he'll never play is Troth or Consequences.

He's a slick operator. He never gives a girl enough rope to make a marriage knot.

He's a gay dog, but he'll never be spousebroken.

He's the type who breaks off an engagement if the girl wants to go too far—like wanting to get married.

His stocks and bonds keep him in steaks and blondes.

He's losing his mind. He just received a letter warning him, "Stop playing around with my wife, or I'll kill you!" The letter's unsigned.

In the hospital recently, a shapely nurse held his wrist to check his impulse.

If he wants to keep his health, he'll have to lose some weight —about 120 pounds of blonde.

He's bored with his current girl friend. He's dating a female spiritualist to try out a new medium.

He knows a great deal about women—mostly from what he's been able to pick up.

He's a real fox—always manages to get what some wolf is after.

He doesn't care to share the best years of a woman's life— just her weekends.

Lots of women in town are urging him to take a memory-training course—so he can remember they're ladies.

Women are amazed at how well he dresses—and how quickly too.

He only goes out with girls who know all about the birds and the bees—and the pills.

He's the original Voice of Sexperience.

Girls are always running through his mind—they wouldn't dare walk.

He believes in love at first sight—it saves a lot of time.

He's had some awful temptations. It required all his strength and will power to yield to them.

People wonder who those women are they see him outwit.

He heard his clergyman say there are 358 sins. He's asking for the list—just in case he's missed something.

It's good that he isn't aware of a scientist's recent statement that no new sin has been discovered in the past 5000 years. It would give him an awful feeling of futility.

He's moving to a place out West where men are men and women are amenable.

His life is just a bed of ruses.

He keeps telling every girl that she has a beautiful figure. He can't seem to touch on some other subject.

The first thing he notices about an attractive woman is the size of her escort.

There have been many times when he decided to take a wife. His big problem has been whose wife to take.

While in Rome once, he picked up a little Italian. All she could say was "yes."

In the summer his car always seems to run out of gas. In the winter he takes girls for dog-sled rides and runs out of dog food.

Once he got beat up for kissing a bride—it was two years after the wedding ceremony.

He's very fond of his relatives, but of all his relations, he likes sex the best.

He doesn't think much of the old saying, "Beauty is only skin deep." He says that's deep enough for him—he's no cannibal.

He's fast going broke, not for a lack—but for a lass.

On an ice-skating rink recently he tried for hours to make a fancy figure, but got his face slapped.

He once got a black eye from a cough—coughing in a married woman's clothes closet.

He went around with a woman who had something that just simply knocked his eye out—her husband.

He needs a heart stimulant every night—a blonde or a redhead.

When he tells a girl he wants to be her good friend, he really means he wants to be good and friendly.

He's master of the art of setting a girl up in an apartment. He whispers a lot of suite things in her ears.

His convertible is called the "Mayflower"—quite a few puritans have come across in it.

He's glad to live in the U.S.A.—a great democracy, where a man has a choice of three governments: blonde, brunette, or redhead.

So far as he's concerned, America is the land of the spree and the home of the knave—the land of milk and honeys.

His favorite song is "I'll Be Seizing You in All the Old Familiar Places."

Girls may have trouble remembering his name or face, but they never forget his hands.

When he meets a girl, he starts to hem and paw.

He met a dazzler lately, and right away he was a different man—he gave her a fake name and address.

He took a girl to Florida to Tampa with her.

He's failing in business because he hasn't learned the difference between stocks and blondes.

He carefully considers the problem of pickups from every possible ankle.

He buys a girl a bikini and looks forward to seeing her beam with delight.

He has a lot of pet theories about women—chief among which is "Nothing succeeds like excess."

People always ask him, "Who was that dame you were obscene with last night?"

He has devoted the best leers of his life to women.

What a nightmare he had recently! He dreamed he was alone on a desert island with a dozen stunning girls—and he was a girl too!

They call him the "Dry Cleaner"—he works fast and leaves no ring.

The doctor advised him to cut out liquor and women, but he only cut out liquor. He says he can always drink when he's old.

He doesn't wear gloves when he goes out with a girl. He feels better without them.

He can read a woman like a book. What they object to is, he uses the Braille system.

The first thing he does is tell a girl she has "hidden charms" —then he starts hunting for them.

Women who go out with him think at first that he has a lot of culture, but they soon discover it's all *physical*.

He's very chivalrous—always wants to protect a girl from men who have ideas, because he has the same ideas himself.

It's not the high cost of living that's aging him prematurely; it's the high cost of loving.

He had a lot of money—but that was four blondes ago.

He never goes out with the NO-it-all type of girls.

The way he chases a skirt he's sure to wind up with a suit on his hands.

Chicks may have no terror for him, but the stork sure does.

His salary has been going to four figures—four shapely dames.

Once he decided to reform. The first week he cut out liquor. The second week, smoking. The third week he cut out women. The fourth week he was cutting out paper dolls.

THE PLAYBOY BOSS

As a boss, he's every pinch a gentleman.

His secretary is brushing up on her shorthand and typing—and also on her jiujitsu.

His father and he are carrying on a business together. His father runs the business—he does the carrying on.

He never paces up and down the office when he dictates—his secretary sits on his lap.

He likes to keep as busy as a bee at the office, with a little honey on his lap.

He has fired several secretaries because of mistakes they *wouldn't* make.

Seeing a shapely new stenographer pass his desk, he phoned his wife: "I'll be a little late tonight. A terrific sales campaign just occurred to me."

His secretary has just found something extra in her pay envelope—the key to his apartment.

He gasps for breath when he dictates to his current secretary —that girl can really run around a desk.

When he hires a secretary, he makes sure to tell her that there will be lots of opportunities for advances.

One girl in the office really has a great future. She's going places —with *him*.

He does his hiring not on the basis of grammar but of glamour.

He's always looking for a secretary who will come through in a pinch.

His idea of the perfect secretary is one who types fast and runs slow.

Although a bachelor, he listed a dependent son on his tax return. When a tax examiner commented, "This must be a stenographic error," he replied, "You're *telling* me!"

Playgirls

She's the kind of a girl you'd give your name to—but not your right name.

She's a home girl—she doesn't care whose.

There's a girl for you who leads a conventional life—she shows up at all the conventions.

She's the sort of girl you want very much to take home to Mother—when Mother isn't home.

Her boyfriend can't deny that she's given him the best weekends of her life.

Her conscience never no's what's wrong.

When it comes time at the altar for her to say "I do," she'll have to be careful not to come out with "I did."

The story of her popularity can be summed up in one word —yes.

She enjoys strip poker games. She shows the boys a thing or two—in fact, everything comes off just fine.

She's leading a delightful sexistence.

At college she was voted the Girl with Whom You Are Most Likely to Succeed.

She's a lover of the outdoors. She doesn't do so badly indoors, either.

Her motto is: To err is human, but it feels divine.

Asked how it happens that she has so many boyfriends interested in her, her answer is simple: "I give up."

She leads a simple, natural life. Her won'ts are few.

The way she dances, she doesn't know the difference between writhe and wrong.

She may not know how to cook, but she sure knows what's cooking.

She's an expert at giving the "Hail, fellow—we'll meet" look.

She owes that mink coat to her Power of Positive Winking.

"Always flirting" describes her to a tease.

Her "no" is like a comma—it doesn't mean a complete stop.

She was getting nowhere with the boys until she decided to get yeswhere.

The fellows all call her "Rumor"—she goes from mouth to mouth.

At college she wore a sweater with a letter given to those who made the team.

She knows how to raise a hem to get a him.

Good girls are born, but girls like her are made.

She's the real "goody-goody" type. When she's propositioned, she says, "Goody, goody!"

Her kiss speaks volumes—but it's far from a first edition.

She went to a bridge party recently, and was really enjoying it, until the cops looked under the bridge.

When she gets married, she should call her home "The Last Lap."

There are times when she's seen at a disadvantage—vertically.

She has a great capacity for love—so emotionally, so feelingly, so affectionately, and so universally.

Everyone thinks she's a Southern belle—she's so free and teasy on the drawl.

She tells bachelors, "Take it from me, don't get married."

She's climbing to success—lad by lad, and wrong by wrong.

She has had no difficulty keeping the wolf from the door— she invites him in.

Everyone knows her to be a lady in her own wrong.

Boy, is she experienced! When she kisses a guy, he knows he's been kissed—*she leaves a note.*

She frequents a bar where she just sits and watches the fellows come buy.

While she's waiting for the right man to come along, she's having a wonderful time with the wrong ones.

She's the answer to a playboy's prayer—to find the unbelievable—a passionate girl who is inconceivable.

The epitaph on her tombstone will undoubtedly read: *At Last She Sleeps—Alone.*

She's looking for a husband. Their wives wish she'd start with a single fellow.

Her old-fashioned mother used to go to the city and stop at the YWCA. *She* goes to the city and stops at nothing.

Her old-fashioned mother repulsed advances by taking to her heels. *She* advances the pulses of heels.

Her old-fashioned mother dropped a handkerchief to attract a man's attention. *She* wears it.

Her old-fashioned mother hurried home to do the dishes. *She* staggers home in her cups.

Her old-fashioned mother made her life a bed of roses. She makes her life a bed of roués.

Her old-fashioned mother dressed like Mother Hubbard. She dresses more like her cupboard.

She'll never make a good housewife. All she knows about lettuce is that it's a proposition.

She was being kept in a Park Avenue penthouse until recently. Her louse expired.

She's so knowledgeable about sex, the birds and bees study her.

Her taste in fellows has a uniform quality—soldiers, sailors, and marines.

She's kissed so many sailors, her lips move in and out with the tide.

She's not such a good dancer, but she can certainly intermission.

She's one for the book—every guy's little black book.

When she demurely asked a fellow, "Who said you can make love to me?" he answered, "Just about everybody."

She recently told a chap, "One false move—and I'll appreciate it."

Men don't meet her—she overtakes them.

She's learned that catching a man is like catching a fish—you've got to wiggle the bait.

Those baby stares of hers are for guys to trip on.

She flies occasionally from temptation, but makes sure to leave a forwarding address.

She doesn't chase men. Does a mousetrap have to chase a mouse?

It's amazing what she can get away with and still keep her amateur standing.

She's a real office cutie. She's not such a good typist or secretary, but the boss can always count on her in a clinch.

She can always get an advance from her boss out of petting cash.

Her boss treats her like a dog—a lap dog.

She was sitting in the lap of luxury until the boss's wife walked in unexpectedly.

On the line in the application blank headed "Sex," she wrote, "Once in a while."

In her latest job, when the boss said, "Let's sit down and get to work," she said, out of force of habit, "Which chair shall we sit in?"

In the office they call her the "Human Switchboard." When she walks across a room, all her lines are busy.

She can't even count on her fingers, but she sure can count on her legs and her hips.

Her boss hired her as his private secretary, but soon found she was a public stenographer.

SOMEONE'S PLAYGIRL DAUGHTER

She's only an astronaut's daughter, but she sure knows how to take off.

She's only an athlete's daughter, but she's always ready to play ball.

She's only a blacksmith's daughter, but she knows how to forge ahead.

She's only a bricklayer's daughter, but she certainly is well stacked.

She's only a butcher's daughter, but there isn't much more she can loin.

She's only a cab driver's daughter, but the fellows all think they auto meet her.

She's only a car dealer's daughter, but she sure has a swell chassis.

She's only a carpenter's daughter, but she knows every vise.

She's only a chimneysweep's daughter, but she soots all the fellows.

She's only a clergyman's daughter, but you can't put anything pastor.

She's only a coal dealer's daughter, but, oh, where's she bin?

She's only a columnist's daughter, but she's always chasing wild roomers.

She's only a communist's daughter, but all the boys get their share.

She's only a congressman's daughter, but she can sure fill a seat.

She's only a crapshooter's daughter, but she can roll you for all you have.

She's only a dairyman's daughter, but what a calf!

She's only a doctor's daughter, but, boy, can she operate!

She's only a draftsman's daughter, but she doesn't know where to draw the line.

She's only a dressmaker's daughter, but she knows how to keep the fellows on pins and needles.

She's only a farmer's daughter, but she sure knows her oats.

She's only an electrician's daughter, but she certainly has good connections.

She's only a fireman's daughter, but she's really going to blazes.

She's only a film censor's daughter, but she doesn't know when to cut it out.

She's only a fisherman's daughter, but the fellows all swallow her lines.

She's only a gardener's daughter, but she knows all the rakes.

She's only a globetrotter's daughter, but she manages to get around.

She's only an insurance broker's daughter, but the fellows like her policy.

She's only a milkman's daughter, but as a necker, she's the cream of the crop.

She's only a musician's daughter, but she knows all the bars in town.

She's only an optician's daughter, but with a couple of glasses she makes a spectacle of herself.

She's only a parson's daughter, but she has her following.

She's only a philanthropist's daughter, but she keeps giving things away.

She's only a photographer's daughter, but, boy, has she developed!

She's only a pitcher's daughter, but you should see her curves.

She's only a plumber's daughter, but she's making the most of her fixtures.

She's only a porch-climber's daughter, but you should see her stoop.

She's only a postmaster's daughter, but she sure knows her males.

She's only a prizefighter's daughter, but she knows all the ropes.

She's only a professor's daughter, but she can give the fellows a lesson.

Political acrobats

When he told his wife he'd been elected, she cried, "Honestly?" He answered, "Why bring that up?"

He chose politics as the most promising of all careers—and is he good at promises!

He's always throwing his hat in the ring. Too bad his head goes with it.

He can stand firmly in midair on both sides of an issue.

Biologists claim there isn't a perfect man on the entire globe. Apparently they haven't read his campaign literature.

Scientists claim that fog can now be made to order. This is hardly news to *him*.

He's very skilled at repairing his fences by hedging.

His latest campaign speech was interrupted thirty times by applesauce.

History repeats itself. In former days politicians dueled—he fences.

Around election time he can be depended on never to leave welfare enough alone.

He'd never run for office if he weren't paid by the year. He'd starve to death on piecework.

He'll stand for anything that will leave him sitting pretty.

He stumps his state both before and after election.

When he first ran for office, he appealed to the voters: "I never stole anything in my life. All I ask is a chance."

With someone like him in the legislature, we can understand why they have a chaplain there—to pray for the country.

He's opposed to a new bill requiring an intelligence test for candidates for public office. He complains that someone is always trying to destroy representative government.

There's a portrait of himself in his office, but it's not a true resemblance. He's shown with his hand in *his* pocket.

It's impossible to confront him with two issues so far apart that he can't straddle them.

He's mastered the 3 P's in politics—Promises, Promises, Promises.

It's untrue that there are 20,000 useless words in the English language. How else could he frame his political platform?

The planks in his platform that look so fine before election start warping very quickly afterward.

He had little to offer except an itch for office—and he was scratched at the polls.

He was defeated because he made a big mistake—he asked the voters to vote a straight ticket.

He told a friend he was defeated because of his youth. Said his friend, "But you're over sixty years and your youth is spent." Sadly he explained, "That's the trouble. They found out how I spent it."

He was elected because of his gift of gab, and was defeated because of his gift of grab.

Screwballs

He has a mechanical mind—too bad some of the screws are loose.

As a child he grew like a little acorn. Now he's come to maturity—he's a real nut.

When he goes to the zoo, he has to have two tickets—one to get in, one to get out.

You have to admit that fellows like him don't grow on trees —they swing from them.

He drinks psychopathic coffee—it's weak in the bean.

He has such a split personality, his psychiatrist told him to go chase himself.

He has such a split personality that his psychiatrist sends him two bills for each visit.

He needs a checkup from the neck up.

His new apartment has made him happier—it has wall-to-wall padding.

Before his first session with a psychiatrist was over, the psychiatrist got on the couch.

Offering candy to his girl friend, he said, "Sweets to the sweet." She thanked him and asked, "Won't you have some of these nuts?"

He's so crazy about baseball, he never dreams about girls. He's afraid he'll lose his turn at bat.

He calls his brother up every night—and his brother doesn't have a phone.

Four psychiatrists have yet to find out what makes him tick—and especially what makes him chime on the hour and half-hour.

He keeps hitting home runs in his head—he has bats in his belfry.

No wonder he flies off the handle—he has a screw loose.

He's going around with a woman who's cross-eyed, knock-kneed, buck-toothed, and with an awful figure—but what lovely nightmares she has!

In one way he's fortunate. He could go completely out of his mind, and no one would know the difference.

He goes from psychiatrist to psychiatrist, always ready to sign for treatments on the dotted couch.

He's been taking so many tranquilizers he no longer worries about paying his psychiatrist's bills.

His case is one that's enriching medical and psychiatric science. He's already paid two brain specialists and four psychiatrists more than $5000 each.

He started with psychiatric treatment slightly cracked. He's finishing up completely broke.

The sign in his psychiatrist's waiting room reads: Worry Now, Pay Later.

He's been going to a psychiatrist to be cured of alcoholism. It's costing him so much, he soon won't be able to afford liquor.

When a psychiatrist told him: "Congratulations! I've cured you of your delusion," he answered unhappily, "So what? Yesterday I was Napoleon—today I'm nobody."

He's girl-crazy. Girls won't go out with him—that's why he's crazy.

Show-oafs

He has such a big mouth, he can eat a banana sideways, or sing duets by himself.

He's like a Christmas tie—loud and useless.

When they go to a party, his wife warns him, "Remember, when the party is over, be sure to go up to the host and apologize."

At almost every party, his wife is sure to be asked by someone, "What does your husband want to be when he grows up?"

They call him the "Mastoid of Ceremonies"—he's a pain in the ear.

He claims he lives by his wits. It's remarkable how a person can live on so little capital.

His wisecracks are always greeted with a tremendous burst of silence.

When he leaves a party, the guests know the meaning of comic relief.

He won't have to wait till he dies to be at his wit's end.

He thinks he's a born wit—he sure must have lost a lot of ground ever since.

He thinks he's a real funnyman, but he couldn't even entertain a doubt.

He thinks the world will beat a path to his door because he's built a better claptrap.

A monkey took one look at him and yelled, "To heck with the Darwin theory—they're not going to make a man out of me!"

He has a cute hobby that burns his friends—hotfoots.

He's perfecting waterproof matches so he can even give hotfoots on rainy days.

His idea of a practical joke is to go into a Home for the Blind and flatten out the Braille.

He's driven a dozen friends crazy by sending them wires reading "IGNORE FIRST WIRE."

He has a well-earned reputation as the death of the party.

Pandemonium doesn't merely reign when he's around—it pours.

There are people who are liked wherever they go—he's only liked whenever he goes.

He claims he lives by his wits—that accounts for that half-starved look on his face.

If you want to see unmatched technique, just watch him making a fool of himself.

As the "life of the party," he needs more effective gags—right across the mouth.

There are people who meet him who never forget a face; in his case they're willing to make an exception.

He has a waterproof voice—no one can drown it out.

He's a live-wire—wired mostly for sound.

There was a minute at one party when a guest didn't recognize him. It was the most enjoyable minute the man had ever spent.

There's something about him at social gatherings that definitely attracts women—to other men

Success hasn't gone to his head—just to his mouth.

He's short of horsepower and long on exhaust.

He's such a braggart, if he can't boast about knowing something, then he boasts about *not knowing it*.

Every year he takes a boast-to-boast tour.

Listening to him makes you think of a river—small at the head and big at the mouth.

He says he'd only marry a girl who can take a joke—that's the only kind who would take him.

At any party he attends, all that the guests want is a place to hang their hats and *him*.

Just encourage him, and you'll be slain by the jawbone of an ass.

He comes into a room shooting from the lip. He wants to hold you spielbound.

He's always out to have the time of your wife at a party.

The surest way to check this "life of the party" is to let him pick up the check.

Snobs

She's so ritzy, she has alligator bags under her eyes.

She won't eat a hot dog unless it's been certified and warranted by the kennel club.

He's proof that stuffed shirts come in all sizes.

He's such a snob, he refuses to work until the government gives him an unlisted Social Security number.

His son has gone into the army, and he's applied for an unlisted serial number for him.

As society swells, he and his wife are the mold on the upper crust.

They don't say that their ancestors came over on the Mayflower. They insist that they had their own boat.

They've moved to Snuburbia.

They can trace their family tree back to the time when their family lived in it.

They even have monogrammed tea bags.

They have a home in a nice location—on the outskirts of their income.

They're buying a home in a restricted development. where no one is permitted to build a house they can afford.

They're trying to keep up with the Joneses, and the bill collectors are trying to keep up with them.

They're moving to an exclusive neighborhood—where the rents are high and the noses are higher.

They can look down on other people, but only because they're living on a bluff.

He's full of rectitude, platitude, and high-hatitude.

He deliberately broke a leg skiing. He wanted a status symbol.

The only thing he ever did was inherit an old family tax loophole.

He wants to know only the people who don't want to know him.

When the doctor was about to give his wife a local anesthetic, he demanded, "Doc, give her the best—*something imported.*"

He looks like something that was stuffed by a good taxidermist.

She holds her head high—too bad she doesn't keep her nose on a friendly level.

She mightn't have such a wrong slant on things if she stopped looking down her nose.

She's as snippy as she's hippy.

She has two nose specialists—one for each nostril.

Tightwads

He's the type who takes things for gratis.

He's a real carefree guy—doesn't care as long as it's free.

Money means nothing to him. When you ask him for some, you get nothing.

All his clothes are tailored with one-way pockets.

He's a strict believer in free speech—like using friends' phones for long-distance calls.

He weighs 175—135 without his money belt.

Amazing how he always manages to be away from the table when the waiter brings the check. No wonder they call him the "After-dinner Sneaker."

He isn't particular how people treat him—just so long as they do.

He's made an art of not picking up the check. You've really got to hand it to him.

He's well known as a dollar-a-year man—it's all he ever spends.

He's just had his dentures tightened so he can put a better bite on his friends.

The longest trip known to mankind is the one his hand takes to his pocket.

Comes December, and he starts dreaming of a tight Christmas.

He's one of those free-loaders who's known from host to host.

He does crossword puzzles vertically so he won't have to come across.

His idea of an enjoyable vacation is to stay at home and let his mind wander.

He saves a lot of money on vacations. He keeps cool all summer by sponging.

He's a man of rare gifts—it's rare when he gives one.

When he donates money to charity, he likes to remain anonymous—so he doesn't sign his name to the check.

He doesn't believe in the popular slogan "Give till it hurts," but he always yells "Ouch!" when he's approached for a donation.

His automobile is so old, his car insurance policy covers theft, fire, and Indian raids.

He's one of those tightwad playboys who tries to make every dollar go as far as possible—and every girl too.

A woman just returned his ring. The envelope was marked "GLASS—HANDLE WITH CARE."

He doesn't always insist that the girl pay the dinner check. He sometimes offers to flip her for it.

When he's out with a girl he has plenty of savoir-faire, but no taxi fare.

He's very unhappy. He's had Blue Cross insurance four years, and hasn't been sick once.

The best definition of an optimist: One who tries to borrow money from guys like him.

An optimist is one who makes the mistake of lighting a match before asking him for a cigarette.

He's one of those two-fisted spenders—both tightly closed.

One of his employees came in a hour early each day for a month, and he charged him rent.

He has people working for him twenty years without ever having asked for a raise—that's why they've been there twenty years.

He's determined not to go without taking it with him; he's bought himself a fireproof money belt.

He even has a burglar alarm on his garbage can.

He recently bought some shirts cheap and changed his name to fit the monogram.

He's the kind who can't be ordered around—unless its a round of whiskey.

His girl asked him for a book of poetry, so he went to a bookstore and asked for a volume of free verse.

He's waiting for a total eclipse of the sun so he can send a night-rate telegram.

The way he nurses a drink it looks like he's drinking from an hourglass.

At his own cocktail parties the whiskey flows like glue.

Of all the near-relatives in the family he's the closest.

When his kids want ice cream because they feel warm, he tells them ghost stories to make their blood run cold.

No one can find fault with his cleanliness. He's been sponging for years.

It's reached a point where he won't even spend the time of day.

He's widely recognized as a man who gives no quarter. Waiters, bellboys and taxi drivers can testify to that.

When he takes a dollar bill out of his pocket, George Washington blinks at the light.

He can make a nickel go so far, the buffalo gets sore feet.

Wet blankets

It's people like him that make you long for the solitary life.

A few minutes with him makes you want to jump for joy—off a tall building.

He's known everywhere as a VIB—a Very Insistent Bore.

When it's time for him to get up and go home, he's full of get-up-and-stay.

He's the kind you bid a welcome adieu.

There are three ways of saying goodbye to him: Adieu, Adios, and Arsenic.

One thing you can expect from him in abundance—and that's redundance.

He claims he can imitate any bird. He's apparently overlooked the homing pigeon.

He's a person who's going places—and the sooner, the better.

He holds people openmouthed with his conversations. They can't stop yawning.

You can always spot him at a cocktail party. He has a highball in one hand and someone's lapel in the other.

He's just what the doctor ordered—a pill.

He's only dull and uninteresting until you get to know him. After that, he's just plain boring.

He's such a bore, he even bores you to death when he's complimenting you.

His stories always have a happy ending. Everyone is delighted when they finally end.

He's so dull, even his dog got bored and left him.

He's good for people's health. When they see him coming, they take long walks.

He umphasizes every other word.

He always has a flood of words and a drought of ideas.

It's not bad enough that he explains everything—he even explains his explanations.

He has his tongue in your ear and his faith in your patience.

He always has a couple of hours to spare, and is constantly on the lookout for someone who hasn't.

The real problem of having leisure time is to keep him from using it.

He can dive deeper into a subject than anyone you've ever known. The trouble is, he stays under longer and comes up drier.

It's true that he's a man of few words. The trouble is, he keeps repeating them.

No one can equal his genius for squeezing a minimum of thought into a maximum of verbiage.

There's one thing that can be said in his favor: it requires no small talent to be as unbearable a bore as he is.

He doesn't need to repeat himself. He gets it trite the first time.

He's a monologist who becomes a monopologist until you become a moanologist.

He serves one useful purpose. Running away from him is the only exercise some of his acquaintances get.

All he has to do is open his mouth, and his foot falls out.

So far as his sense of humor is concerned, he's living on the wrong side of the cracks.

By the silence in the room, you can safely conclude that he has just told a joke.

Some people provide happiness wherever they go; he, whenever he goes.

He's like a summer cold—you just can't get rid of him.

He has occasional flashes of silence that make his conversation brilliant.

His parties are so dull that a guest who dropped dead at one was the life of the party.

One advantage of going to his dreary parties is that you can get home at a decent hour.

On leaving one of his parties, a guest usually says, "I've had a most enjoyable evening. Sorry this wasn't it."

He says he'd go to the end of the earth for his friends. They only wish he would, and that he'd remain there.

Encountering three guests strolling together at a resort hotel, he asked, "What's going on?" "We are," they chorused—and did.

It's not that he doesn't know how to say nothing. The trouble is, he doesn't know when.

If he should remark, "There's something I've been intending to say, but I just can't seem to think of it," be sure to suggest, "Probably an appointment you're already late for?"

Even as a child, he was such an insufferable bore that when he was nine years old his parents ran away from home.

"Please don't bother seeing me to the door," he said to a weary host. "It's no bother," was the answer. "It's a real pleasure."

Wives

BABBLERS

In his entire life he never spoke as fast as when he proposed. He must have sensed it was his last chance to do any talking.

She speaks 140 words a minute, with gusts up to 180.

The one and only time she stops talking is when her mother starts.

He murmured as he sat at the dinner table, "How tranquil it must have been in the Tower of Babel!"

He married her because of her beautiful mouth. He wishes now she wouldn't keep it open so much.

When he goes to a dentist, he has her alongside the chair babbling away, so he won't feel any extra pain.

It's no help to him when she lets her mind go blank—she neglects to turn off the sound.

A doctor told them he needed rest and quiet, and prescribed a tranquilizer—to be taken by her.

She says, "I just don't understand my husband. He hardly ever talks, unless he has something to say!"

Out on a golf course with her once, he found a trap on the course that was exasperating—she just wouldn't close it.

She asked the doctor to look at her tongue to see if it was coated. He shrugged, "No need to—you never find grass on a racetrack."

They've been married fifteen years, and he loves her still.

He'd be willing to forget the fact that she set her trap for him when they first met—if she'd just shut it now.

He wouldn't object to her having the last word—if she'd only get to it.

Queried by one of those radio-survey phone calls, "To whom are you listening?" he replies, "To my wife—who else?"

In any argument with her he always gives in. What's the use? —it's just his word against thousands of hers.

He knows now why Adam was created first—to give him a chance to say something.

He's just phoned the doctor: "My wife has dislocated her jaw. If you happen to pass by in a week or so, you might drop in— no hurry."

He's an outstanding linguist. He's mastered many tongues but not hers.

At bedtime, when she asks, "Is everything shut up for the night?" he patiently replies, "Everything else, dear."

He understands why she got that double chin—too much work for one.

Once she rebuked him: "What's the idea? You yawned seven times while I was talking to you." "I didn't," he said. "I was just trying to say something."

From the day they were married he hasn't been on speaking terms with her—only on listening terms.

On their latest anniversary she asked, "Can't we celebrate?" He was tempted to reply, "Yes, let's have two minutes of silence!"

The only time she never interrupts him is when he talks in his sleep.

THE BALL AND CHAIN

Before he married her, he thought she was a shrinking violet. Now he knows the word should be "shrieking."

He wishes she were his mother—so he could run away from home.

She's a bridge fiend. Only a fiend could kick as hard as she does.

She claims they're happily married. The fact is, *she's* happy, *he's* married.

He should have been warned when he attended the funeral of her first husband—the corpse had such a relieved look.

When he agreed to marry her, it was a load off his chest—her father and two husky brothers got off it.

He was really fooled when he asked her to marry him and she said she was agreeable.

When he complains that she's driving him to his grave, she sneers, "What did you expect to do, walk?"

When she told him the man who married her would get a prize, he should have asked for a look at it first.

During their courtship she purred that she was saving herself for him. Now he wants to know why, at 165 pounds, she has to save so much.

Before they were married, her chin was her best feature—now it's a double feature.

She's resorted to henna, and he's resigned to Gehenna.

He doesn't have to worry about making a fool of himself—she's doing the job for him.

She's the beneficiary of his $100,000 insurance policy, and she wants to know what excuse he can give her for living.

He recently wired a hotel to reserve "a suitable room where I can put up with my wife."

He well remembers the night, five years ago, when he had a wreck in his car—he's sorry he married her.

A friend told him, "I just got a cute little poodle for my wife." He sighs, "I wish I could make a trade like that!"

He recently phoned his boss to say he couldn't report for work because his wife broke an arm—his.

For his last birthday she gave him a present that really made his eyes pop out—a shirt with a collar two sizes too small.

She sneers, "I had to marry you to find out how stupid you are." He replies, "You should have known that the minute I asked you."

She often berates him: "Before we were married, you told me you were well off." He answers, "I was, and didn't know it."

Once she screamed, "I should have taken my mother's advice and never married you. How she tried to stop me!" "Holy mackerel," he exclaimed, "how I've misjudged that woman!"

There's no doubt who's the boss in their house—she's taken complete charge of the controls on the electric blanket.

He's often asked why he has that number F-83659 tattooed on his back, and he explains: "That's not a tattoo—that's where my wife ran into me when I opened the garage door."

He came home one night, and found his partner making love to his wife. Amazed and dumfounded, he said, "Herman, I must—but you?"

She recently asked an insurance agent: "If I take out a $500,000 insurance policy on my husband's life and he should die the next day, what would I get?" He answered, "Life."

His daughter, hesitating to accept a proposal, told him, "Dad, I hate to leave mother." "That's all right, dear," he said, "just take her with you."

He says that drink is the curse of his marriage. Once it made him shoot at her—it also made him miss.

He sued for a separation, but in court she denied that they weren't getting along very well together. "We did have an argument, judge, and I shot him," she said, "but that's as far as it went."

He was recently run over by a hit-and-run driver. When a cop asked him if he'd gotten the car's plate number, he said, "No, but I'd recognize my wife's laugh anywhere."

He's getting a little leery—she's just bought him a deerskin coat to wear on his next hunting trip.

She read his fortune on a weight card: "It says you're magnetic, a born leader, and widely recognized for your strength of character—it's got your weight wrong, too!"

THE GETTER HALF

He took her for better or worse. She took him for everything.

The outcome of their marriage depends on his income.

She's really his "better half." When she asks him for money, he'd better have it.

She loves him for what he is—well-to-do.

He always has a voice in what she buys—the invoice.

On his birthdays she always sends him a card reading "Money Happy Returns."

They have a joint bank account. It's in two names—her married name and her maiden name.

She runs up expenses so fast it leaves him breathless.

She's his treasure so long as he remains her treasury.

Running a house is a matter of checks and balances. The more checks she writes, the worse his balance gets.

She'll get back that warm feeling for him—when he buys her a fur coat.

There's one thing about him that she loves—he wonders how long it will take her to spend it.

He keeps a goldfish bowl on his desk. He likes to see something opening its mouth without asking for money.

When he leaves for a business trip, she wheedles, "Be sure to write—even if it's only a check."

She's worried about his insomnia—she hasn't been able to go through his pockets for months.

He tells her he can't face those bills she's run up. She says, "You don't have to face them—just foot them."

Instead of sending his suits to the cleaner, she industriously removes the spots herself—five spots, ten spots . . . .

She was his secretary before they were married; now she's the treasurer.

Their ship of matrimony isn't moving so smoothly, because she won't stay away from the sales.

He's convinced there's no life on the moon. There are no charges for calls there on her phone bills.

The things she buys all the time for the house makes him realize how few things it lacks.

She was determined to marry a man clever enough to make a lot of money, and dumb enough to spend it all on her.

She's disturbed because lately she can't seem to balance her budget. According to her figures, she's spending less than he's earning

He keeps reminding her, "Any day now we're liable to be on a pay-as-you-went basis."

There's no doubt she knows how to make a dollar go far—so far that he never sees it again.

When he proposed, he declared, "I'd go through anything and everything for you." So far, he's only gone through his bank account.

The gag about the absent-minded husband who sent his wife to the bank and kissed his money goodbye doesn't apply to him. It isn't absent-mindedness in his case—it's a fact.

He doesn't worry when she isn't at home for several days—where else would she be but shopping?

A friend told him, "My wife dreamed last night she was married to a multimillionaire." "You're lucky," he sighs, "My wife has that dream in the daytime!"

They both like the same thing. The trouble is, he'd like to hold on to it and she likes to spend it.

She calls him a "good egg"—sure, but wait till he's busted.

He'd better hang on to his capital if he doesn't want her to lose interest.

Once he told her he might be going broke. "Don't worry, dear," she said, "I'll always love you even though I'll never see you again."

On the verge of bankruptcy one time, he asked a friend to break the news to her gently. "Tell her I'm dead," he suggested.

He gave her the world with a fence around it, and she turned around and gave him the gate.

HOUSEKEEPERS

The meals she cooks are putting color in her husband's face —purple.

When it comes to housekeeping, she likes to do nothing better.

She's had him on frozen food so long, his stomach is sending out blizzard warnings.

He's provided her with a modern kitchen—now all he needs in it is an old-fashioned wife.

She doesn't have to hire domestic help—she seems to have married it.

If death ever approaches, his final wish will be for her to cook his last meal—then he'll feel more like dying.

Where there's smoke, there she is—cooking.

She smothers the steak in onions, but it still tastes as if it died a hard death.

What a cook! She's burned so many slices of bread that their toaster has been declared a fire hazard.

One time she purred: "Dear, what will I get if I cook another dinner like tonight's?" He answered, "My life insurance!"

She feeds him so much fish, he's breathing through his cheeks.

Her cooking is really something to write home about—for his mother's recipes.

He's her second husband. She keeps wanting him to eat everything her first husband did—but he refuses to commit suicide.

He deserves a decoration for eating one of her meals—a purple heartburn.

His is a real surprise marriage. When he comes home to a well-cooked meal and kind words, boy, is he surprised!

She says she's too weak for housework. He's not strong either for her idea of housework.

When they met she told him she'd been to a cooking school —he thinks she must have learned in ten greasy lessons.

He sure knows how to settle her hash—with bicarbonate.

It always amazes him that she's able to see right through him when she can't see a button missing from his coat.

Right after marriage, she decided what to do to have soft, white hands—NOTHING.

She gets mad when he says the soup is cold. Indignantly she asks, "What do you want me to do—burn my thumb?"

All she knows about cooking is how to bring *him* to a boil.

Before marriage she turned his head with her charm—now she turns his stomach with her cooking.

She serves him blended coffee—today's and yesterday's.

There are enough grounds in his coffee cup for a divorce.

Ever since their marriage, they've gone through thick and thin. When it comes to cooking, she's thick and he's thin.

One night she whispered, "there's a burglar in the kitchen. He's eating the casserole we had for dinner." He said, "Go back to sleep—I'll bury him in the morning."

She's not a cook—she's an *arsonist*.

Since their marriage, he's learned a great deal about reincarnation—only they call it hash.

Some wives can cook but don't. His wife can't cook but does.

She has one fixed theory in the kitchen—if it doesn't move, wrap it in aluminum foil.

Once she cried, "The dog ate the meatloaf I made for you." He said, "Stop crying. I'll buy you another dog."

He no longer gets his morning dish of instant oatmeal—she lost the recipe.

When he pleads to be surprised for dinner, she obliges—she soaks the labels off the cans.

He's had all he can bear of her cooking—he's threatening to go home to her mother.

She's served him so many TV dinners, he's thinking of looking for a new sponsor.

When she tells him, "Woman's work is never done," he counters, "That's right—and your housekeeping proves it."

Her kitchen is so messy and cluttered, when bread pops out of the toaster, he'd be late for work if he tried to find it.

Is she lazy? He defies anyone to produce another housewife who washes dishes in bed.

He married her because he wanted someone to cook and keep house. Trouble is, she married *him* for the same reason.

He's given up asking her to straighten up the house. She wisecracks, "Why—is it tilted?"

He always has the last word with her—in the mornings anyway. He says, "Oh, don't get up. I'll have breakfast downtown."

Sometimes she tells him she has a marvelous meal planned for him. "I'll tell you about it on the way to the restaurant," she says.

She's really a terrific housekeeper. She's been divorced three times, and in every settlement she keeps the house.

STRAYERS

She's happily married—her latest boyfriend likes her husband.

One time while he was on vacation, she wrote him: "Now be sure to go out with no one but men, and I'll do the same here back home."

She insists that at the bottom of her heart she loves her husband—there's a boyfriend at the top

Even after ten years of marriage her husband finds her entertaining—when he comes home unexpectedly.

She was told by a fortuneteller, "You should be happy—a nicer man than your husband you have yet to meet." She replied, "How exciting! When?"

She married him for his money. Now all she's interested in is a little change.

Accused of having been seen with another man, she protested, "Dearie, it was only my husband—you know there's no one but you!"

A friend said, "Your husband is brilliant-looking. I suppose he knows everything." She replied, "Don't be silly. He doesn't even suspect."

She frequently boasts about the "straight and narrow." She's undoubtedly referring to her girdle.

She's the type who considers herself too good to be true.

Once her husband caught a man embracing her, and he yelled, "Now I know everything!" "Oh, yeah?" she sneered. . . . "When was the Battle of Vicksburg?"

Teaching his young son to count, he asked, "What comes after 10?" Answered the kid, "The man next door."

Writers

He's putting everything he knows into his next literary work. It's sure to be a short story.

It's a first-grade novel. The only trouble is, most readers have gone beyond the first grade.

You can read yourself to sleep with his novel—it's a great yawn.

He should have put a finishing touch to that story—a match.

He must have written that play on a tripewriter.

His book is bound to be a Best Smeller.

In writing it he must have used a dictaphony.

His books will be read long after Shakespeare, Dickens, Hemingway, and Faulkner are forgotten—but not until then.

Reading his novel is like eating an artichoke—you have to go through so much to get so little.

As a mystery novel, it's just run-of-the-morgue.

He claims he reaches thousands of readers—good thing they can't reach him.

They call him the "Pharmacist." Every book he writes is a drug on the market.

His preface states that the characters bear no resemblance to any person living or dead. That's precisely what's wrong with it.

He claims he puts fire into his writings. He'd be better off to put his writings into the fire.

He's just written something that will be accepted by any magazine—a check for a year's subscription.

He's taken up writing as a career and has already sold several things—his watch, typewriter, overcoat, and furniture.

"The play of the future" is what he calls his latest brain child. Another like it, and he won't have any future.

No fewer than five characters die in his mystery novel and are interred in the plot.

The story has as much action as a snake's hips.

His novel is an indefinite idea in infinite ink.

His novel should win a Pulitzer prize—at least the first two letters.

The book will leave its mark on literature—like chicken pox.

He wanted to be a novelist badly, and he's achieved his ambition—he's a bad novelist.

He writes books nobody will read, and checks nobody will cash.

He's one author who's sure to be flooded with pan mail.

Nicknames

They call him ACCORDIONIST: He plays both ends against the middle.

They call her AFTER-DINNER SPEAKER: If she speaks to you, she's after a dinner.

They call her ANGEL: She's always up in the air, harping about something.

They call her ARCHER: She knows how to keep her beaus in a quiver.

They call him BEAN: Everyone strings him along.

They call him BIOLOGIST: He crosses an intersection with a convertible and gets a blonde.

They call her BOTTLENECK: If a fellow opens a bottle, she's ready to neck.

They call her BUSINESS WOMAN: She's interested in everybody's business.

They call him BUTTON: He's always popping off at the wrong time.

They call him CAESAR: He's a man of great nerve and wonderful Gaul.

They call him CATERPILLAR: He got where he is by crawling.

They call him CHARACTER ACTOR: When he shows any character he's acting.

They call her CHEWING GUM: She's Wrigley all over.

They call her CHORUS GIRL: She's always kicking.

They call him CLASS-CONSCIOUS: He has no class, and everyone is conscious of it.

They call him CLIFF: He's a big bluff.

They call him CLOCK: His hands are always moving over figures; they go around girls so fast, it alarms them.

They call him COLD: You can't get rid of him in a hurry.

They call her CONVERTIBLE TOP: She's been a brunette, a redhead, and a blonde.

They call him COOKIE: He has such a crummy look.

They call him COP: When he meets a girl, he wants to make a pinch.

They call him CORN: In school he was always at the foot of the class.

They call him CORKSCREW: He's so crooked.

They call her CROWBAR: She's not so much to crow about, but she doesn't bar a thing.

They call her CRYSTAL: She's always on the watch, and gives you a glassy stare.

They call him DETECTIVE: Girls say his hands have built-in search warrants.

They call him DON JUAN: The girls "Don Juan" to have anything to do with him.

They call him DRIP: You can hear him, but you can't turn him off

They call him DRY CLEANER: He's a wolf who works fast and leaves no ring.

They call him EGG: He's too full of himself to hold anything else.

They call him EXCLAMATION POINT: He's always blowing his top.

They call him FIGHTING QUAKER: He quakes more than he fights.

They call him FISH: He gets into trouble because he can't keep his mouth shut.

They call her FLOWER: She's often potted.

They call her FORTUNETELLER: As a gold digger, she can tell a man's fortune.

They call her FRUIT SALAD: She's as slippery as a banana and as sour as a lemon, and when she's squeezed, you get hit in the eye like a grapefruit.

They call him GARBAGE MAN: He has that certain air about him.

They call him GEOMETRY: He's always found in a triangle.

They call him GIRDLE: He's sure been around women.

They call him GOAT: He's always butting in.

They call her HAZEL: She's a real nut.

They call her HOME GIRL: She's not particular whose home.

They call her ICE CREAM: She's sweet but cold.

They call her INSTANT COFFEE: She's easy to make.

They call her IODINE: She's a drug on the market.

They call him LACE: You'll always find him around a skirt.

They call him LEMON SQUEEZER: He always dances with a wallflower.

They call him LIGHTNING: He conducts himself properly.

They call her LILAC: She can lilac anything.

They call her LIVE WIRE: The way she dresses, there isn't much insulation.

They call him LUKE: He's not so hot.

They call him MAGICIAN: He can turn anything into an argument.

They call him MATCH: He loses his head when he gets lit up.

They call him MATHEMATICIAN: He likes to work with figures —females', that is.

They call him M.D.: He's Mentally Deficient.

They call her MELODY: She's real sharp, knocks guys flat, and boy, does she know the score!

They call him MIRACLE WORKER: It's a miracle when he works.

They call him MOTH: He's been found in many closets.

They call her MOTOR MECHANIC: She's always taking off attire.

They call her MUSCLES: She's in every fellow's arms.

They call her MUSICIAN: She's a snob full of airs.

They call him MYTH: He's a myth-fit.

They call her NAPKIN: She's always in some fellow's lap.

They call him NAT: Short for G-N-A-T.

They call him OCEAN: He's all wet.

They call her PEACH: The tighter you squeeze her, the mushier she gets.

They call him PHOTOGRAPHER: When he's with a girl, he puts out the light. The idea is to see what develops.

They call him PIE: He has lots of crust.

They call her PLYMOUTH ROCK: She has a shape like a Plymouth and a head like a rock.

They call him PNEUMATIC DRILL: He's such a bore.

They call her RADIO STATION: Anybody can pick her up, especially late at night.

They call her RESOLUTION: She's hard to keep.

They call him RIVER: The biggest part of him is his mouth.

They call her RUMOR: She goes from mouth to mouth.

They call him SPIDER: He's always living in suspense.

They call him THEORY: He hardly ever works.

They call him TRAVELER: When he takes a girl out, he always tries to touch points of interest.

They call him TRUCK: He always has a load on.

They call her TURKEY: She's stuffed in the right places.

They call her WHEATCAKE: She sure is stacked.

They call him WHEELBARROW: He needs to be pushed.

They call him WIGGLE: He wears his hat all the time because he's afraid his wig'll come off.

They call him WINNIE: He has a voice like a horse.

They call him WRESTLER: He's always throwing his weight around.

Squelches

Look, Dr. Jekyll, you're getting under my Hyde.

You've convinced me about reincarnation—now tell me what part of a horse you were in a previous existence.

I can't actually blame you for your ancestors, but I sure must blame them for you.

Let's play Building and Loan. Just get out of the building and leave me alone.

Whatever is eating you must be suffering from indigestion.

There's nothing the matter with you that a nice, first-class funeral couldn't fix.

If Moses had known anyone like you, there would have been another commandment.

You could make a good living hiring yourself out to scare people with the hiccups.

You impress me as the type of person who always wants to save face, so why don't you stop shooting it off?

Excuse me while I go out for a cup of coffee. I have to steady my nerves before I take another look at you.

I'll bet you're the one who goes to libraries just to tear the last chapter out of mystery novels.

You really have an open mind—and a mouth to match.

Look, I'm not going to engage in a battle of wits with you—I never attack anyone who's unarmed.

You make me wish I had a lower IQ so I could enjoy your company.

You know, I'd like to send you a Valentine, but I haven't figured out how to wrap lace around a time bomb.

I'm really pleased to see you're back—particularly after seeing your face.

Tell me, is that your lower lip, or are you wearing a turtleneck sweater?

You've got the sort of face I don't want to remember, but can't forget.

You're something that one only meets in a nightmare.

It isn't simple to figure out what you've got, but whatever it is, take my advice and get rid of it.

I wouldn't fret so much if I were you—after all, we can't all be mentally sound.

I understand you were an infant prodigy. It's too bad you've continued to act like an infant long after you ceased being a prodigy.

Why don't you leave here and go to the zoo? You'll be less conspicuous there.

It's not the ups and downs in life that bother me—it's the jerks like you.

You remind me of some of those new dances—one, two, three, jerk!

I'll bet you're called a big thinker—by people who lisp.

You have a fine personality—but not for a human being.

It's an experience to have someone like you at this party. May I be the very first to shake you by the throat?

You may think you're a gay buck, but you're only two bits.

Why don't you go and get lost somewhere where they have no Found Department?

I haven't decided yet exactly what piece of my mind to give you, but stick around, I've got quite a choice.

It's no use asking you to act like a human being—you don't do imitations.

I hear they're naming a cake after you—a crumb cake with a lot of crust.

A crumb like you should have stayed in bread.

I can't forget the first time I laid eyes on you—and don't think I haven't tried.

I understand when you were a kid your mother sent your picture to Ripley, and it was promptly returned, marked, "I don't believe it!"

I'm just palpitating to know where you've been all my life— and when you're going back there.

Listen, baboon, don't accuse me of making a monkey out of you. Why should *I* take all the credit?

You sure are a squirrel's idea of Utopia.

You're just perfect at any party as an M.C.—a Mental Case.

You couldn't even entertain a doubt.

It's easy to understand why people like you made Oscar Wilde.

You appear to be as happy as if you were in your right mind.

Why don't you pal around with a half-wit so you can have someone to look up to?

I must say you exemplify the spirit of brotherly shove.

I'd like to help you out. Just tell me which way you came in.

On your way out, could I drop you off somewhere—like a nearby bridge?

You've convinced me of the truth of the old proverb, "Distance lends enchantment."

Look, I've got Christmas ties that aren't as loud and useless as you are.

Why don't you go and have your jocular vein cut?

I've known calamities in my lifetime, but never a vocalamity like you.

You may think you're the big cheese at parties, but you only smell like it.

You remind me of a clarinet—a wind instrument.

I'm going to send you a present—as soon as I can figure out how to wrap up a Bronx cheer.

The longer I know you, the more I depreciate you.

There are plenty of manholes in this town, so why did you have to drop in here?

Your Early American features fascinate me—you look like a buffalo.

Anytime you happen to pass my house, I'll appreciate it.

You may be a tonic to your family, but to me you're a pill.